T

Also by Connie Schultz

Life Happens

...and His
Lovely Wife

...and His Lovely Wife

A Memoir from the Woman Beside the Man

Connie Schultz

RANDOM HOUSE NEW YORK

Published in the United States by Random House, an imprint of The Random House Publishing Group, a division of Random House, Inc., New York.

RANDOM HOUSE and colophon are registered trademarks of Random House, Inc.

Grateful acknowledgment is made to the following for permission to reprint previously published material:

The Columbus Dispatch: Excerpt from an article by Jonathan Riskind and Jack Torry (*The Columbus Dispatch*, September 3, 2006). Reprinted by permission of *The Columbus Dispatch*.

Dayton Daily News: Excerpt from "Brown's Wife Understands the Consequences of His Win" by Jessica Wehrman (*Dayton Daily News*, November 13, 2006), copyright © Dayton Newspapers, Inc. Reprinted by permission of the *Dayton Daily News*.

IRVING BERLIN MUSIC COMPANY: Excerpt from "An Old-Fashioned Wedding" by Irving Berlin, copyright © 1966 by Irving Berlin. Copyright renewed. International copyright secured. All rights reserved. Reprinted by permission of Irving Berlin Music Company.

TMS REPRINTS: Excerpt from a May 2006 story by Knight-Ridder reporter Steve Thomma, copyright © McClatchy-Tribune Information Services. All rights reserved. Reprinted with permission of The Permissions Company on behalf of TMS Reprints.

ISBN 978-1-4000-6573-8

Library of Congress Cataloging-in-Publication Data

Schultz, Connie.
. . . and his lovely wife: a memoir from the woman beside the man / Connie Schultz.
p.   cm.
Includes index.
1. Political campaigns—United States—Case studies.   2. United States. Congress.
Senate—Elections, 2006.   3. Elections—United States.   4. Brown, Sherrod.
5. Schultz, Connie.   I. Title.
JK2281.S37 2007
324.9771'044–dc22   2007013187

Printed in the United States of America on acid-free paper

www.atrandom.com

2 4 6 8 9 7 5 3 1

First Edition

Book design by Susan Turner

To every woman who has ever felt anonymous

In memory of my parents, Chuck and Janey Schultz

contents

introduction

THE FIRST TIME I HEARD IT, I LAUGHED.

Oh, come on, I thought. *He didn't just say that.*

It was December 2005 and we were at a restaurant in southern Ohio, where a hundred or so Democrats and a handful of young campaign workers had gathered to hear my husband, Sherrod Brown, announce for the seventh time in two days why he was running for the United States Senate.

The party chairman of the county stood up at the lectern and in a loud, booming voice introduced "Congressman Sherrod Brown—and his lovely wife."

By Week 40 of the campaign, I had been introduced or mentioned that way nearly a hundred times. But this was the first time, and it took some getting used to: My only identity during the campaign, it seemed, was going to be a nod to my marital status, in case anyone wondered just who *was* that middle-aged woman standing next to the congressman who was now a Senate candidate.

"How cliché can you get?" I grumbled as we walked to our car a few minutes later.

"Well, he didn't know better," Sherrod said, wrapping his arm around my shoulders. "They don't know you down here like they do in Cleveland."

Hmm. Yes, Cleveland. That would be the city where I had been writing for years at *The Plain Dealer*, the largest newspaper in Ohio. Cleveland, the same city, it turned out, where I was introduced as "his lovely wife" for the fourteenth time—and yes, by then, I was keeping count. That night, Sherrod and I were at a political dinner, where some of the most enlightened people I know had gathered to rally for change.

"Congressman Sherrod Brown is here," a woman—a *woman*—announced from the stage, "and he's here with his lovely wife, Connie."

"Wow," Sherrod whispered. "Did she just say that?"

I stopped counting once we hit the fifty marker. I knew I was not the point at these gatherings, and I was so proud of the man who was. Sherrod had spent his entire political career fighting for people who feel ignored, mistreated, and betrayed by the country they love. Now he was running for the Senate, and I got goose bumps watching the crowd cheer for him.

Also, I realized I was getting cranky about something I could not change. If I couldn't rely on a sense of humor, I was in for one long year on a campaign trail that had already begun to test my every assumption about how far women have come in this country. I couldn't just dismiss this *no name, no career, just his lovely wife* as a holdover from the older generation, either. A young woman who worked for the campaign, noting my irritation, turned to me with eyes wide and said, "What's wrong with being his lovely wife? I don't, like, get it."

Sometimes, others helped me keep my sense of humor about the vaporizing identity so many other wives knew about only too well. My friend Jackie Cassara would call and leave messages "for the lovely wife," punctuated by that guttural chuckle of hers that always makes me laugh. And playwright David W. Rinkels, who laughed out loud when he heard the title of this book, shared this story about a "lovely wife" from long ago:

"You know who first said that?" he asked. "It was a radio announcer. He said, 'That was a beautiful song by George Gershwin and his lovely wife, Ira.'"

At least I was in good company—me and George's brother, Ira.

When a county chairman in southwest Ohio introduced me as "Sherrod's lovely wife, Candy," I gave him points for originality and moved on. By then, Sherrod had been running for more than five months, and I was so busy, and so used to what had become the standard intro, that I just stood there and waved, as if being called Candy were the most natural thing in the world.

My name, by the way, turned out to be an issue unto itself. Sherrod and I married in 2004, when I was forty-six. Seemed silly even to think about changing my name, or silly to me, anyway. I doubt I will ever forget the first time I met the wife of a senator who had all kinds of opinions on what I should and shouldn't do. We were wading in a swimming pool, where I announced to the gaggle of wives that Sherrod and I had just become engaged. It wasn't long before I regretted opening my big mouth. Sherrod, then a congressman, heard this woman shriek from the middle of the pool: "You're going to keep your *job*? You're going to keep your *name*?"

When I explained that I had built a career as a journalist with this name, not to mention an identity and a life, she laughed.

"Honey, my husband is my career," she said.

No one else around us said a word.

When Sherrod decided to run for the Senate, I decided to take a leave of absence from the job I loved as a newspaper columnist. I had been used to a certain degree of attention and reward for what I did, not for who I married. All that changed in the time it took me to clean out my desk and hit the campaign trail. I went from being a woman paid to give her opinion to a wife spouting her husband's views everywhere she went, from chicken dinners and pig roasts in nearly all of the eighty-eight counties in Ohio to high-dollar fundraisers in Beverly Hills and Manhattan. Sherrod and I agreed on all the issues that mattered, but it still felt odd that my answer to every question in front of a crowded room or a TV camera started with the words "Well, Sherrod feels" or "Sherrod has always believed." It was quite an adjustment.

The day after I decided to take a leave from *The Plain Dealer,* I sat alone in my kitchen and wrote five giant words in my journal: WHAT'S TO BECOME OF ME? Writing wasn't just what I did, it was who I was. I didn't know what I thought about something until I put pen to paper, fingers to keyboard, and I couldn't imagine how I would make sense of the world unfolding in front of me if I wasn't writing it down and thinking it through at my computer.

As I looked back on our short life together, I realized I should not have been taken by surprise. There were glimpses into my future that I had chosen to ignore.

When Sherrod and I were dating, I had met many congressional spouses, but found them to be exclusionary. I had been a newbie who was engaged but not yet married. That alone disqualified me from official membership in the Congressional Club. This was declared by the president of the club in front of thirty or so other wives gathered for a meeting at one of the congressional retreats.

"You can apply after you're married," she said. "If you do, you'll be a member for life. But you must join while your husband is in Congress. Some women never did and then wanted in after their husbands were out of office, but it doesn't work that way. No exceptions."

They saw themselves, it seemed to me, through the lens of their husbands' lives. I once made the mistake of clearing my throat, raising my hand, and saying that, while I knew who their husbands were, I didn't really know much about *them.*

"Surely," I said, "a room full of women is a room full of talent."

They proceeded to go around the room, and one by one, they described the geography and demographics of their husbands' congressional districts and whether they had a difficult race for reelection. This was after Tom DeLay's redistricting stunt, so the women from Texas were particularly animated, since many of their husbands were facing tougher races in reconfigured districts. I learned very little about those women that day, but I never doubted there was a lot more to them than what their husbands did for a living. So much of what constitutes a woman remains hidden from public view. As my friend Karen Long always said to her children, "Anonymous was often a woman."

After the meeting, the wife of a longtime congressman pulled me aside.

"I hear you're a writer," she said.

I nodded and offered my hand, which she grabbed for a nanosecond before putting her hands on her hips. "What's said in that room stays in that room. We have each other, and that is the only real support we have. We need each other and we need to know we can speak freely."

Then she walked away.

To this day, I can't recall a single comment made in that room that would have elicited even a smidgen of scrutiny from the public, let alone a gasp. Reporters would have yawned. The most candid confession came from a wife with young children who said she felt like a single mother most weeks—a complaint heard 'round the country from the wives of workaholic, or just hardworking, husbands.

"I am never going to one of their meetings again," I later growled to Sherrod. "The only thing we didn't talk about was how to bind our feet."

About six weeks into the campaign, I started to regret my harsh assessment of those congressional wives, and I was sorry that I hadn't seen why they needed one another so much. Truth be told, I wish I had made the effort to become friends with a few of them, even the wife who carried her tiny dog in a custom-made purse everywhere she went. At least, I thought, she had figured out how to always have someone around who cared about her, and only her. There were many days during the Senate race when I felt that the only living creatures who saw me as something other than a prop or a problem were our own pets, two black cats, Reggie and Winnie, and a sausage of a pug named Gracie.

Gracie always greeted me like a long-lost lover who'd sworn off life itself until my return. I'd walk through the door and immediately she'd start running figure eights across the center hallway, barking, barking, barking, as if to say, "Oh, my God, it's you! It's you!" If I stepped out to fetch the mail and returned sixty seconds later, she'd do it all over again.

Reggie, the male cat, rushed to the door whenever he heard my voice because the mere sight of me meant that food was on its way. What's not to love? Winnie, though, was the oldest and wisest of the pets, and she would have none of this excitement. Whenever I dragged myself through the door after another long day on the campaign trail, she'd look askance, glancing up from licking her paws only long enough to cast a wary eye as if she, too, wondered what had become of me.

What I didn't realize then was that I could write my own playbook. I didn't have to follow someone else's rules on how to be a political wife. In fact, I could just keep on being Sherrod's wife and do what I have always done: talk to people, take notes, and share their stories—and my own. It took a while for me to get there, but once I did, I never looked back. The road up ahead offered a lighted path I couldn't see when I was way back there, wallowing in all that fear.

Around the same time, my nineteen-year-old daughter, Caitlin, did what she said I had done for her so many times in her life: She gave me a writer's nudge to keep going. One night, she was sitting at my computer when she called me in from the kitchen.

"Hey, Mom, I have a song for you that I know you're going to like."

This was rare—having her home from college, and sharing her music. I sat down next to Cait, drinking in the light that is my daughter, as she played a song by Natasha Bedingfield titled "Unwritten."

The song is about filling the pages of your own life and risking a leap into the unknown to write your story. " 'Today is where your book begins,' " she sang.

I sat there and held Cait tight, unable to speak at first. How did my baby ever get to be so wise?

"You're never going to stop writing, Mom," she said, smiling. "I've known you all my life, and that is what you do." Later, she gave me the CD with that song, and I played it in private moments, as if it were my own soundtrack, throughout the campaign.

Slowly, I came to terms with what it means to be married to a candidate running for statewide office. We no longer lived the kind of life that squeezed neatly into Week-at-a-Glance planners. Campaign life was more like triage, where you tackled one crisis after another, right up to Election Day.

Returning to my reporter's roots helped. Early in the campaign, I started carrying a Moleskine notebook everywhere I went. Every week I filled up another notebook with thoughts, conversations, and stories from the road. I had returned to my familiar, my safe place, where the act of putting pen to paper helped me make sense of the world whizzing by.

In recent weeks, I have been getting to know some of the Senate wives—and husbands—who made major sacrifices so that their spouses could run. To a person, they have been nothing but encouraging, and even excited, when they found out I was writing this book.

"Don't be too careful in it," one said, as several others nodded. "Let them know what campaigning is really like." I was so touched by their candor—and their trust. If there was a consistent theme, it was this: Please don't whitewash.

Their comments reminded me of a book I had read a decade ago by Elsa Walsh titled *Divided Lives: The Public and Private Struggles of Three Accomplished Women.* I have never forgotten the admonishment in her introduction.

When women writers told their own stories, she said, they were "insufficiently honest and intimate. . . . It was as if women in their own books viewed admissions of pain, anger, or confusion—or even just telling the true story about their roles as wives and mothers and friends—as betrayals of one of their central responsibilities as women."

Her words have had a profound impact on me, both as a columnist and now as the writer of this book.

Ultimately, this is a story about a marriage—my marriage. In so many ways, I'm your everywife—or at least every wife who loves her husband. I listen to him when he needs to talk, chastise him when his priorities get lopsided, and share my highest vision of him when he's discouraged. And I hoot and holler like the bobby-soxed cheerleader I once was whenever he moves the marker closer to his own finish line. Nothing exceptional in that. I meet wives like me every day.

What was different in this marriage, in this time, was that my husband was seeking one of the most powerful and public jobs in the country. He was running for the United States Senate in a state that journalists and politicians call the bellwether for the country. Millions of eyes turned to Ohio about twenty seconds after Sherrod announced he was running, and the glare of that scrutiny never dimmed for the next eleven months.

Such constant, sometimes threatening, surveillance affects a marriage. We knew that. How much it would change us we wouldn't know until the campaign was over.

I've been as honest as I can in this book. Sherrod read it all, and he never asked me to change a story or delete an observation.

That tells you a lot about our marriage.

This is the story of how we got there.

...and His
Lovely Wife

one

Trash Talk

TWO WEEKS AFTER SHERROD DECIDED TO RUN FOR THE SENATE, I was hanging out at home with our dog, Gracie, when a white van pulled up in front of our house and slowed to a stop next to the bags of garbage piled at the end of our driveway.

It was trash day, and we were so new to this neighborhood that for a moment I thought maybe we'd moved to a place where they use vans instead of garbage trucks to pick up the trash. What did I know about the genteel far west side of Cleveland? I was fresh from two decades on the gritty east side, where no two homes looked alike and trash day meant dodging redesigned golf carts that zipped into the driveway and scooped up everything in sight faster than you could scream, "Wait, no, not the lawn furniture!"

This new neighborhood was way more sedate than that, if you didn't count the roar of Weedwackers, leaf blowers, and ride 'em lawn mowers. Still, everything sure *looked* calm on our sapling-lined street. Everything matched, too, which is why for weeks Sherrod and I kept pulling into the wrong driveways when we came home from work. It felt like America as you might imagine it if nobody but the Pilgrims had been allowed to migrate.

My radar, though, kicked in when the two men in the van jumped out and I noticed that they were wearing suits. I don't mean jump-suits. I'm talking dress pants, suit coats, and ties. And each of them had just grabbed two bags of our garbage.

"Uh-oh, Gracie," I said to our aging, half-deaf, nearly blind pug. "I think we've got a problem."

Gracie had followed me from her bed under my desk to the CD player four steps away because she can never get enough of me, which really matters sometimes, like when you've just realized that two men in suits are trying to steal your trash and you suddenly feel very vulnerable, and very much alone.

The only reason I noticed them at all was that I was leaning over my CD player in front of the window to replay one of my favorite Bonnie Raitt songs, "Something to Talk About." Normally, I wouldn't feel the need to name the artist or the song, but if it weren't for Bonnie Raitt I wouldn't have been in front of the window. Even now, I feel a surge of gratitude toward Bonnie just thinking of how she helped me catch in the act two men in suits trying to steal our trash.

I'm repeating myself, I know, what with the men and the suits and the trash and all, but really, the first time you see something like that out your front window and not in a movie theater you feel the need to say it a few times to let it sink in.

"Gracie," I yelled, "those two men in suits are trying to steal our trash!" I ran to the front door and threw it open.

Even with Gracie's considerable disabilities, she could grasp the seriousness of the situation, probably because I started screaming, and I've been told, sometimes not so nicely, that I have a voice that carries.

"Hey! Hey! Drop that trash! Drop that trash!"

On cue, Gracie started barking so hard only one of her paws was touching the ground. That got their attention. The men in suits took one look at me and the beast, dropped the bags, ran to the white van, and tore off.

"You're kidding," Sherrod said when I finally reached him after calling his cell phone, his BlackBerry, his desk phone, and his scheduler.

"Do I sound like I'm kidding?"

"Oh, my God."

"Yeah."

"Did you get their license?"

"What?"

"Their license plate number? Did you get it?"

I wanted to say, "Oh, sure, I whipped out the binoculars we don't own, focused the infrared ray we also don't have, and nailed the suckers."

Instead, I started to cry.

"Who would do this to us?" I blubbered. "Who would care about our trash?"

Sherrod hesitated, then sighed.

"I'm sorry, honey," he said. "Welcome to the campaign."

I WAS THE LAST PERSON WHO WANTED SHERROD TO RUN FOR THE Senate.

No kidding. Dead last.

Sometimes, when I was in Washington, I felt the need to explain that I am not the kind of political wife whose life revolves around her husband's career, and usually the person on the receiving end of this information would look at me as if I'd just admitted I needed the Fork of Shame in a restaurant where everyone else was using chopsticks. This was when Sherrod was a congressman. When you are a woman married to an elected official in Washington you are always, first and foremost, a political wife, and you are expected to toe the company line in a town where the commerce is power and politics. In such a world, the standard public version of the political wife is sleek, silent, and supportive, as seen and unheard as a Victorian child.

So I had a problem. My voice carries, remember? I've also spent all of my adult life as a feminist and a journalist, most recently as a newspaper columnist, sounding off, speaking my mind, giving my opinions without waiting to be asked. I had been getting all kinds of rewards for drawing attention to myself: a salary, health care benefits, my own mug shot at the top of the page twice a week. The thing is, if I can't get others to notice me, they'll never pay attention to what and who I care about, like hourly workers' right to a living wage, innocent men holed up in prison, a law that requires every man to own at least one denim shirt. Okay, I made up that last one, but I can dream can't I?

I don't mean to suggest that a woman who is a feminist and a columnist accustomed to lugging around her own megaphone can't fall in love with a congressman, and even marry him. In fact, I'm living proof that this is exactly what she can do, although an awful lot of people like to point out that we're not your typical combo platter. They don't mean to suggest we're special. Most think we're odd, if not overly optimistic. In any case, I'm a wife paid to give her opinion, so I'm your basic nightmare as a political wife, not to mention for any political consultant.

Not for Sherrod, though, which is one of the reasons I married him. He happens to love my opinions—most of them, anyway—and we tend to agree on most things, too. He is forever pushing me to speak my mind. He also shamelessly gushes on my behalf. Even total strangers tell me how proud he is of me. They know this because he often manages to work me into speeches about job-killing trade agreements and the doughnut hole in Medicare Part D. Now, that's love.

When we married in April 2004, I knew that I was marrying a member of Congress, but I didn't feel as if I was marrying a congressman. I fell in love with Sherrod, a smart, passionate, funny guy who claimed within weeks of meeting this longtime single mother that he knew he'd found the love of his life. The feeling was mutual, much to the shock of everyone I knew—especially me.

Like many women, I'd lived numerous lives by the time I met Sherrod. For eleven years I was a married, stay-at-home mom who wrote freelance stories at my kitchen table. Then, in the time it took me to say "But I want a career, too," I became a single working mother, and I'd been doing that for another eleven years when Sherrod showed up. By then, I had figured out it was best to pave your own road to happiness, and mine took me to a place where, for the most part, I was fairly content.

I did have the occasional pang of loneliness. I recall a time when my daughter, Caitlin, who was nine at the time, couldn't sleep. She asked if she could climb in with me. Now that she's twenty and I'm lucky if she'll even make time for lunch with me, I'm so glad I never said no when she believed just lying next to me would solve all her problems. She snuggled into bed with me that night, bringing our dog and two black cats with her, and was sound asleep in the time it took her to tell me she loved me. A long time later, I was still awake, lying flat on my back and thinking, "There are five beating hearts in this bed, and not one of them is a man's."

My dear friend Bill Lubinger once asked me, "Is it hardest to be alone when you have bad news?"

"No," I said, "it's harder when you've got good news."

Overall, though, life was hectic but rich. My son, Andy, was already grown and pursuing love and his doctorate degree at The Ohio State University. (If I don't include "The" in the university's name, we'll be noting my mistake in the paperback edition of this book. The things academia obsesses over.) I took care of my daughter, tended my friends, and held my mother's hand as she took her last breaths. From that moment on, I also tried to be a good daughter to my grieving father, a retired factory worker who had always hated his job and most of his life and now he was mad at God, too, for taking Mom away so soon.

"Why does *she* have to go?" he asked me outside her hospital room two days before she died. "It was supposed to be me."

How do you answer a question like that? For five years and running since then, I'd been trying.

So, by the time Sherrod sent me his first e-mail asking where in the world *The Plain Dealer* had found me, I'd done plenty of living and was glad of the adventure. For the record, I'd never laid eyes on Sherrod before, but I had read his book, *Congress from the Inside.* I had never shaken his hand or interviewed him or included so much as a paraphrased quote from him in any story I wrote. If I had, I wouldn't have gone out with him. Some stories you're glad you missed, which I didn't know until I was forty-five and slid into the restaurant booth opposite Sherrod Brown on January 1, 2003.

He showed up wearing four days' growth of facial hair because he was afraid of looking too eager. He also wore a sweatshirt from Lorain Community College. He didn't even own a shirt from his alma mater, Yale, which he told me almost immediately and which earned him big points. He also brought two pages of his favorite quotes. He had typed them himself and then folded the pages into the back pocket of his jeans, which had holes in the knees.

I was in love by the time we ordered coffee. Sherrod, ever competitive, swears he knew I was the one as soon as I arrived, after I dropped my coat and then nearly head-butted him when we both bent over to pick it up.

We were engaged by Thanksgiving. We married on my mother's birthday the following spring. Our children—Caitlin and Andy, and Sherrod's daughters, Emily and Elizabeth—walked us down the aisle at Pilgrim Congregational United Church of Christ in Cleveland. Sherrod is Lutheran, so we ended up with three pastors—Pilgrim's pastors, my friends Kate Huey and Laurie Hafner, and Sherrod's pastor from First Lutheran Church in Lorain, Linwood (Woody) Chamberlain. At our reception, Sherrod said when a journalist marries a congressman, you need three ministers.

I had lived in a rented duplex in Shaker Heights, on Cleveland's east side, for eleven years, while Sherrod lived in his congressional district in Lorain on the far west side. After we married, he needed to continue living in his congressional district, but my daughter, Caitlin, was a junior in high school, and we did not want to further yank the yarn on her unraveling life by making her move and change schools. Also, most of her memories revolved around life with her single mom, and no one filled a house—or a life—quite like the irrepressible Sherrod.

"He takes some getting used to, Mom," she said early in our courtship. This was right around the time he decided that our precious pug, Gracie, had a name that didn't match her face, so he renamed her Rufus. To Caitlin's horror, Gracie immediately took to the new moniker.

"Your name is *Gracie*," Cait would tell her beloved pug. *"Gracie."* The dog would wag, wag, wag her tail—until Sherrod called "Rufus!" Then off she'd go to her new best friend.

Cait was growing increasingly fond of Sherrod, though, which I first discovered while we were watching C-SPAN one evening, waiting for Sherrod to give a speech on the floor of Congress. The coolest people turn into C-SPAN nerds once they're related to a member of Congress. You also find yourself referring to people you can't stand as "my friend across the aisle." Strangest thing.

As soon as Sherrod popped up on the screen, Caitlin turned to me and said, "You know, Mom, I do care about Sherrod."

I know thin ice when I'm sliding on it, so I just tiptoed. "That's nice, honey," I said. "I'm glad."

"Yeah," she said, nodding her head as she stared at the screen. "If he died? I'd cry."

So, FOR A YEAR AND A HALF, WE KEPT TWO HOUSEHOLDS GOING, which meant we were forever leaving something on the other side of town. When Cait graduated from high school in June 2005, we merged. By the end of that summer, we had moved together into a development, chosen because it was near the airport and only a half-hour drive to my job in downtown Cleveland.

Our children's lives were humming along. Caitlin left for college in Ohio that September, and Elizabeth returned to Columbia

University, where she was a senior. Emily was married to Michael Stanley. They lived in Brooklyn, New York, both of them working at jobs they loved. Andy had brought to our wedding a remarkable young woman from Long Island named Kristina Torres. He claims that when he asked if he could bring her, I immediately asked, "Is she worth $115?"—referring to our cost per plate at the wedding reception sit-down dinner. I was simply trying, in a mother's subtle way, to establish whether this was a serious relationship. They have since set a wedding date, and I like her. Definitely worth the $115.

Our children were off living their lives, and we could finally settle into our own. For the first time, I felt that I was Sherrod's full-time wife, and that person evolved in the moments hidden from public view. Sherrod's wife twirled the curls of his hair around her fingers in the darkened movie theater and listened to him play "Let It Be" on the piano late at night. She took long walks with him even in the rain and sat like a girlfriend on the front stoop waiting for him to pull into the drive. Sherrod's wife had Sherrod all to herself, at least once in a while, in those private, unscheduled moments that incubate a marriage and keep it alive.

Then the earth shifted.

Suddenly, Sherrod was considering a run for the Senate.

A Democrat had not been elected statewide in Ohio for fourteen years, but the political climate was changing dramatically in our state, and the gale winds were threatening to topple the Republican Party.

Republican Bob Taft had become the first Ohio governor charged with a crime after he failed to report gifts and golf outings. He was convicted of violating Ohio ethics laws and ordered to pay $4,000 and apologize to the state. One widely publicized poll of governors' popularity ranked him last.

Tom Noe, a Republican fundraiser and party activist in the Toledo area, oversaw the state's rare-coin fund investment with the Bureau of Workers' Compensation. Noe made headlines across the country after the Toledo *Blade* exposed his role in what was soon dubbed "Coingate." Noe was headed for conviction on charges of theft, money laundering, forgery, and corrupt activity. In a second scandal, he was charged with illegally funneling $45,400 to President George W. Bush's reelection campaign. The Bush campaign had originally honored Noe with "Pioneer" status, but after he was indicted, many prominent politicians, including Sherrod's potential Republican opponent, Senator Mike DeWine, scrambled to return the money Noe had raised for them, or to donate it to charity.

Finally, we had the nonstop coverage of Republican congressman Bob Ney. He represented the 18th District in southern Ohio until he decided not to, which came after he pleaded guilty to charges of conspiracy and making false statements related to the Jack Abramoff lobbying scandal.

So much Republican scandal, coupled with Americans' growing opposition to Bush's war in Iraq, made even the most reticent of Democrats on the state and national scene start talking about perfect storm this and sea change that—often casting a hopeful eye in Sherrod's direction.

At first, some Ohio Democratic Party officials tried to persuade Sherrod to run for governor. It was a proposition loaded with history, both political and personal.

In 2001, Sherrod considered running for governor against Bob Taft after the Republican majority threatened to take away Sherrod's congressional district. Sherrod's only electoral loss up to then had been to Taft in Sherrod's 1990 bid for reelection as secretary of state, but this time it was Taft who looked vulnerable. Sherrod had barely whispered his possible candidacy for governor before the Republicans folded on the redistricting scheme, drawing an even safer district for Sherrod in the end. Journalists felt robbed of a feisty rematch and branded Sherrod as a guy who always leans but never runs.

If Sherrod ran for governor, I would essentially have to run for Ohio's First Lady, the mere suggestion of which provoked rounds of hysterical laughter among friends who claimed to love me. After several glasses of wine one evening we all agreed that the best way for Sherrod to have a successful run for governor would be to ship me off to Europe for six months. First Ladyhood and I just weren't a good fit. Poor Sherrod. I still remember his look of utter horror when, in a state of heightened anxiety brought on by three successive calls to our house in one night urging him to run, I screamed, "Okay, but if you win, I'm never going to give any gift shaped like the state of Ohio!" An understandable outburst, I think, when you consider we have a basement full of baskets, pie tins, Christmas ornaments, clocks—you name, we got it—all given to Sherrod by elected officials and shaped to resemble the great state of Ohio.

Fortunately, Sherrod didn't want to be governor. He loved the stuff of national politics, and eventually a good friend and Democratic colleague, Congressman Ted Strickland, announced in 2005 that he would run for governor. His wife, Frances, was the perfect candidate for First Lady, too. She had a doctorate in education, was the embodiment of grace, and wrote political songs that she sang while playing her guitar all over the state of Ohio. Sherrod's staff eventually started suggesting that maybe I should come up with some kind of talent—someone proposed that I learn how to play spoons—but I was destined to be a far less entertaining candidate's spouse.

Sherrod made it clear from the beginning that even if he decided he did want to run for the Senate, he would not do it without my unequivocal support.

"I won't do this unless you want me to," he said over and over. "And I don't mean you finally shrug your shoulders and say, 'Oh, all right, go ahead.' That's not good enough. You have to want me to run, because I'm not going to do this without you."

For a long while, he was not sure he wanted to risk giving up the job he loved for one that was far from certain to be his no matter how hard he campaigned. And, truth be told, aside from his family, there was not an endless string of people begging Sherrod to get in. No matter how many politicians announce their races with angst-ridden assurances that they are only surrendering to the will of the people, they are usually giving in only to the relentless call of their own ambition. That isn't as bad as it sounds. Often, it's an ambition to do good in the world, but even then you have to be mighty driven and fairly full of your own potential to believe that, out of millions of options, you are the one who should lead.

Most local people who liked and respected Sherrod, including party activists and the overwhelming majority of his constituents, wanted Sherrod to stay put. He was a seven-term Democratic congressman, a true progressive in a seat that even Republicans begrudgingly conceded was his until he didn't want it anymore. If the Democrats took the House in the 2006 midterm elections, he would chair the powerful Health Subcommittee of the Energy and Commerce Committee. Finally, he would have the chance to overhaul a health care system that benefited insurance and drug companies at the expense of the health of too many Americans.

For years, Sherrod had organized bus trips to Canada for senior citizens so they could buy affordable prescription drugs. He had refused the congressional health care plan, vowing never to take it until all Americans had health care. Noble gestures, but they didn't do anything to get to the heart of America's health care crisis. For Sherrod, the chairmanship would finally give the tiger some teeth.

He couldn't have it both ways, either. He had to choose. To run for the Senate, Sherrod would have to surrender his seat in Congress and take on a two-term Republican senator in a state that had twice delivered victory to George W. Bush, most recently in 2004, when I watched my husband slump behind the wheel of our parked car on Election Night and hold his head in his hands as one phone call after another assured him that early reports of exit polls had been wrong, wrong, wrong and we were about to give Democrats across the country a reason to hate Ohio all over again.

I still remember the postelection bumper sticker we spotted in New York City: "Have you mugged an Ohioan lately?"

National leaders, though, were prodding Sherrod to run for the Senate. Senator Chuck Schumer, head of the Democratic Senatorial Campaign Committee, and Senate Minority Leader Harry Reid courted him—and wanted an answer by July 2005.

"If you need the answer now, it has to be no," Sherrod told them. When Schumer kept pressing with continued calls, Sherrod told him that he was concerned about the impact such a race would have on our marriage and my career.

"She just won the Pulitzer this year, Chuck," Sherrod said. "She'd probably have to leave the paper, and she's worried about what that could do to her career."

Sherrod was reluctant to tell me Schumer's response, but I pushed.

"You aren't going to like it," he said.

"I want to know."

Sherrod sighed. "He said, 'Well, Connie had her chance at the brass ring. Now it's time for her to support you.' "

I wanted to ask Schumer what exactly Sherrod had sacrificed for me to win a journalism prize, but I'd never met the man. Later, much later, I got to know Schumer, and I came to appreciate his willful disregard for perceived obstacles. No one championed Sherrod more than Chuck Schumer.

One of the most moving pleas came from a friend of Sherrod's, Dr. Jim Kim, the director general's top deputy at the World Health Organization and a close associate of Dr. Paul Farmer, a pioneer of AIDS treatment in Haiti. Sherrod and Jim became friends after they traveled together to a TB prison in Siberia in 2002. The prison's success rate in treating prisoners with tuberculosis provided a benchmark for Sherrod in his tireless quest to fund public health programs around the world for infectious diseases, such as TB, malaria, and HIV. He saw with his own eyes how the right drugs, strictly administered at relatively little cost, could save the lives of thousands of people who had surrendered all hope.

That trip to Siberia also forged a deep bond with Jim Kim. Sherrod admired his selfless commitment, frequently recounting how Jim had insisted that Sherrod wear a surgical mask but refused to wear one himself when meeting with the prisoners. Jim didn't want to do anything that might suggest he thought he was different from the

patients he was helping. To him, the risk of appearing distant or arrogant was greater than any risk of infection.

In September 2005, Jim was on the faculty of Harvard University's medical school when he asked to meet Sherrod for dinner to talk about the Senate race. Sherrod assured him that he wasn't running, but agreed to meet with him. Immediately after their three-hour talk at a restaurant on Capitol Hill, Sherrod called me, and I will never forget the excitement in his voice or the weight of his words.

"Jim said, 'You could make such a difference in the world.' He really thinks my being in the Senate could save lives."

Another relentless tug at Sherrod's sleeve came from one of his closest friends in Congress, Bernie Sanders of Vermont. Bernie is a socialist who ran as an independent, but he and Sherrod have a lot in common, from the unruly hair on their heads and the rumpled shirts on their backs to the passion for social and economic justice that united them in battle day in and day out on the House floor. Both opposed the war in Iraq, free trade agreements, and any attempt to privatize Social Security and Medicare. They championed universal health care, an increase in the minimum wage, and countless other measures designed to bolster the poor and the middle class. They had fought together side by side throughout Sherrod's fourteen years in Congress, and now Bernie was moving on. He was running for the Senate—and he didn't plan to go it alone.

"Think about what we could do together," he said to Sherrod, night after night. "You and me, in the Senate."

Sherrod respected Bernie as a mentor and loved him like a brother, and Bernie's relentless whispers in the Brooklyn accent of his youth followed Sherrod home every weekend. Months later, Bernie told me that the only reason Sherrod gave him for hesitating was me.

"He kept talking about this wife he loved," Bernie said, wrapping his arm around my shoulders. "This marriage he had, how much he cared about his wife. Uhh, on and on."

And then there were the journalists. Political reporters and columnists were forever asking Sherrod if he was running, but their interest wasn't always driven by a passion for change. Some were political junkies looking for reasons to get out of bed, and nothing tugged on the bedclothes like the promise of a partisan slugfest. When word first got out—and word always gets out—that Sherrod was thinking of running for the Senate, reporters across the state started calling even as they let out a collective groan of "There he goes again." Some of them were sure Sherrod was only toying with them, their same accusation when he decided not to run for governor.

Sherrod was also feeling pressure from his colleague and dear friend Ted Strickland, who had decided to run for governor. Strickland was telling everyone, including any reporter within spitting distance, that Sherrod should run for the Senate. Ted told Sherrod that running together would help them both in different parts of the state.

The greatest pressure to run came from Sherrod's family. His mother, Emily Campbell Brown, and his brothers, Bob and Charlie, wanted him to run. (Sherrod's father, Charles, a family doctor, died in 2000.) They are a political family, driven by their desire to change the world and energized by the rough-and-tumble of a campaign. Sherrod's mother was a civil rights activist in Mansfield, Ohio, and she raised her three boys to serve. All of them went to Ivy League colleges, and all have been involved in politics their entire adult lives.

Charlie, a lawyer, was West Virginia's attorney general in the 1980s and is now a public-interest lobbyist in Washington. Bob, also a lawyer, had worked for President Jimmy Carter and on Capitol Hill. Sherrod, the baby of the family, was not a lawyer. He majored in Russian studies at Yale, and then won his first election in 1974, the year he graduated from college. Sherrod was a senior when the Richland County Democratic Party chair at the time, Don Kindt, asked him to run for Ohio tate representative. Kindt expected for Sherrod to run and lose, and then later win a seat on the city council in Sherrod's hometown of Mansfield. Sherrod had other plans. He campaigned hard, knocking on more than twenty thousand doors before defeating the incumbent state rep.

Sherrod served four terms in the statehouse, then ran success-fully for two terms as secretary of state before Bob Taft beat him in 1990. Two years later, Sherrod became the congressman for Ohio's 13th District, replacing the retiring Don Pease. After fourteen years in the House, most of it spent in the minority, Sherrod was feeling restless.

While Sherrod's brother Bob wanted Sherrod to run, he didn't push. "I'm not the one whose life will be hell for a year," he said. "I'm not the one whose marriage will be tested."

Charlie, though, did push, and hard. In September, when it was clear he had yet to convince his younger brother that he should run, he sent an e-mail to me titled "Sherrod championing your career":

"It's great to see Sherrod . . . continuing to champion your ca-reer," he wrote, "as in fact all we Browns have tried to do for you. Cer-tainly I have."

He continued, "Now is the time for all of [us] to champion Sher-rod's career. . . . The issue is not whether he has a 51 percent chance to win; he chose a career in politics, and who ever knows that answer. What should be clear is that running alone will open up fantastic ca-reer options, which he can't get in the House."

Charlie went on to insist that it was Sherrod's "duty" to "live his potential rather than ducking it."

He ended with this: "I ask you, Connie, to urge Sherrod to run for the Senate."

The constant drumbeat was beginning to take a toll on me, and on our marriage. I was starting to shut down, avoiding the topic whenever possible. Sherrod was feeling pulled in a direction that would take him away from me, from us. That was my fear, anyway, and for a while, fear reigned.

"Can't we just talk about it?" Sherrod asked in mid-September.

"Which part of 'it' do you want to talk about?" I said. "How we'll be apart for an entire year? How I will lose my job and have to give up my career? How you could lose your job? Or how our entire lives will be splayed for public consumption and the Republican attack machine?"

Sherrod never yelled, never got angry. He was trying to figure this out, and I was responding only with my fears. I was tired of change, and the stress that came with it. I wanted to settle down into a normal life, or at least our version of normal. We had finally started living like a real married couple—one set of house keys, one house. We had one master bedroom, and his-and-her sinks in our new bathroom. We called the same front door home, and for the second time in less than two years we were giddy newlyweds. I was scared of losing what two longtime single parents had managed to find together in middle age.

Then one afternoon, for no reason I can remember, I stood in the middle of our high-ceilinged family room and thought, "This place is nicer than my parents' wildest dream for their own lives."

And that is when I started to change my mind.

Sherrod and I fell in love not because of shared space, but, in part, because of our shared vision for the world. We earned our living in very different ways, but we fought for the same people, the same ideals. We met right after he voted against the war in Iraq and I had been writing columns to oppose it. When we first started dating, one of our rituals was to compare ugly mail on Fridays. For the first time in our lives, we had strong partners in each other to lean on, which lightened the load for both of us. Now we risked getting too comfortable, too steeped in home and hearth, instead of using that support to embolden us for the world out there, where it mattered.

Sherrod was torn about running. I knew that. But I watched as he encouraged others to run for office. I listened as he told them this was the time and Ohio was the place. And I studied his face whenever he talked to Strickland on the phone. I knew that if Sherrod didn't run, he would always wonder what might have been. I didn't want that weight tied around our marriage, or my own heart.

I talked to one of my most trusted advisers, my direct editor, Stuart Warner. Stuart edited my narrative series that was a Pulitzer finalist in 2003, and he was the editor of my columns when I won in 2005. Nobody believed more in my abilities or worked harder to drill them from the rock than Stuart. He also shared my passion for the profession, believing as I did that it was still a crucial component of democracy. I thought he'd wince when I told him that Sherrod was thinking of running. Instead, he motioned to an empty meeting room where we could talk privately.

He closed the door and said, "You aren't going to want to hear this."

I stared at him and waited.

"Sherrod should run. This country needs him to run, and he needs you by his side to do it. You'll be a tremendous asset. Look at what you believe in. Look who you've been fighting for your entire career. That's who he'll be running for, and they will vote for him and he can win. You can always come back to this work if you want. Or you can move on to something bigger. You have nothing but options, but this is the right time, maybe the only time, for him to run."

I was stunned, but I was also listening.

I needed to talk to Jackie.

Jackie Cassara is one of my closest friends. She is Ethel to my Lucy when she isn't being Auntie Mame, which is most of the time. She once stitched and framed for me Rosalind Russell's best line from that play: "Life is a banquet—and most of you poor suckers are starving to death."

Nobody looked out for me more than Jackie. It was Jackie who read Sherrod's first e-mail to me and immediately announced that he was the man I would marry. On our way to my low-key wedding, she blasted the CD she'd burned for me consisting entirely of wedding show tunes, including "An Old-Fashioned Wedding" from *Annie Get Your Gun*. Merrily, we belted out Ethel Merman's lines:

I wanna wedding in a BIIIIIG church
With BRIIIIIIDES-maids and FLOWWW-er girls.
A lot of ushers in TAAAAIL coats,
Re-PORRRRR-ters and pho-TOG-raphers.
A ceremony by a bishop who will tie the knot and say:
"Do you agree to love and honor?"
Love and honor, yes, but not obey!

One of my favorite photos, taken right before our wedding, shows Jackie walking next to me in the church hallway with a clipboard in her hand, issuing orders to the very end.

The day we met to talk about the Senate race, though, started out a bit more somber.

"So, he's going to do it?" she said, her dark brown eyes burrowing into me as I stirred my coffee.

"I think he's waiting for me," I said.

"And what are you waiting for?"

I shook my head, unable to speak, and she reached across the table, grabbed my hand, and smiled.

"Honey, you're bigger than all of this," she said. "Bigger than your job, bigger than your fears, bigger than any attack those nuts out there want to fire at you and Sherrod."

"I'm worried about my career."

"You're always going to write."

"I'm worried about our marriage."

"You two are so in love it makes me sick, makes all of us sick. I'm not kidding, we look at you and we throw up."

At that, I laughed.

"Besides," she said, "I'm friends with a Pulitzer Prize winner, and that's been nice. Really. But now I want to be friends with a United States senator. Could you make that happen, please?"

One person not thrilled at all with Sherrod's renewed contemplation was Paul Hackett, an Iraq War veteran and a lawyer who nearly won the 2nd Congressional District seat in a special election after Rob Portman resigned to become U.S. trade representative in late summer of 2005. Sherrod had given Hackett money and lent him a campaign staff member. When Sherrod thought he wasn't running for the Senate, Democratic Party leaders started courting Hackett. He was telegenic and outspoken, a newcomer who attracted a lot of attention for his off-the-cuff swipes at Republicans in general and George W. Bush in particular, calling him a "son of a bitch" in one interview and a "chicken hawk" in another.

Hackett was unpredictable, which made him the darling of the media and lefty bloggers. *The New York Times*'s James Dao described him as "garrulous, profane, and quick with a barked retort or a mischievous joke."

Sherrod had initially encouraged him to run, but pulled back when he became concerned about Hackett's viability as a candidate. By September, Sherrod was sure Hackett could not beat DeWine. Hackett had not announced his candidacy for the Senate, but he had made it clear that he was seriously considering it—and he was in no mood for Sherrod Brown's change of heart. Sherrod could get in if he wanted, Hackett told reporters, but it wouldn't change his mind about his own race.

On the first Saturday in October, I did something that makes Sherrod and me laugh now, but it really mattered at the time. I was a big fan of the television series *The West Wing*, and I owned the first six seasons on DVD. Sherrod had never been a fan of the show, complaining that the characters talked too fast and that he was distracted by the "errors in fact." He also didn't have a TV set in his Washington apartment, which further diminished his chances of becoming a *West Wing* groupie.

I pulled out Season Two, slid the first disc into the DVD player, and asked Sherrod to watch the first two episodes with me.

The first scene opens on mayhem as several in the presidential party are shot. It's dramatic, but it's not why I wanted Sherrod to watch. The first two episodes are full of flashbacks that explain how Jed Bartlett, played by Martin Sheen, finally decides to work up the nerve to run for president. And he decides to run for all the right reasons, none of which have to do with his comfort level or whether he can win.

It takes him a while to get there, and at one point his wife, played by Stockard Channing, lectures a campaign staffer that the reason her husband is so irritable with everyone is because he's scared.

"He's not ready yet," she tells him. "He'll get there, but he's not ready yet."

In the final scene, we see how Jed Bartlett gets there, and maybe Sherrod and I were just too old to be watching a middle-aged actor have an on-screen epiphany, but we both teared up at the end.

I flicked off the TV and took Sherrod's hand.

"You have to run, don't you?"

"I really do, don't I?"

I nodded, and we held each other for a while. Then we laid down our ground rules for the grueling year ahead:

• Sherrod would run as an unapologetic progressive. No tiptoeing to the middle of the road, no caving to consultants who wanted to remake him into what Sherrod called "Republican Lite." His message, not polls, would drive his campaign. Sherrod was going to take to the voters his fight for the working men and women of Ohio.

• We would learn from the mistakes of the Kerry campaign. Sherrod would run in all eighty-eight counties of Ohio, which included some of the most conservative pockets in the Midwest. And whenever the Republican attack machine opened fire, we would fight back—hard. No lying down for the kind of vicious Swift Boat ads that had challenged John Kerry's war service and his patriotism.

• Our marriage would remain a top priority. We would be apart during most weeks, especially for as long as I could stay at *The Plain Dealer,* but on weekends we would travel together. And whenever possible, Sherrod would sleep in our home.

He also promised to keep making my coffee in the morning, but I didn't consider that a deal breaker.

Sherrod made a few calls to family and supporters before announcing his race the following week. Reaction was swift, and devastating.

Shirley Fair, a longtime constituent who adored Sherrod, summed it up best. She walked up to me at a pancake breakfast and started to cry.

"Shirley, what is it? What's wrong?"

She grabbed my hand and squeezed hard. "Why is he doing this?" she said, nodding toward Sherrod. "Why is he leaving us? Why is he running?"

"He'll make more of a difference in the Senate, Shirley," I said, putting both my hands on her shoulders. "He's not leaving you, he's just going to have a bigger district."

Shirley just shook her head.

"We're all afraid," she said, the tears streaming down her cheeks. "We're afraid he cannot win."

It didn't take long for us to realize that Shirley had lots and lots of company.

two
Now What?

It takes more than a supportive spouse and family to wage a successful campaign for the U.S. Senate.

We knew that.

In fact, you could take all that we knew about the upcoming campaign and it would almost match in size, scope, and importance everything we didn't know.

We knew, for example, that Ohio was a big state of more than eleven million people. What we didn't know was how it would feel to travel that state many times over folded into a made-in-America Chrysler Pacifica. Nothing against the Pacifica; it got us everywhere we needed to go in Ohio, and safely. It's just that no car is made to double as a restaurant, hotel, office, supply center, and conference room. The only thing we didn't do in the car was go to the bathroom, no matter how lost we were in rural Ohio. We also conducted ourselves like mature adults when it came to public displays of affection, which most grown-ups aren't too terribly interested in anyway after spending five hours in the car.

We also knew that Sherrod had to raise at least $14 million, most of which would go to television advertising in the last weeks of the campaign. What we didn't know was how much of that would come from the Democratic Senatorial Campaign Committee and how much Sherrod would have to raise on his own.

We knew that to raise that kind of money, Sherrod would have to be on the phone a lot. What we didn't know was that he would have to average 201 calls a week.

We knew that Mike DeWine and the Republican Party would run a nasty campaign against Sherrod. What we didn't know was what tactics they would use and just how personal they would get.

Finally, we knew that Sherrod needed the support of the national Democratic leadership, especially Senators Chuck Schumer and Harry Reid. We knew Schumer was celebrating Sherrod's entry into the race. What we didn't know, but found out fast, was that Reid was mighty unhappy with Sherrod.

As soon as Sherrod decided to run, he flew to Washington and met with Reid. It was short, and painful.

Reid had wanted Sherrod to get in far earlier, back in July, but Sherrod and I weren't ready then. So Reid had encouraged Hackett to get into the race, and Reid was understandably upset with Sherrod now.

"Harry said I've created a real mess with Paul Hackett, and I'm going to have to fix it," Sherrod told me over the phone.

Schumer called Sherrod later and insisted that this was a temporary stumble.

"Sherrod, don't worry about this," he said. "You're going to be fine, it'll all work out, I'm thrilled you're in."

Sherrod sighed and thanked him.

"But Sherrod?"

"Yeah?"

"You *are* going to have to fix this mess with Hackett."

Sherrod was deluged with reporters' calls and speculations that he had lied to Hackett and was indecisive. Many of them erroneously reported that Sherrod had entered the race after Hackett announced, when in fact Hackett had yet to declare his candidacy.

Sherrod cited "family concerns" to explain his delay in entering the race.

I pleaded with Sherrod to tell reporters it was my fault that he had waited, but he would have none of that.

"No one is entitled to the Democratic nomination," he said. "That's what primaries are for. And no one sets my timetable but me. I'm not going to apologize for putting family first. And I'm not going to be the kind of jerk who blames his wife."

Hackett's spokesman, Karl Frisch, told the *Dayton Daily News*, "We welcome him to the race. It's been a long time since he lost a statewide campaign."

Even some of Sherrod's most ardent allies felt they had to part company with him, at least for a while. The most heartbreaking of these temporary breaks was with Congressman Tim Ryan, who represented Youngstown and part of Akron and was one of Sherrod's closest friends in the House. Elected at age twenty-nine, he was a two-term congressman from the blue-collar Youngstown area whom Sherrod had actively mentored. Sherrod had initially told Ryan he was not running, and when the Democratic leadership of the Senate asked Ryan to help recruit someone to run against DeWine, he pushed Hackett. Ryan felt he had given his word to Hackett, and told reporters he had to continue to support him. By the end of the campaign, Ryan was constantly at Sherrod's side, but for now, the air between them was chilly.

Sherrod called DeWine to tell him he was seeking DeWine's seat. It was a stiff but civil conversation. Paul Hackett, though, took the news of Sherrod's decision to run as if a dagger had been thrust through his shoulder blades. The *Akron Beacon Journal*'s cartoonist, Chip Bok, drew Hackett with a giant "Sherrod Brown" pin as big as a sword stuck in his back.

When Sherrod had called Hackett to tell him he was running, the conversation had not gone well. Hackett was understandably steamed, and right after Sherrod declared his candidacy, Hackett made it clear that he was in, too.

"My advice to Sherrod is, 'Come on in, the water's fine,' " he told bloggers and reporters. He also said to anyone who would listen—and that would be everybody, it seemed—that Sherrod had gone back on his word.

The coverage was starting to get to Sherrod. "Hackett's making it sound like I betrayed him."

"Should you respond?"

Sherrod shook his head. "I'm running against Mike DeWine. He's the Senate incumbent, he's my Republican opponent, he's the guy I have to beat."

I admired his resolve and wished it would rub off on me. Everything felt so personal, and so permanent. I wondered how we would survive all the attacks and turmoil, but Sherrod kept assuring me it would pass. While I was constantly tracking every mention of Hackett, Sherrod was focused on beating Mike DeWine. Whenever reporters asked about Hackett, Sherrod immediately pivoted to DeWine.

Local political bloggers called Sherrod everything from a traitor to a washed-up has-been. The last thing we needed, they said, was another "career politician."

Two liberal writers felt compelled to launch spirited defenses of Sherrod. David Sirota, a rising star among progressive writers, penned blogs and op-ed pieces championing Sherrod as a national leader in the fight against unfair trade agreements. Sirota was derided for months after that by other bloggers who insisted he was a flack for Sherrod, even though Sirota never received a single penny from the campaign.

Ezra Klein, a writer for *The American Prospect* magazine, trumpeted Sherrod's progressive record in their December issue:

Brown is arguably the most prominent elected Democrat in Ohio. More important to the stereotypical netroots participant, he's an unabashed liberal. Earlier this year, he led the fight to reject the Central American Free Trade Agreement (CAFTA), rendering a Republican president's trade deal nearly unable to clear the Republican-controlled Congress. . . . That's par for the course with Brown, one of the House's most effective, articulate spokesmen for progressive causes. A Cleveland Democrat, Brown is pro–gay marriage, pro–gun control, pro-labor, pro-choice, pro–universal health care—and unabashedly active on all these fronts, Ohio's reddish tinge be damned.

Markos Moulitsas Zúniga, the eight-hundred-pound gorilla of the blog world with *Daily Kos,* ignited another firestorm when he professed neutrality but suggested that Hackett withdraw from the race. His readers disagreed, and, in a poll, came out for Hackett 84 percent to 15 percent.

In our campaign, tension was growing between staff members who believed in the magic of the Internet and those who preferred traditional means of voter outreach. Sherrod was just growing increasingly annoyed. Some of the staff and consultants—I could never keep track of how many there were, because we still didn't have a campaign manager and so no one person was accountable for everything—encouraged him to reach out to bloggers, but he wanted to talk issues while they wanted to hammer him for running in the first place. He was frustrated, too, that they were unwilling to acknowledge his relentlessly progressive history. Sherrod had voted against the war in Iraq, for example, but most of them seemed not to care. Hackett had changed his position on the war—from opposing troop withdrawal to, a month later, supporting it—but the bloggers loved him.

Meanwhile, concerned colleagues at *The Plain Dealer* were pulling me aside and advising me to keep my mind and my options open. Better not quit your job too soon, they advised. Have you thought about what you might want to do if you don't return to the paper? they asked. Have you and Sherrod thought about life after the campaign?

It didn't take long for me to realize most of my colleagues did not think Sherrod could win. Astute journalist that I am, I figured this out after about a dozen or so of them came up to me and said, "Do you really think he can win?"

Until that moment, it had never occurred to me that Sherrod wouldn't win. He'd been in Ohio politics for more than thirty years. He knew how to run in Ohio, and he knew how to win. He had run for elected office fourteen times, and lost only once, in 1990.

My own armor of certainty suffered some dings, though, with the onslaught of fretful colleagues. I didn't dare share their concerns with Sherrod. Whenever he asked what I was hearing in the newsroom, I'd tell him the latest complaints addressed on *The Plain Dealer*'s "Daynote," a regular e-mail missive in the newsroom that encouraged meaningful discussion about our daily efforts but also included answers to such vital and anonymous questions as "Why does the water taste funny in the water fountain?" and "How come the smokers don't have to stand across the street?"

Then came the plagiarism incident. A pro-labor blogger, Nathan Newman, who actually supported Sherrod, suddenly took center stage in Ohio's Senate race for the worst of reasons. Sherrod had wanted to challenge DeWine and force him to reconsider his vote of support for Bush's latest Supreme Court nominee, Samuel Alito, whose record on workers' rights was, to Sherrod, abysmal. Instead of an original letter being drafted (or at least one that cited its sources), staff missteps led to a section from an entry on Newman's blog being included in the letter, with no attribution. Without attribution or prior permission, it was in direct violation of office policy.

Sherrod knew nothing about the lifted material. He signed the letter, and off it went to DeWine. The DeWine campaign leaked the story to various newspapers around the state.

Four days later, *The Plain Dealer*'s Steve Koff wrote a story that ran on page A4 titled "Brown's Alito letter lifted from blogger."

"Brown's language was crisp—and was plagiarized," Koff wrote.

Sherrod and I did not know this kind of story was coming. We found out about it like hundreds of thousands of other readers, by opening our morning *Plain Dealer.*

The next day, the wire services carried the story that most other papers had chosen to ignore. One of the Cleveland TV stations teased the story twice before airing it, then led with the claim that Sherrod had "signed it in his own hand, which is plagiarism." They filmed the piece right outside *The Plain Dealer.*

In response, there was my husband, on the screen in our own living room, angrily accusing *The Plain Dealer* of "tabloid journalism"—not once, but twice.

Immediately, I called him.

"You make my life harder in the newsroom when you do that," I said. "You have a right to be angry, but I don't work for a tabloid and I hate when you say that. Some people will see that as attacking your wife, not just her employer."

"Sorry."

It was a short call.

That evening, Sherrod sent a second letter to DeWine, this one carefully crafted under the watchful eye of communications director Joanna Kuebler.

This time, no word from the DeWine office.

Over the next two days, three more pieces about the plagiarism incident ran in *The Plain Dealer.* Koff's follow-up included passages from Sherrod's second letter to DeWine, and quoted blogger Newman saying he was fine with Brown's copying his work without giving him credit, which only made me groan.

That same day, *The Plain Dealer*'s Jim Strang, who relished telling me that he lived in Sherrod's congressional district but had never voted for him, weighed in with an unsigned editorial titled "Rep. Brown's purloined letter." It was a litany of complaints against Sherrod: his "dilatory decision" to enter the race, a recent miscast vote that he quickly corrected from the House floor, and then the letter.

Okay, I told myself. At least the letter was behind us.

Or not.

The next day, *Plain Dealer* cartoonist Jeff Darcy ran a six-panel cartoon on the editorial page titled "MORE SHERROD BROWN PLAGIARISM."

Panel one: Sherrod as Hamlet, holding a skull and opining, "To be a Senate candidate, or not to be . . ."

Panel two: Sherrod forging his signature to the Declaration of Independence.

Panel three: Sherrod giving a speech, parroting JFK's "Ask not what you can do for your country . . ."

Panel four: Sherrod as Nixon, his hands up in peace signs, declaring "I am not a crook!"

Panel five: Sherrod as Charlie Brown, mortified that he has just cast a wrong vote, which had nothing to do with plagiarism, but who was I to quibble?

Panel six: Sherrod wearing a shirt with "Hackett" crossed out and "Brown for Senate" added, after having shot himself in the foot, over the caption, "Brownie, you're doin' a heckuva job."

It was the Nixon caricature that did me in. And so I did a stupid thing. I sent an e-mail to Darcy.

You certainly have the right, Jeff, to depict my husband in any way you choose. Today's cartoon, however, broke my heart. For 30 years, Sherrod has fought for those who would have no voice and no future without him and the few other elected officials who champion the most unpopular of causes. Your cartoon attempted to liken him and all he stands for to one of the most corrupt politicians in our lifetime.

I won't pretend your cartoon wasn't devastating, at least to me. I've been one of your biggest fans. I've been silent about all the rest of this week's coverage about a staffer's mistake, even though I thought it was blown entirely out of proportion, and probably because he is married to me. But today's cartoon, by you, was a sucker punch. I would never, ever have expected you to depict Sherrod in such an unfair and ugly way.

Just so you know, Sherrod remains a hero to so many. Especially to me.

Darcy never responded, but it made its way to editor-in-chief Doug Clifton. When I found out that Clifton had forwarded it to my department supervisor—who told me she defended me as a loyal wife—I dragged myself into Clifton's office.

"I know I shouldn't have sent that note to Darcy," I said.

Clifton nodded. He looked weary, not angry.

"It's only going to get harder here for you, Connie, and you're going to have to keep your feelings out of this."

"Or I'm going to have to leave," I said.

"Yeah," he said, nodding. "Let's hope that doesn't happen."

Later that evening, Joanna sent an e-mail to Sherrod that gave both of us a chance to take a deep breath and reminded us of what has always mattered most.

This is so beside anything relevant, but in light of our day, I thought I would share. I was at the store tonight and the cashier, who I know by face, chatted with me in our normal exchange of pleasantries. She saw my ID and asked where I worked. I told her I work for a Congressman from Ohio. We exchanged laments about our day and joked about finding a money tree.

I started to walk away when it occurred to me that I didn't know her name, despite my having "chatted" with her for more than two years.

I stopped, turned around and introduced myself. Her name is Chantale. We shook hands.

As I left the store, it honestly occurred to me that I learned that from you and Connie. And how much better the world would be if we all did that more.

I say this only because we are having a really rough time, but in the end, you guys are to the core something that is so rare, and what you both have makes a difference in the world.

I printed Joanna's e-mail, folded it into a tight square, and tucked it into my wallet for the long months ahead.

three

"I Want You to Be Wallpaper"

THE TURMOIL FOR ME AT *THE PLAIN DEALER*, BOTH INSIDE MY head and in the newsroom, seemed to increase with each passing week of Sherrod's campaign.

"I want you to be wallpaper," said Doug Clifton.

Doug was concerned that my presence, however passive, at Sherrod's campaign events could be interpreted as *Plain Dealer* support for Sherrod's candidacy. I told Doug most people would think I was standing alongside my husband because I was his wife. Besides, for the three years I'd been writing a column, I had been the far right's punching bag. It wasn't as if my politics were a mystery to even the most casual reader.

Yet I could appreciate Doug's skittishness. He was the one who would get the plaintive e-mails from readers—both inside and outside the newsroom, as it turned out—and, ultimately, the burden of me rested with him. I kept fighting this urge to apologize to him for falling in love in the first place. Instead, I assured him that I would abide by his dictate and blend into the background as best I could, even though what he suggested was quite a departure for me.

For the first four months of Sherrod's race, I looked far less engaged in the campaign than did the political groupies who aimed their cell phone cameras at us everywhere we went. I was wallpaper.

This did not, however, stop bloggers—and occasionally a colleague—from claiming otherwise. In early December, *Plain Dealer* reporter Bill Sloat, who lived and worked five hours away in Cincinnati, wrote Clifton an e-mail after he saw a story in the Cincinnati *Enquirer* that mentioned I had attended a church service where Sherrod spoke.

Clifton said Sloat told him he had no idea Sherrod and I were married, and that our marriage was going to complicate the life of every *Plain Dealer* reporter covering Sherrod's race.

"Will each reporter on the political beat eventually end up having to explain that what Connie does on her own time is her own business (as it is, of course)?" wrote Sloat. "Is it time for *The Plain Dealer* to explain that publicly, and up-front, now that the campaign has started?"

"Does he not read the paper he writes for?" I asked Clifton, who had called me into his office. I found it curious that Sloat had told Clifton he didn't even know Sherrod and I were married. *The Plain Dealer* had mentioned our marriage in several stories. In November 2005, I had devoted an entire column to our engagement after Clifton insisted that our society writer, Sarah Crump, cover it in her column.

Clifton shrugged his shoulders. "I think he raised important issues and I should write about them. We have to make sure readers know that we're aware of potential conflicts and that you and I agree on the boundaries."

Clifton's column, titled "Happy Couple Raise Issues in Newsroom," ran on *The Plain Dealer*'s op-ed page on Thursday, December 8, 2005. Doug showed it to me first, which I appreciated, and he didn't throw me out of his office when I said, yet again, that I thought an entire column about my marriage was overreacting.

Clifton outlined the potential conflicts, for me and for the paper. He mentioned Sherrod's primary race against "a promising young Democrat" named Paul Hackett. The "Brown-Schultz marriage will go from—for us—a sometimes ouchy, low-visibility one to one that is likely to become increasingly painful."

After several paragraphs about the unfortunate position I'd put him in, Clifton ended by assuring readers we all knew how to do our jobs:

> I have neither the ability to influence Sherrod Brown's conduct, nor the intent. But I do have influence over Connie and, happily, we're on the same page.
>
> She has a keen understanding of the delicate position she—and our paper—are in. She understands that she can't both campaign for her husband and write a column. And I understand that she is a supportive spouse who will be at her candidate husband's side from time to time.
>
> If there comes a time when Connie feels her obligations as the wife of a candidate require a more visible presence on the campaign, she will take a leave of absence. Meanwhile, look for Connie in her twice-weekly column, not campaigning for Sherrod Brown.
>
> And understand that Connie's relationship with candidate Brown will have no influence—for or against—our coverage of his campaign.

Clifton's column got wide coverage in media circles, and I received many supportive e-mails from journalists—mostly women—from around the country. The basic theme of the letters: Don't you give up your career.

Once Clifton's column appeared, I never stopped having to answer the insult wrapped in a question, universally posed only by men: Can Connie Schultz write her own opinions when she's married to Sherrod Brown? I know he didn't intend for that to happen, and I don't hold it against Clifton. But it did make me cranky for a long, long time.

FOR THE NEXT FEW WEEKS, I REMAINED IN THE BACKGROUND AT public events, but I was increasingly involved behind the scenes in the campaign. I took on so many additional responsibilities while trying to maintain a full-time schedule of column writing—not to mention navigating the increasingly rocky terrain of permissible topics—that the pace started to take a toll on both my nerves and my energy.

I was straddling two worlds, not taking up residence in either of them, and feeling lost much of the time. When I look back on it, I can see that what I most feared was that the Connie I knew—the writer I had known for years—was evaporating. I looked at the long road ahead and thought, *Wow, I could lose the marriage I cherish, the career I love, and the me I know, by the time this campaign is over.* It seemed like a lot to lose.

Gone were our late-night talks about everything, big and small, that had filled our days. No more walk-and-talks around the neighborhood, no end-of-the-week surprises when Sherrod would burst through the door shouting "I caught an early plane!" Most nights now, when he wasn't in session in Washington, he didn't drag through the door until almost midnight, if at all. Ohio is a big state, and often he stayed in a hotel so he wouldn't have to get up before five to get to the next day's first event. He wanted to be home every night, but doing so would wear him out long before the May primary took place.

Our entire life together had shifted. Now every conversation, no matter where it started, ended up being about the campaign. It was all politics, all the time, and it takes extraordinary discipline to maintain that level of focus without feeling that you've lost sight of everything else that matters in life. Every day, we told ourselves this race could help change the direction of the country. Most days, that was enough.

Instead of charging ahead to sort out all that was happening, I chipped away at myself, refusing to even admit how scared I was. My range of column topics got more and more narrow for fear of looking as if I were using my newspaper column to stump for my husband. My conversations with colleagues became fewer and narrower, too, because I had morphed from a colleague to a source. I didn't want to put them in a position of learning something through friendship that they knew they should put to use as journalists.

I also surrendered our social life to a scheduler, who was now planning our every night and weekend. Sometimes that was the hardest part of my life to give up, and I didn't always deal with it well. One incident in particular comes to mind.

It probably didn't help that I first learned about it after spending a grueling weekend folded in the backseat of the campaign car. Add to that a full day camped out at University Hospitals for my father's surgery on one of his two blocked carotid arteries. Even if I had spent the previous three days curled up in bed with a week's supply of Dom Perignon and Bugles—my idea of comfort food—I doubt I would have been a good sport about this one: The campaign had scheduled an out-of-town fundraiser on our second wedding anniversary.

I seldom asked for personal time with Sherrod. This was an exception, and one I didn't think needed much explaining beyond my saying, "Please keep this date open." I realize this may mark me a sappy romantic, but I think a middle-aged couple ought to celebrate the day they thumbed their noses at the failure rates of second marriages and declared their devotion for as long as they both shall live. Considering that we were forty-six and fifty-one at the time, we figured the odds were in our favor on that one.

As happens so often in campaigns, this snafu was somebody else's fault. The scheduler blamed the fundraiser and the fundraiser blamed the scheduler, and behind my back they both blamed me for being impossible to deal with.

What bothered me most was my reaction to this depressing news: Instead of feeling blue because my husband would be away on our special day, my mind immediately rocketed to the possible press coverage. What if a reporter found out that the Senate candidate who was supposed to be so in love with his bride blew off their anniversary to raise money? So what, some would say. But you never knew what could become a snarky item in a metro brief or on a newspaper's blog.

I imagined the press call: "You say you're running a values-driven campaign, Congressman, but you're dumping your wife on your anniversary? What kind of family values are those?"

"Is this why you kept your own name, Ms. Schultz? . . . Ms. Schultz?"

Two days later, I discovered that Sherrod was also scheduled to be in New York on April 19, the night we were to celebrate the publication of my first book. Random House was publishing a collection of my columns, *Life Happens,* and I had asked them to launch the book tour at Joseph-Beth Booksellers in Cleveland, out of loyalty to the town I called home. Hundreds of people were expected to attend—*in Cleveland, which is in Ohio, which is where he is running for senator,* I emphasized to the campaign scheduler and fundraiser, who were too busy blaming each other again to listen to the not-so-lovely wife, who was just impossible to deal with anyway.

When I told Sherrod, he shrugged his shoulders. "I don't know how this happened," he said.

The following week, I went to a private lunch before a "Women of Excellence" panel discussion with three prominent Cleveland women. One of the panelists turned to me and asked, "How does a marriage survive a Senate race?"

Still stinging from the botched wedding anniversary, I wanted to say, "I'll let you know."

Bad idea. So not the political-wife thing to do.

So, instead, I tried to sound as if I had it all figured out. "It's important for a couple to be cognizant of the pressures and mindful of the need to recalibrate when things get out of hand," I said as they all nodded.

Oh, hell, I thought. *Even I don't believe me.*

"Actually, I want to bounce something off you," I said to the three women I had just met. They leaned in, and I told them about the scheduling problems.

"That has to change," one of them said.

"You have to set the ground rules right now," another said. "No one screws with the wife."

"Yeah?" I said, quickly warming to my new sistahs.

"Yeah," they all said, nodding their heads and waving their forks in the air.

"Yeah," I said, waving my own fork now. I made a mental note to call Sherrod as soon as I was back in the car.

By the time I pulled out of the parking lot, though, Sherrod was calling me.

"I changed the schedule," he said, sounding as if he'd just won a seven-way primary. "I told them no to both, baby. We're going out to dinner for our anniversary, and I'm going to be front and center at your book signing. You won't be able to miss me: I'll be the tired guy trying not to cry at the sight of you."

FOR NEARLY FOUR MONTHS, I TOLD MYSELF THAT NO SENATE RACE, not even my husband's, was going to interfere with my column, which ran twice a week. It felt like the only thing left of my previous life, and I clung to it. My usual practice was to write first drafts by 11 A.M., then e-mail them to my editor and my computer at work. I'd drive the thirty minutes to the newsroom in downtown Cleveland for the final edit. Most other days I was either out interviewing or working the phone in the newsroom.

That schedule worked fine before I was sitting in on one early-morning conference call after another for the campaign during the week and then spending entire weekends on the road with Sherrod. Twice in early February, I drove into the *Plain Dealer* parking garage, turned off the car, and promptly fell asleep. It gets mighty cold during Cleveland winters, and I could count on shivering myself awake within a half-hour or so. I also started dozing behind the wheel in shopping centers a lot after work. I tried telling myself there was nothing at all unusual about falling asleep in various parking lots around northeast Ohio, but one conversation with a close friend, Dr. Gaylee McCracken, cured me of that little bit of magical thinking.

Gaylee has known me for nearly thirty years, and she is a woman used to being in charge. When I was about to separate from my first husband, she walked through my house with a pad of stickers to mark everything she thought I should take with me. When she found out I was dating Sherrod, she Googled him and gave me a full report.

She married young, was one of Cleveland's top-tier civic volunteers while raising two children, and was also a talented silkscreen artist. Her giant prints of seashores and flowers—many with images of human genitalia tucked into waves and petals—hang throughout my home.

Soon after Gaylee turned forty, she started feeling her life was missing something. Most women I know respond to such needling midlife urges by joining book clubs or learning sign language. Gaylee went to medical school. Eight years later, she was a full-time internist who fired patients if they didn't stop smoking after a year and during her annual reviews was always reprimanded for taking too long with her patients, who adored her.

I was not her patient, as I decided long ago that I didn't want a friend trying to make small talk while she had my legs up in stirrups. However, I'd been going to my own doctor, Patricia Kellner, for so long that she'd become my friend, too, so Gaylee wasn't exactly dissuaded from taking a medical interest in my comings and goings. She knew I'd had chronic asthma since I was sixteen, and starting about thirty seconds after Sherrod declared his race for the Senate, she regularly checked in to make sure I was taking care of myself. For a while, I lied to her with impunity, assuring her that I was keeping up with exercise (*so* not) and vitamins (not a one) and getting plenty of sleep (not even close). Then one evening, right around six, her call woke me up—in the car.

"Con?"

"Yeah," I said, trying to figure out (a) whose voice was on the phone and (b) when did it start to snow?

"Were you asleep?"

"Um, well, yeah. Just a little nap."

A driver in the car next to me slammed her door and pressed that annoying little key chain button, thus prompting her horn to trumpet to the entire world that her locks were securely engaged.

"Are you in a car?"

"Um, well, yeah."

"You're sleeping in your *car*?"

"Only for a few minutes."

"Where are you?"

I thought we'd just established that. "In my car?"

"*Where* in your car?"

"At Heinen's."

"Were you getting groceries?"

"That was the plan."

"Oh, my God."

"I'm fine."

"You're not fine," she said. "You're sleeping in the middle of a parking lot at six o'clock at night."

"Actually, I'm not really in the middle, I'm more on the side, near the Home Depot."

"This is funny?"

"Apparently not."

From that moment on, Gaylee was on the case. Her dozens of phone messages throughout the campaign usually began, "Not that you think you actually *need* me, but I am wondering how you're doing, and if you don't call back soon I'll assume you're asleep in a car somewhere. . . ."

By January, we were desperate for some good news in the campaign, and it came delivered by lanky, six-foot-one John Ryan, who agreed in mid-January to become Sherrod's campaign manager. Our campaign was a mess. We were hiring people willy-nilly, and

Sherrod was still getting hammered by bloggers and some Demo-cratic activists for opposing Hackett in the upcoming May primary. The fundraising machine was all but hibernating. We knew it, the press knew it, every Democrat we ran into knew it. John Ryan knew it, too, but it didn't stop him from taking one of the biggest leaps of his career.

We'd had a hard time finding a campaign manager. At first, Sher-rod had interviewed candidates, many of them high-profile, who were recommended by the national Democratic Party. All of them were from somewhere other than Ohio. One by one, they assured us they weren't coming to our state any time soon. Either they couldn't bring themselves to work in that state that had broken so many Kerry supporters' hearts, or they simply didn't think Sherrod could win. They never said that outright, of course, but they'd say things like, "Wow, you've got a tough race ahead," or, "Whew, you're going to need an *awful* lot of money to beat Karl Rove."

To this day, we don't know how we finally got the sense to turn to John Ryan. We've known him for years, and that's what we always call him, John Ryan, two names, like John Boy from *The Waltons*. Can't explain it. It's just who he is to us.

Well, he's that, and so much more.

For one thing, he was the devoted father of three daughters, and Sherrod often said John Ryan seemed to love his girls as much as Sherrod loved his. That mattered to Sherrod, who would throw him-self across train tracks for his Emily and Elizabeth. Like Sherrod, John Ryan regularly brought his girls to political events, so they often ran into each other with daughters in tow.

Sherrod grew close to Ryan because of their mutual passion for workers' rights and social justice. John Ryan was only twenty-one when he was elected president of the local union of the Communica-tions Workers of America. In 1996, he became president of the Cleve-land AFL-CIO. Ryan transformed their grassroots political operation into a well-oiled machine that backed candidates and issues that reg-ularly won. He was an ardent, in-your-face union activist who also knew how to get along with people in the business community. *Crain's Cleveland Business* named Ryan the fourth most influential Clevelander in their 2003 Top Forty listing.

One of my favorite John Ryan stories involves a discussion he had with his union activist father, Arthur, toward the end of his life. Arthur was in his mid-eighties, suffering from dementia and living in a nursing home. John Ryan regularly visited his dad late at night, after work and his many meetings, and one evening he showed up looking especially tired. He was volunteering nearly full-time for a county-wide Democratic candidate, and his father asked if he was getting paid overtime.

"What's that, Dad?"

"Overtime. You getting overtime for that?"

"No, Dad."

"You know what you need, son?"

"What's that, Dad?"

"You need a union."

I knew John Ryan from my time as a reporter and a union member with the Newspaper Guild–CWA. I didn't know a reporter who didn't trust him, and so it was easy to build a friendship once I started dating Sherrod. I continued to like him even after he spent months trying to cajole Sherrod into running for governor.

"Guv'nor," he'd say, whenever he ran into us.

"Mrs. Guv'nor," he'd add, nodding at my furrowed brow and then laughing in his high-pitched giggle.

One evening, after yet another candidate for campaign manager had turned us down, Sherrod and I were sitting in our family room and John Ryan's name came up. I don't know why, or how, and Sherrod can't remember either. We do, however, applaud ourselves now for our momentary flash of genius in a bumbling campaign at the time.

"John Ryan believes in you," I said.

"John Ryan believes in the work," Sherrod said.

"You can trust him."

Sherrod nodded. "Nobody works harder than John Ryan."

Sherrod walked upstairs to his office and made the call. He came downstairs, his face clouded.

"He's thinking about it," he said. "He's not sure he's up to it."

The following account of my subsequent and immediate call to John Ryan comes from him. I swear I don't remember this conversation, but I'm just as certain that John Ryan would never lie. Besides, it sounds like the act of a desperate wife.

According to John Ryan, I picked up the phone and dialed his cell number.

"John Ryan?"

"Hey, Connie. Hi."

"I know Sherrod just called you, and I know what he wants you to do."

"Okay. Well, I'm going to give it a lot of thought—"

"Look, John Ryan. If this is about your family, then I understand why you can't do this. But otherwise, I don't want to hear it. We need you."

And then John Ryan says I hung up on him.

John Ryan called the next day and said his wife, Jeanne, said he should do it.

For the rest of the campaign, when anyone asked John Ryan why he took the job, he said, "Catholic guilt and Connie Schultz's call."

In keeping with the theme of our campaign, almost everyone told us we were nuts: No labor guy from Cleveland could possibly run a successful campaign for the U.S. Senate.

That's what they said.

We are happy to report that they were wrong.

AFTER *THE PLAIN DEALER*'S COVERAGE OF THE PLAGIARISM INCIdent, I distanced myself from any and all at the paper who would be covering Sherrod's race. That included the entire editorial board and all the politics writers. In a couple of instances, this meant altering relationships with those I considered friends. It just seemed better for them, and for me, if we avoided talking altogether. I had gone from being a colleague to a potential source in the time it took Sherrod to say "I'm in."

At the end of January, *The Plain Dealer* launched its new political website, which included a blog called *Openers,* designed to make our coverage more immediate. Gone were the days when newspapers could keep a loyal readership simply by publishing a morning newspaper. The Internet, with its breaking-news immediacy, had changed that landscape, and newspapers were slowly learning how to compete.

Local political bloggers groused that *The Plain Dealer*'s chief motive was to neutralize their relevance, but that presumed *The Plain Dealer* had been paying much attention to them in the first place. At that point, they were gnats on the screen door. Later, some area bloggers, such as Jeff Coryell of *Ohio 2006* and Chris Baker of *Ohio 2nd,* would distinguish themselves as astute, sometimes newsbreaking, observers on Ohio's political scene. Others would write themselves into irrelevance.

Openers was actually a part of Doug Clifton's strategy for *The Plain Dealer* to dominate the mainstream media's coverage of Ohio's statewide elections. We knew from the 2004 election that our statewide races, particularly those for governor and the Senate, would be fodder for political writers around the country. Clifton was determined that no one would beat us in our own backyard.

As for the bloggers, the only thing Clifton seemed to care about was the vitriol they unloaded with predictable regularity on *The Plain Dealer.* Publicly, he said he didn't care about bloggers, but I was having a hard time believing that in light of his column about my marriage to Sherrod, which cited a passage from an anonymous blogger as his reason for writing it in the first place.

The Plain Dealer's blog allowed *Plain Dealer* political writers to file dispatches from the road throughout the day, encouraging political junkies to visit the newspaper's website regularly. It also provided a forum for audiotaped interviews with candidates. Paul Hackett's interview with the editorial board, which was rescheduled after he canceled the first time, was taped and then posted on *Openers.*

Immediately, Sherrod's campaign staff protested because, several weeks earlier, Sherrod had initiated a meeting with the *Plain Dealer* editorial board to discuss what he considered to be their unfair coverage of the campaign. An audiotape of that spirited discussion, though, had not been posted on the website.

Despite the suspicions of the campaign staff, this oversight was not, as it turned out, evidence of malice or a conspiracy against Sherrod. When a staffer called *Openers* editor Jean Dubail to ask why, his answer was simple: No one had taped Sherrod's interview because it was not yet common practice. I knew Jean well, as both a respected colleague and a friend. I didn't for a moment doubt his word.

Nevertheless, Hackett's audio did give him a leg up on coverage, which rankled some of Sherrod's staff. Privately, I worried that we were becoming hypersensitive to every hiccup in the press.

Much more disconcerting to me personally was *The Plain Dealer*'s decision to link to local political blogs on *Openers.* One of the links on the site was ardently pro-Hackett and regularly bashed Sherrod and me, at one point running a post referring to my "tits" in response to a lighthearted column I'd written about blogs. Another blogger predicted that DeWine supporters would "dismantle Connie and leave pieces of her bleeding at the roadside."

In early February, I sat at my desk in the newsroom and let sink in what was unfolding. With one click, *Plain Dealer* readers could devour whatever lies, mischaracterizations, and attacks bloggers felt like writing about us on any given day.

I understood that no newspaper covering Ohio politics could ignore the blogs. I also understood it was time for me to leave.

I talked to Karen Sandstrom, my longtime friend who had become my supervisor at the paper the previous year. She was sick over some of the blogs, but, like me, felt that *The Plain Dealer* couldn't ignore them. She was sympathetic, but she also knew that I had already been struggling mightily over what I could and, increasingly, could not write about in my column.

"I wrote about *pantyhose*," I said, wincing at the recent memory. She smiled. "It was very funny."

"I can't do funny all the time," I said. "I can't stop writing about all the things that really matter."

"No one said you had to," she said, but she started nodding her head as soon as I began rattling off the list.

The war in Iraq was a cornerstone of Sherrod's campaign.

Overworked pharmacists were trying to help senior citizens make sense of the new, impossibly complicated Medicare prescription drug plan. Great column, but Sherrod was holding news conferences in pharmacies around the state blasting the Republicans for passing legislation that was driven by the drug companies.

Voter registration, which I had championed in a series of columns in 2004, was off-limits, even as Republican secretary of state Ken Blackwell, now a candidate for governor, tried to push for more restrictions. His Democratic opponent, Congressman Ted Strickland, was Sherrod's close friend.

"Yeah," Karen said, nodding her head. "Doug would never let you write about that now."

I stared at her for a moment, then silently nodded. We both knew what was happening. *The Plain Dealer*'s website wasn't the reason I had to leave. It was just the final push I had known was coming: The website had forced me to lift the shade from the window to see how the landscape had changed. I could not be the columnist I wanted to be as long as Sherrod was running for the Senate. Slowly, but ever so surely, I was losing my voice. I could not give readers the column of substance they deserved, and I wasn't the journalist I wanted to be.

Before I went to see Clifton, I stopped by the desk of my editor, Stuart Warner. He had warned me that this day would come, but he had also urged me to think about what Sherrod's race could mean for the state and the country. Stuart and I had had many long talks about the importance of this race, and how Sherrod would need me with him on the road.

"You're going to be his secret weapon," Stuart had said more than once. "You'll do more good on the road than you can ever accomplish here." He never said it without scowling, though, because he knew how much I loved my job, and working with him. He was my editor, my mentor, and my friend.

"You'll never stop being a journalist," he had written in an e-mail to my home the previous week. "It's in your blood."

He looked at me now and didn't even try to smile. He knew what was coming. "I know this is hard for you, but it's the right thing to do," he said. "We're going to be covering the race more, and Sherrod is going to need you."

That night, Sherrod greeted the news with shock—and anger. Not at me, but at my profession. He was forever insisting that no one could possibly question my ethics or credibility, and I knew he meant that, but I also knew he was struggling with considerable guilt over the impact his decision to run was having on my life.

"There's no way you should have to stop writing about what matters to you," he said. "This is bullshit."

"It's not," I said, "and you know it's not. I have to avoid even the appearance of conflict, and that list of topics is growing too long."

He looked stricken, and I felt defeated. We had both known it would come to this, but his love for me and his faith in my integrity had never let him consider it a real possibility. His refusal to accept this inevitability had led to more than one argument, always unresolved.

"I'm so sorry," he said. "I didn't want to think this could ever happen to you."

The next day, on February 10, I met with Clifton to tell him I would write for the following week and then take a leave of absence for the rest of the campaign. To my surprise, he said he hadn't expected me to leave so soon. Like my supervisors, he grimaced when I told him what some of the bloggers were saying, and he nodded when I told him I wasn't having any fun anymore writing my column.

"You'll come back, right?" he said, after agreeing that I would write an exit column. "You have to say in that column that you'll be back in November."

Sherrod had left for Washington that morning. After speaking to Clifton, I went home that afternoon and didn't leave the house for the next two days. I needed to sit with my decision and think about what it would mean.

Then, the following Monday night, the campaign received stunning news. John Ryan and press secretary Joanna Kuebler were wrapping up a meeting at our home when an Elyria *Chronicle Telegram* reporter called to ask Sherrod one question: "Is it true that Paul Hackett has dropped out of the race?"

Sherrod had heard no such thing, and told him so.

Moments later, Joanna's cell phone rang. A campaign staffer read a breaking news story on *The New York Times*'s website: Two days before the primary filing deadline, Hackett was out. He was angry, too, claiming that Senators Chuck Schumer and Harry Reid had pressured him to get out of the race. He was done with politics, he told *New York Times* reporter Ian Urbina.

The Plain Dealer soon reported that Hackett's own pollster said that Sherrod was ahead by an almost 2-to-1 margin. With those kinds of numbers, Hackett couldn't possibly raise the money he needed to wage a primary race. And without Hackett, the Democratic field was clear for Sherrod. There would be no primary.

Sherrod greeted Hackett's news with relief.

"Well," he said, "at least Hackett's behind us now."

He couldn't have been more wrong.

STUART WARNER CALLED ME EARLY THE FOLLOWING MORNING.

"Would you reconsider your leave of absence? The coverage will die down for a while now that there's no primary."

Karen Sandstrom also asked me to stay longer. "Doesn't this change things?"

For a whole twenty-four hours, I thought maybe they were right. Maybe I could continue to write a column for a while.

Then one of my oldest friends at the paper, editorial writer Joe Frolik, wrote a blistering attack on Sherrod—without identifying himself as a longtime family friend. Our families had celebrated many birthdays and holidays together. His take on the race was a two-fisted thrashing of Sherrod, a litany of my husband's flaws through Joe's eyes.

I had no idea it was coming until I woke up that morning and turned to our op-ed page. The lengthy column, wrapped around a large photo of Sherrod and his friend Congressman Ted Strickland, was titled, "Brown Has a Little Time to Get Back on His Game."

When I arrived at the newsroom, several colleagues and a couple of editors mentioned the column to me. All of them said they were surprised by the vitriol, and they raised the same question ricocheting in my own head: Why wasn't that writer held to the same standard of full disclosure as I? Why didn't he reveal his family's long-term friendship with the candidate's wife?

When I read Joe's column now, all these months later, it doesn't ignite the rage I felt at the time. He is a smart and gifted writer, and I wish him well. But his column still stings. I had tried to step as carefully as possible in the newsroom after Sherrod announced his candidacy. I had stopped attending newsroom meetings about political coverage, to avoid even the appearance of scouting for the campaign. I knew that Sherrod's race would be scrutinized at every turn, which is what good journalists do—and I worked with some of the best. But I could not accept that after more than twenty years of friendship, there was no warning that my friend's column was coming. And if I could not accept that, it was time for me to go.

I told Stuart and Karen Sandstrom that my decision was final: The next day's column would be my last. Even friends in the newsroom who had argued earlier in the week that I should stay until the summer now agreed there was no way I could.

Stuart asked to speak to me privately. I thought he was going to lobby me to change my mind, but he was doing what he has always done for me in the newsroom. He was looking out for me one last time.

"If you don't remember anything else I've told you in the last four years we've worked together, I want you to remember this," he said. "The media are not your friends anymore. The people here are not your friends. They are journalists covering your husband's race, and your history with them does not matter."

I hated that he said that, and I hated that he was right. I felt as if I were losing an entire community of friends.

The day before my last column ran, *The Plain Dealer*'s reader representative, Ted Diadiun, announced my impending departure in the "Daynote," a daily in-house e-mail to the newsroom:

> A FOND (AND TEMPORARY) FAREWELL:
>
> As you will read in her column tomorrow, Connie Schultz will be on sabbatical through the end of the political campaign in order to avoid the inevitable charges of conflict of interest while her husband, Sherrod Brown, campaigns for the U.S. Senate. The energy she brings to both the newsroom and the pages of *The Plain Dealer* will be sorely missed.
>
> This might be a waste of typing energy, but it would sure be nice if our readers could learn this news from Connie before somebody sends it to Romenesko and the blogosphere. That said, in the office pool for how long it will take for the news to get out there, "Daynote" claims 30 minutes after this posting.

Ted was off by twenty minutes. Ten minutes after he hit the send button, Jim Romenesko, who edits one of the most popular journalism blogs in the country on the Poynter Institute's website, called my direct line at *The Plain Dealer*. "I wanted to beat the thirty-minute deadline," he said, chuckling. "On principle, you know."

My column was posted that evening on the *Plain Dealer*'s website and ran in the next day's paper, on February 16. I wrote it in less than an hour, probably because I'd had plenty of time to think about what I wanted to say. I didn't want anyone to think I had been forced to leave. It mattered to me as a journalist, and as a feminist, that this was my decision, my timing. I also didn't want a lot of women readers blaming Sherrod. I laid out my reasoning—and my life—as clearly as I could, hoping that no one would read imaginary motives between the lines. I wrote about how much I loved my job, then laid out the conflict:

> I still want to write about what's on my mind, but that is becoming increasingly difficult. Each passing week brings more limitations in my choice of topics because there is a concern that some will accuse me of using my column to stump for my husband.
>
> As a woman and a feminist, the suggestion that I am merely parroting my husband both amuses and offends me.
>
> As a journalist, however, I am sensitive to even the appearance of conflict. I am also keenly aware of the difficulties my remaining in this job could create for my colleagues, some of whom are dear friends, who must cover the Senate race.
>
> As a wife, I feel the pull to be the partner my husband deserves. Sherrod has been incredibly supportive of my career at every turn. Not once has he ever asked me not to write about an issue, even when he knew it might create problems with some of his constituents.
>
> I want to be just as unequivocally by his side now. I cannot play a significant role in his campaign as long as I work at this newspaper.
>
> Now comes the hard part.
>
> What may not feel great for me is better for everyone around me. So, this column is my last for a while. I'm taking a leave for the duration of the campaign.

I assured readers that this was my decision, and that I planned to return to the paper after the election. I ended by reminding them of some of the people who had driven my work as a columnist:

> In the meantime, please remember to ask who gets the money in the tip jar at the coat check and at the bar.
> Tip restaurant servers in cash whenever you can.
> And if you or someone you love is thinking of settling down with another human being, keep in mind what my mother always told us girls:
> "Don't marry him 'til you see he how treats the waitress."

Over the next few days, hundreds of readers weighed in, almost all of them incredibly kind. Even those who made sure I knew they usually didn't agree with me politically wished me well, although occasionally making it clear they weren't so sure about Sherrod. "I'm going to miss the column," wrote one man who worked for an insurance company. "I don't think you'll be gone for long. I think Sherrod is going to have a tough time beating DeWine. Maybe he should try being a house husband!"

One of the most meaningful notes came from my colleague John Campanelli. John was at least a decade younger than I, the devoted father of two elementary-age children, and a gifted writer. I knew him as the funny guy who sat in the row in front of me, but I didn't realize we had working-class roots in common until he wrote this e-mail, which he sent as soon as he heard I was leaving:

> I'm going to say this now, because it's safe to assume that things might get kind of hectic next week (and because it's so much easier for me to express things with a keyboard).

> My grandfather came to Cleveland in 1922, made a living with a strong back, hauling cinders from the mills and then selling them to concrete companies. He didn't make it past third grade in Italy, but he never resented "the guys in the ties" like some of the other laborers did. He sacrificed plenty so his son, my dad, could go to college and be one of

those guys in the ties. My grandfather and father taught me about pride in work and pride in city—as much as a suburban kid can feel, anyway.

And I can tell you that I have never felt a greater pride for my city and paper, the one I delivered as a kid, than when that guy—because of you—came forward and confessed to the rape that had been pinned on Michael Green. That feeling was then eclipsed when you won journalism's highest honor.

I want to thank you for that. That's just really, really cool.

Working in the same newsroom with you has been an honor.

John's letter reminded me of where I come from, and why those roots mattered. I wasn't losing my job, nor was I facing the kind of daily grind that wore my father out. I was about to take a leave of absence from a job I loved so that I could help my husband run for the United States Senate. What a privilege.

On Tuesday, February 28, I drove out of the *Plain Dealer* parking garage for the last time in 2006. I pulled my gray Pontiac Vibe into a carwash about a block away, blasting Bruce Springsteen as the suds poured down my windows. When it was finished, I pulled to the side of the lot, got out of my car, and dried off my bumper with one of my gloves. Then I reached into the glove box and pulled out what I'd been waiting for weeks to stick to the back of my car.

It was a red, white, and blue bumper sticker: "Sherrod Brown for U.S. Senate."

I hit the highway, focused on the road ahead.

four

My Husband, the African American Woman

JACKIE AND I WERE HAVING DINNER IN CLEVELAND WHEN A WAITress came up to me and said, "Ms. Schultz, I'm sorry to bother you, but did you know that Fox News is saying your husband is Shur-ROD Brown, and that he's a woman?"

"That explains so much," Jackie said, shaking her head.

I threw a cherry tomato at her and thanked the waitress for the update.

Radio talk show host Rush Limbaugh had also weighed in on Ohio's Senate race with his usual brand of wisdom. Paul Hackett had dropped out, Limbaugh said, because the Democratic bigwigs wanted Sherrod—which he, too, pronounced "Shur-ROD"—who was African American.

Reporters, talk show hosts, and bloggers were having a lot of fun with all this. So, when I gave a speech the following day to about 150 women, I thought it was best to come clean.

"Well, as you all know by now, Rush Limbaugh said my husband is African American."

Laughter, mixed with a few gasps by those who listen only to public radio.

"And Fox News said he is a woman."

More laughter, now mixed with much shaking of heads.

"So, you see, I'm even more liberal than you thought. I'm actually married to an African American woman."

Oh, we hooted and hollered over that one. Nothing like a room full of rowdy women to clear your head.

I may have been making jokes, but our new campaign manager, John Ryan, was all business.

John called a mandatory meeting for all staff.

"I want you there, too, if you can make it," he said in a phone call to my cell. "Sherrod has to be in Washington, but I want everyone to understand how serious these ground rules are, and your being there will drive it home."

"Ah, yes, Frau Schultz, that will scare them."

"Connie."

"I'll be there."

It would be one of only three times I would show up at the headquarters during the campaign, bloggers' claims notwithstanding. ("She's running everything!" one blogger declared. This came on the heels of Sherrod's telling *The Plain Dealer* that his wife was a chief strategist. Like that's not true in *every* healthy marriage.)

Aside from these three visits, my physical absence from headquarters was deliberate. I'd heard too many horror stories about overbearing political wives, and I wanted to make it clear to everyone that Sherrod and I trusted John to hire the people we needed to do the job. The last thing John needed was a hovering wife who threw her weight around just because she could. John said he was asked many times during the campaign what it was like to work in a campaign with two strong-willed people at the helm, and he always told them that

Sherrod and I never tried to strongarm him or undermine him. Why would we? We wanted John because he was a proven organizer and leader, and we knew he would worry so we wouldn't have to—which his subsequent new crop of gray hair clearly proved is exactly what he did. Nobody sweated the small stuff like John Ryan, and we relied on him every single day.

One of the policies we established early with John Ryan was that Sherrod and I, not the campaign, would pay for all of my flights and our kids' flights. We did not think it was fair to take contributions from people who supported Sherrod's race and then use some of those funds to fly his family around, and we made sure that everyone on staff knew this was our policy.

At the meeting, John asked everyone to introduce themselves and invited a variety of staffers to speak before he laid down the ground rules for the campaign. The room grew silent as he rattled off the list:

- Every e-mail can be subpoenaed. Use good judgment. Don't write anything you wouldn't want to read in the next day's newspaper.
- Never, ever use government e-mail for campaign communications. No campaign e-mails to the congressional office, and vice versa.
- No government staff may work for the campaign during office hours.
- Everyone should learn where the panic button is located in the office, as well as the code word if someone feels threatened by a visitor. You yell it out, someone else knows to call 911. (This came about in part because of several attacks on Kerry workers in Ohio in 2004.)
- No woman walks unescorted to her car at night.
- Everything you do and say is for public consumption.

"For a lot of people, you're the closest they'll ever come to meeting Sherrod," John said. "Remember that. When you're out there talking to people, when you're in here answering the phones, whenever you open your mouth on behalf of the campaign, you represent Sherrod Brown. Remember who he's fighting for, and live up to that promise every single day."

I looked around the room at all the young faces, many of which I was still trying to name, and wondered what brought these people to this place, at this time, for this candidate. I hoped they were there for all the right reasons—including the eleven million people of Ohio who deserved better than what they were getting from their government.

As it turned out, almost to a person, that's exactly why the staff were there.

CAMPAIGNS ARE LIKE LITTLE COMMUNITIES, WITH ALL THE ATTEN-dant problems of small-town life. Gossip, office romances, personal crises, and behind-the-scenes conniving—it was all there, and far more easy to discern than most of the staff realized. Sherrod certainly didn't need to know about all that. In the process of protecting him, though, I lost my closest confidant.

To get Sherrod focused, Ryan developed a system that removed Sherrod from much of the day-to-day concerns and pulled me in, to the point where I would tell Sherrod about developments and problems only on a need-to-know basis. Let Sherrod focus on the big things: raising money, giving speeches, holding news conferences.

Some staff members tried to expense their parking tickets? Please don't tell Sherrod.

An employee posted anonymously on a nasty blog? Dumb thing to do, don't let it happen again. Sherrod remained unaware.

But when we hired a staffer who claimed he was twenty-five and an ordained minister, and then found out that he was neither? Oy. Gotta tell Sherrod that one.

Never did I think I'd be in this position with my husband, but as the campaign wore on, I saw how important it was to insulate him from much of the day-to-day missteps and mini-crises.

Ryan's list of priorities for Sherrod gave him more than enough to worry about, particularly if he was ever to meet the monthly and quarterly fundraising goals. Heaped onto this stress were initially impossible demands.

Kimberly Wood, our Ohio campaign finance director, was young and talented and shared Sherrod's commitment to social and economic justice. She knew how to raise money, too, but she had yet to learn how to deal with Sherrod in a way that didn't make him want to pull out his eyebrows. She meant well, but she had a habit of pushing him in ways that he felt suggested he wasn't trying hard enough. As he kept reminding her, "Kimberly, nobody wants to win this race more than I do." To which she would always respond, "I know. I know. Sorry." And then she'd push him even harder.

The chief role of campaign fundraisers is to identify potential donors and then provide the candidate with call sheets listing their names and phone numbers. The call sheets must be updated regularly, ideally on a daily basis, so that there's no such thing as "downtime" on the campaign. The only exceptions to fundraising calls were when he was attending fundraising meetings or fundraising events or giving speeches or media interviews. Sherrod wasn't expected to call when he was asleep, but he was encouraged not to make sleep a habit.

By February, Sherrod was getting frustrated with his fundraising team, and not because he didn't understand the importance of raising money. Many days, that was all he did. But he was making up for lost time after a late and difficult beginning, and it seemed that all he heard from our team was how his efforts weren't enough. They were young drill sergeants, and the concept of positive reinforcement was often lost on them. But there was a bigger problem, and that was how to get Sherrod refocused after he'd spent so many weeks worrying about everything. Now we had John Ryan, but by the time John became campaign manager, Sherrod had already spent too much time and energy weighing in on the minutiae. Meddling had become a habit. He was fretting over staff hires and salaries, campaign material and media coverage, and regularly placing phone calls over what was and wasn't getting done.

Ryan, who was concerned about fundraising, called me. He'd known Sherrod for nearly two decades, and he knew no one campaigned harder than Sherrod. What he wanted to do was break Sherrod's habit of weighing in on all aspects of the campaign.

"We have to get him focused, Connie," he said. "He has to make more fundraising phone calls, and Kimberly wants him to have someone from her team with him all the time to help dial and answer the phone." We agreed that I would wait to talk to Sherrod until after his meeting the next day with Ryan and Kimberly.

Ryan laid out his marching orders for Sherrod in a memo, which he updated at least weekly and sent to the two of us throughout the campaign: "Your brain, energy and commitment must be fully focused on three activities you do well: speaking to voters, media and raising money."

In a meeting at our home two days later, he told Sherrod that the campaign must target swing voters, and that Sherrod would have to raise an impossible amount of money, between $14 million and $17 million.

"If we have enough money, you will win," he said,

Months later, when our own polling showed Sherrod steadily pulling ahead, Ryan finally admitted to us that early in the campaign he did not think Sherrod could beat DeWine no matter how much money he raised.

"So you lied to us?" Sherrod said in mock horror.

"No," Ryan said, grinning. "You never asked if I thought you could win."

Ryan's first priority with the campaign was damage control. He had to, as he put it, "unhire" some people who had been hired without Sherrod's knowledge, and at high salaries. This included two of the national fundraisers. Ryan agreed with Sherrod's assessment that they weren't doing their jobs, and he promptly fired them. They were replaced by Kim Kauffman, a tireless Democratic fundraiser who, like our Ohio fundraising director, Kimberly Wood, shared Sherrod's political vision—and always returned his calls and e-mails, which was a dramatic improvement.

By mid-February, Sherrod was averaging about fifty fundraising calls a week. Ryan and Kimberly met beforehand to develop a script for their conversation with Sherrod.

"We're going to set a goal for Sherrod," Ryan told her. Later, he admitted it hadn't occurred to him that he should explain to Kimberly that Sherrod would be the one to set the goal, with their help. Instead, Kimberly suggested to Sherrod that he had to start making four hundred calls a week. Fortunately for Kimberly, she announced this in a restaurant, over lunch, surrounded by lots of potential voters. Unfortunately for her, she didn't realize just what button she had pushed. Sherrod is a math whiz. He loves numbers. The dictionary stand in our kitchen holds not a dictionary, but an encyclopedia of baseball statistics. This is not a man you want to bully with numbers.

"Kimberly," Sherrod said, "that is not humanly possible." Kimberly, of course, disagreed. Like most good fundraisers, she thought her part of the campaign was the only thing that mattered. This was in direct conflict with our field staff, who thought voter contact was the only thing that mattered, and our communications staff, who were convinced that press coverage was the only thing that mattered. To be fair, they all were willing to concede that maybe there should be a little time set aside for "those other things," as long as it didn't conflict with what really mattered.

After a spirited discussion, Kimberly finally agreed with Sherrod that perhaps two hundred calls a week was a more reasonable goal. That way Sherrod could at least leave a message with the potential donors he called—at least 65 percent of the time his first call was to a secretary or voice mail—and he'd also have time actually to talk to them if they returned his call.

Sherrod refused, however, to let someone else place his calls. "I've never done that," he said. "I never did that in my office, and I'm not going to do that now. It sends the wrong message, that I think I'm too important to dial my own phone." I told Ryan I didn't see Sherrod budging on that one, and I agreed with his decision. From the beginning, Sherrod and I insisted that he would never compromise his core values, and this was one of them.

A deal was a deal. From March 1 through November 5, Sherrod averaged 201 calls a week, and in that time the campaign raised more than $7 million.

Sherrod dialed his own phone, every single time.

MY FIRST SPEECH FOR SHERROD WAS ONE I DIDN'T EVEN KNOW I would be giving until an hour before I was scheduled to go up on-stage at the Ohio Democratic Party's endorsements meeting in Columbus, the state capital. I was on my way there, but my plan was to watch my husband accept the party's endorsement and then go to dinner with him. Instead, I was on the phone with John Ryan, who called to tell me that Sherrod was running late and they needed me to speak for him.

It was fairly uneventful, if you didn't count the two men who told me they hated Sherrod for running against Hackett, and the fretful party chairman, Chris Redfern, who pulled me aside right before I stepped onstage to ask if I'd ever given a speech before. I assured him I wouldn't embarrass him or anyone else and proceeded to thank everyone for supporting my husband, even though I knew full well there were plenty in that auditorium who thought Sherrod could not win.

I looked out at the crowd and decided to tell them a story about the man behind the office. In late 2003, the Medicare drug bill, which Sherrod had opposed, finally passed in the middle of the night, by one vote. Sherrod and many other Democrats had fought hard against the bill, which they believed would hurt the many senior citizens who would no longer be able to afford adequate health care. Even the Republicans knew that most Americans opposed the bill, and so the vote was held open against House rules into the early morning hours, until enough members had been browbeaten or threatened into changing their votes.

Sherrod finally left the House chambers around six in the morning, and he called me from a street corner in Washington, his voice raw.

"What's wrong?" I asked.

He drew a deep breath, and kept pausing between words. "I just crossed paths," he said. "I just crossed paths with a chambermaid. She had to be in her sixties, she was wearing her uniform and standing at a bus stop."

I waited for him to finish.

"I couldn't look her in the eye," he said, his voice breaking. "I couldn't look at her because I knew what we'd just done to her."

The crowd grew silent as I shared that story about Sherrod. "That's my husband," I said. "And that's your next senator."

Later that evening, Sherrod and I were finally together and decided to stop at the Blue Danube Tavern in downtown Columbus before checking into our hotel for the night. The place was packed, and Sherrod pulled out of his inside breast pocket a stack of campaign brochures and started working the room. A few moments later, he came back with a stunned look on his face.

"What happened?"

"It's gonna be a long campaign, baby."

He had stopped at a table of middle-aged women who had clearly been eating and drinking for a while. All but one of them were friendly, but that one was a real doozy.

"Are you a Democrat or a Republican?" she asked Sherrod.

"Democrat."

She flipped the brochure back at him.

"I guess you find Democrats repugnant," he said.

· She nodded.

"Well, the Republicans have done such a fine job running Ohio," he said.

She scowled at Sherrod. "At least they don't fuck everything that moves and then deny it."

Proving once again why he, and never I, could be a candidate for elected office, Sherrod just walked away. When he recounted the story, I immediately whirled around to get a look at her. She stared right back at me, but her dinner companions looked away.

"I could take her," I said.

"Honey."

"Well, I could."

We looked at each other and laughed. Not hard, mind you, but we managed a chuckle.

Long campaign, indeed.

THE NEXT DAY, WE STOPPED AT A BOB EVANS RESTAURANT ON THE way back to Cleveland. Sherrod loves Bob Evans, or at least he did as long as he could order their vegetable stir-fry. Recently, though, they had dropped it from the menu, and whenever we were hungry we searched for a Bob Evans so that we, and any staff member unlucky enough to be with us, could fill out a complaint form requesting the return of vegetable stir-fry.

I blame the waitress named Michelle. I don't remember which Bob Evans she worked at, but I will never forget the spark she lit under my husband when she answered his question about the vegetable stir-fry.

"If you want it back, you have to fill out a complaint card."

"Will that do any good?"

She nodded her head with the authority of a woman who's seen things. "That's what happened with Italian dressing. Enough people filled out the complaint card and they brought it back."

From then on, Sherrod put us all to work. "We have to fill these out," he said, passing out the cards to all of us at the table. "Tell them we want the vegetable stir-fry back on the menu."

Sherrod always wrote the same thing: "Please bring back the vegetable stir-fry."

I always wrote the same thing, too: "Please bring back the vegetable stir-fry so that my husband will stop complaining and I can eat my fruit plate in peace."

During this particular Bob Evans stop, an elderly woman wearing a cobalt blue sweater that matched her eyes approached Sherrod as he munched on a roll.

"Congressman?"

Sherrod looked up and smiled.

"My future son-in-law lives in Franklin County," she said. "For three years, he's been trying to get his Social Security. I don't know if this is something you can help with?"

Sherrod ripped off a corner of his placemat and wrote down his name and government office number. "I'm not promising anything, but we'll see what we can do," he said.

She smiled. "I'm hoping he'll be my son-in-law down the road."

"Well, I'm not talking to him about that," Sherrod said, grinning.

"Well, okay, then," she said.

I watched her walk away and couldn't help but think of the angry woman we'd encountered less than twenty-four hours ago.

Sherrod, though, had other things on his mind.

"Did you fill out the complaint card?" he said as we gathered our belongings to leave. "Remember, the people brought back Italian dressing, and the people can bring back vegetable stir-fry, too."

Despite our best lobbying efforts, though, we have yet to see vegetable stir-fry at a Bob Evans. Sherrod, however, remains hopeful.

five

Focus

WHEN SHERROD CALLED FROM THE BED IN OUR TINY WASHINGTON efficiency, his voice sounded even huskier than usual. It was early March, seven-thirty in the morning, and he was clearly sick. And exhausted.

"I don't want to move," he said. "I don't want to do anything."

This was not the Sherrod I knew. I'm the one who rolls out of bed and, too often, right onto the floor. He springs to life like the first robin sprinting across the lawn.

The day before, he had visited the doctor, who prescribed cough syrup with codeine to control the hacking and give him a chance to sleep. Normally, Sherrod won't even take Tylenol for a headache, but he was worn out from coughing throughout the previous night and running nonstop all day along the Capitol's marble floors and stairways, which he insisted on climbing for the pedometer steps.

The codeine, though, had offered no reprieve. Two doses, at bedtime and then in the middle of the night, couldn't keep him from tossing and turning most of the night. I had a feeling more than the head cold was impairing his sleep.

"You're worried all the time, that's probably why," I said.

"Yeah," he said. "This morning John Ryan sent me an e-mail. Looks like Hackett was on *The Daily Show* last night."

He hesitated for a moment.

"They said Hackett was twenty points ahead in the polls when he dropped out."

"You're kidding," I said. Paul Hackett had actually *trailed* Sherrod by at least that much by the time he dropped out of the race, but that wasn't the point. We were paying too much attention to every poll that popped up—and to Hackett's continuing coverage. He was out of the race, but not yet out of Sherrod's head.

A recent column by *Newsweek*'s Eleanor Clift had suggested, as other journalists had, that Hackett had dropped out because Democratic Party officials were circulating rumors meant to impugn his military service in Iraq.

"The only way the Republicans can win in Ohio," she wrote, "is if the Democrats blow it, and they're working at it. Democratic Party leaders pressured Iraq war veteran Paul Hackett to withdraw from the Senate race (in favor of a veteran congressman) with undercover operatives launching a whisper campaign about Hackett's service that was reminiscent of the Swift Boat Veterans for Truth campaign against Kerry—and equally reprehensible."

Who were these "undercover operatives"? And what were the rumors? It was much easier to suggest than to report. Some journalists repeated Hackett's charge that Sherrod knew about the rumors and encouraged their dissemination, which was false. The only time a staff person approached us with even the hint of a rumor about Hackett's service in Iraq was in December 2005, while Sherrod and I were meeting at national Democratic headquarters in Washington. Immediately, Sherrod cut this person off in midsentence.

"I don't want to hear anything about this, and I don't want you or anyone else on my campaign involved in spreading any of these rumors about Paul Hackett. Period." When we later suspected he had violated Sherrod's order, he was fired.

All of this was catching up with Sherrod. "You aren't feeling well," I told him. "You had a fever two nights ago, you've got a bad cold, and everyone's on you all the time about fundraising. It's hard to have perspective right now."

I reminded him that we weren't alone in this race. "If you're meant to win, God will help make it possible. We have to have faith."

"I need to have better call lists," he said, referring to the donor contact lists regularly generated by our fundraising team. "That's what I need." His response threw me, coming from the man who still played songs from a Lutheran hymnal on our piano in the living room to relax.

I tried to remember the last time he'd done that, and came up empty.

Then I tried to recall the last time I'd heard Sherrod whistle. He used to whistle all the time—at his desk at home, in the kitchen, walking the dog, even in the shower.

For weeks now, he'd been silent.

"I really, really love you," I said.

"Thanks," he said quietly. "I love you, too." I knew he had to get ready for a breakfast meeting, so we agreed to talk later in the day.

I hung up the phone and pushed away from the kitchen table, no longer hungry for the English muffin in front of me. I walked down the hall to my office. What was happening to us?

Signing on to the computer, I started searching my e-mail for Google alerts, looking for references to *The Daily Show.* There it was, lodged between the daily morning newspaper alerts and spam. It turned out to be not a newspaper story, but an account by a blogger who described himself as "a magazine editor, a freelance writer, a capitol hill staffer, a game designer and a history professor" and proud contributor to another blog titled *The Elitist Pig.* What he didn't mention was his championing of the far right on many other blogs, which only five minutes of research revealed.

Nevertheless, he now had the political blogosphere's attention. "Today I was reminded yet again," his blog entry began, "that you don't really 'get' the news unless you watch *The Daily Show* on Comedy Central." He repeated Hackett's accusation that Democratic leaders "did everything they could to persuade him not to run and eventually tried to sink his campaign with dirty tricks during the primary."

I tried finding an actual clip of the show. I checked out the *Daily Show* site. Nothing. I clicked onto a blog search engine, and started typing various word combinations in search of the video clip.

Then I caught myself.

What was I doing? I was getting all worked up about something we should just ignore. Sherrod was running for the Senate because he cared about what was happening to so many Americans who were suffering under their own government's policies, and those Americans should be our focus. Sherrod knew that, and so did I, but somehow we kept letting ourselves get distracted by static.

I needed to get a grip.

I remembered what Jack Dover, Sherrod's beloved chief of staff in the congressional office, told me over a recent dinner in Washington. It was a rare moment to relax. We were waiting for Sherrod to show up, so Jack had ordered a bottle of merlot and I could feel the warmth rise in my cheeks as I settled back and enjoyed the time alone with him and his wife, Agnes, a lawyer who is as smart and kind as they come. She nodded sympathetically as Jack leaned over and forecast my future:

"You are going to be such a different person at the end of this campaign," he said.

"What do you mean?" I said.

"You'll see."

I remember wishing he'd said that with a smile.

Now, here I was, only a few weeks later, pounding the keyboard in search of more distractions.

Such a different person. The memory made me shiver.

I logged off the computer and pushed away from my desk.

Focus, I told myself. *Focus.*

ONE WEEK LATER, SHERROD OFFERED A GLIMPSE INTO THE FEAR that I hadn't quite known was haunting him.

Joanna, our driver Walter O'Malley, and I were in the car with him, driving back to Cleveland. Sherrod had given a speech to 250 progressives in Solon, a suburb southeast of Cleveland. Something had happened to Sherrod in that room, and we were all trying to figure out what. For the first time in weeks, he was on fire.

We had been astonished to find a standing-room-only crowd in this suburb, which was known as much for its lack of diversity as for its tremendous growth in the last two decades. Sherrod poked his head into the room, turned around, and started laughing.

"Can you believe this?" he said, his eyes wide. "In *Solon?*"

Sherrod was lively and quick during his short talk, ending his speech by promising two headlines in newspapers across the country on November 8:

"The first headline, in *The New York Times* and the *Los Angeles Times,* in the *Chicago Tribune* and *The Miami Herald,* is going to say, 'Democrats take back the House and Senate.' "

The crowd cheered.

"The second headline is going to say, 'Ohio Turns Blue.' "

That brought the crowd to its feet. Sherrod glanced over at me and grinned. Then he started taking questions, and as he answered, the audience grew more animated.

One man stood up and asked how Sherrod planned to defeat "DeWine the moderate." Sherrod lunged: Mike DeWine, he said, was no moderate.

"Mike DeWine voted for the Iraq War," he said. "I voted against it." The audience exploded.

"Mike DeWine voted for the energy bill. I voted against it." More cheers.

"Mike DeWine voted to privatize Social Security. I voted against it." Applause, more cheering. Clearly, though, the war was his home-run line.

I leaned over to Joanna, who had the same immediate response.

"He needs to reverse the order on that," I said. She showed me the sheet of paper in her hand and laughed. "War last, not first," she had written.

I watched my husband in front of those cheering people and smiled at the change that was unfolding right before my eyes. He was more relaxed, no longer tripping over his words. He was defiant one minute, funny the next. In a wise, measured voice, he talked about how he and the Democrats would be different. Not once did he stumble, nor did he get that weary look on his face when someone challenged him.

I looked over at Walter, who flashed me his thumbs-up grin. He saw the change, too.

The crowd gathered around Sherrod afterward, and many of them approached me, too, buzzing about his "great speech" and how excited they were to work for him. One man, an African American businessman still wearing his three-piece suit and tie, told me he had never heard Sherrod speak before. "Now that I've heard him, I want to help him," he told me. "I filled out a volunteer card. Count me in."

On the drive home, Sherrod listened for a few minutes from the front seat as Walter, Joanna, and I offered our post-speech review, peppered with praise for how strong he seemed.

"You had them hoppin' like popcorn in a skillet," I said. He rolled his eyes and grinned.

"What's changed?" I asked him. "You were a lot gutsier tonight."

Sherrod nodded, leaned back into his seat, and looked through the windshield straight ahead as he spoke. "I've been afraid," he said.

Walter and Joanna were silent. I was surprised he was willing to admit any fears in front of staff members, even Walter and Joanna, two of our most trusted confidants.

"Why?" I asked.

I was wondering if he would repeat what he had been sharing privately with me during our early morning talks at home in recent days. It was always in that quiet time, when the neighborhood was still dark and we could hear the hoot owl calling from the trees out back, that Sherrod would occasionally reach over, grab my hand, and softly say, "I woke up scared today."

The first time this happened, I let it rattle me. I was used to Sherrod the warrior. He had always been up for the fight when it came to politics.

Since the campaign had started, he had admitted to occasional fears, but they revolved around the mammoth task of fundraising. Could he raise the $10 million to $14 million everyone said he needed to win? It sounded bigger than both of us.

A few times lately, though, he had also admitted that he was worried that one little mistake on his part could result in an avalanche of bad press that would bury him. We'd talk it through until the clock warned us we were running out of time, and then he'd leave for another day of battle—armed with his briefing book and a steaming bowl of oatmeal.

On our way home from the rally in Solon, though, he talked about a different kind of fear.

"I'm afraid of letting down all these people counting on me," he said. "All the people showing up at these events who tell me they're there because they believe I can win. All the people on the campaign staff, and the ones who work in my government offices."

"Honey," I said, but he cut me off.

"Think about it," he said. "Think about how many people won't have jobs if I lose. Think about all those people who were so heartbroken after 2004 and here they are again, willing to believe. Think what it will do to them if we lose."

This was the Sherrod I knew all too well, the youngest child, the baby brother, the man who was always trying to meet everyone else's high expectations.

"No one doubts that you are working harder than anyone else to win," I said.

Joanna chimed in, too, illustrating the compassion and strength that made us increasingly grateful that she was on board. "And we're in this with eyes wide open," she said. "Every last one of us knows how hard this race is going to be, Sherrod. We know it, but we're believers. You're the one who always says, 'It's not about me. It's not about any one of us. It's about the people of Ohio, and what they deserve.' "

Sherrod was quiet for a moment, still staring out the window.

"Thanks, guys," he said.

Walter glanced over at him, flashed him a grin.

"Besides, boss," he said, "you're going to win."

Sherrod reached over and squeezed Walter's shoulder.

"Thanks," he said.

He eased back into his seat, and for the rest of the drive, he just stared through the windshield, focused straight ahead.

six

April No Foolin'

IN MARCH, OUR CAMPAIGN NOT ONLY STARTED TO HUM, IT WAS actually snapping its fingers a bit.

Public polls showed Sherrod steadily gaining on Mike DeWine, which was bad news for the two-term Republican senator and was constant fodder for political reporters, who loved covering the polls even if most of them still thought there was no way Sherrod could win.

John Ryan was stripping away every last penny of waste he could find in our budget, with the help of the newly hired Judy Zamore, who managed the campaign's finances as if they were her own. She became one tough compliance officer, forever scrutinizing office practices to make sure we obeyed every campaign finance law down to the last comma.

Sherrod started virtually every weekday by calling four to six radio stations around the state. Typically, he made the first call between six and six-thirty, and almost everyone put him on the air for at least a minute or two. If they didn't have any questions, he told them what they ought to be asking, and the interview rolled on.

Joanna and her team worked themselves ragged scheduling as many news conferences as she could cajole local television stations into covering—which turned out to be a lot. She is a dramatist at heart, which she claims comes from growing up in Los Angeles, and with the help of staff and volunteers, she was great at conjuring up compelling visuals. Sherrod would stand in front of a closed factory or a set of railroad tracks, surrounded by working men and women, and talk about how current trade policies had betrayed America's workers and crippled their communities. Or he'd stand behind a lectern set up in a nursing home or community health center, surrounded by nurses, doctors, and patients, and talk about the hundreds of thousands of Ohioans who have no health insurance.

I was initially skeptical of these press events, after having spent so many years in a newsroom full of journalists, including me, who groaned at even the mention of covering yet another staged news conference. The dramatic cut in staff at most local broadcast stations, though, made news conferences an easy hit for the evening's newscast. It was not unusual for two or three TV cameras to show up each time, often with reporters along. Some of them, feeling the pinch of cutbacks in their own newsrooms, occasionally whispered their support for Sherrod after the interview. One cameraman slapped a Sherrod Brown sticker on his camera.

We had so much going on in the campaign that our daily schedules were snapped into three-ring binders and color coordinated so that we could distinguish at a glance among fundraising events, news conferences, media interviews, rallies, Democratic Party dinners, and votes in Washington. We also had different colors assigned to my events and Sherrod's events, as distinct from our joint appearances, so that we could easily see when we'd be together and apart.

Sherrod insisted on having my schedule included with his because he always wanted to know where I was headed. Frequently, after looking at my schedule on the way to his own events, he would call on my cell phone to tell me a story about someone I was about to meet. Many times, he would give me a funny political story or a long-ago memory of an event in the region, making it possible for me to connect with the crowd and single out individuals who had known Sherrod for years.

So much to think about, but at 6:05 in the morning on April Fool's Day, Sherrod and I were about to illustrate why this was the perfect name, indeed, for the day that would launch Month Five of the Sherrod Brown Senate campaign.

We stood side by side in our bathroom, facing a day that would begin with an hour-and-a-half drive to a rally in my hometown of Ashtabula and then take us south along five hundred miles of highway before we ended up at yet another hotel right about midnight. Sherrod was scheduled to speak at two rallies, one news conference, and two dinners where we would welcome hundreds of people over chicken cordon bleu, heavy on the bleu.

We were also only days away from another major fundraising deadline, and we weren't sure that Sherrod would make his goal. At the same time, we were trying to caution staff and volunteers not to get too excited over the latest public polls that showed Sherrod either gaining on Mike DeWine (Rasmussen) or leading by 8.9 points (Zogby International). Our own private poll showed us gaining but still behind.

Prioritizing is so important in campaigns, and in that spirit we spent our few precious private moments as husband and wife focused on the most pressing issue of the day: We were arguing over how to use the toothpaste.

Sherrod would say *he* wasn't arguing but merely trying to show me "how to use a stupid tube of toothpaste," and that it was I who took umbrage.

Imagine that: a forty-eight-year-old woman getting testy because her husband thought she needed a lesson on how to brush her teeth. Would his suffering never end?

"There is a reason," he said, "that these tubes have snap tops."

I could not have been less interested in this primer. I had reached the point in life where I was pretty settled on what I would and would not be open to when it came to expanding my horizons. The art of the snap top? I would leave that mountain unscaled.

"How old am I?" I asked.

"Chronologically?"

A male voice wafted up from the center hallway. "Um, I'm going to go start the car," Walter yelled.

"See what you did?" I said, now aiming the tube directly at Ohio's Democratic nominee for Senate. "You embarrassed Walter."

"Put the tube down."

"Make me."

"Connie."

"*Sher*-rod."

By my calculations, one good squeeze and I could nail him right between his narrowed eyes.

Then I caught a glimpse of myself in the mirror: nostrils flared, pupils dilated, face flushed fuchsia.

What was I doing?

This was *not* about toothpaste.

This was about control, and what little of it was left in our ever-contracting lives.

The night before, we had commiserated like two old people on a park bench, trying to figure out how it could be that we hired a bunch of staffers young enough to be our children who now thought they were the boss of us. They were directing our every move: how to speak and when, where to go and when to leave, what to wear and when to change it. We weren't even deciding anymore what music would be playing on the radio of our car, which we almost never drove anyway. And somehow we had been reduced to negotiating for the scant private time we had as a couple. Really, we were a knee-bend away from begging.

Sherrod and I looked each other in the eyes and suddenly it hit us. I set down the tube and he pulled me into his arms.

"This isn't about toothpaste," I said.

"No," he said, laughing. "It's about all these kids bossing us around."

I sat down on the edge of the bathtub. "How did this happen to us?"

Sherrod shrugged his shoulders and grinned. "Welcome to the campaign."

We left for the day declaring a toothpaste détente.

No staff intervened.

IN RETROSPECT, OUR FIRST DAY IN APRIL WAS PREMONITORY IN small, and not so small, ways. The curtain over the window parted for just a moment, allowing us a peek at the road up ahead. Our rumble over a tube of toothpaste gave us a funny story, but also a warning that the only way to make sense of what you're feeling is to stop in your tracks every so often and take a good look at yourself. Mirrors help. So do old friends like Jackie, who took one look at an exhausted me on the evening news and left this message: "Constance. Saw you on TV. You look like hell. When's the last time you had a day off? Call me."

My habit of note taking since Sherrod had announced his candidacy had turned into an obsession, as if writing it all down would ensure that parts of me would survive somewhere, if only on the page.

There were other glimpses out the window that day. We met men and women whose stories wove their way into our narrative for the rest of the campaign. And a rare moment with my father became his final act of heavy lifting that would carry me toward the finish line.

We didn't know any of this about that day when we were smack in the middle of it. At the time, it was like any other Saturday on the trail, if you didn't count our supreme "gotcha" moment with our April Fool's prank on campaign manager John Ryan regarding an imaginary crisis. He might have gotten angry at us, too, if he hadn't just pulled off a similar April Fool's stunt at the expense of Kimberly

Wood. Other than these shenanigans, we seemed to be having a normal campaign day.

Our first event was a minimum-wage rally in Ashtabula, a small working-class town on the shores of Lake Erie, about an hour east of Cleveland. My father, my sister Toni, and my brother, Chuck, still lived there. My other sister, Leslie, lived in nearby Conneaut. Dad and Toni planned to attend their first Sherrod speech.

I can never drive to Ashtabula without remembering why I left. By the time I was nine or ten, I had already figured out it was the kind of town most folks passed through on their way to somewhere else. Small towns seem to grow two kinds of kids: those who can't imagine leaving, and those who can't imagine staying. I was the latter, and when I left for Kent State University—ninety minutes and a whole world away—I knew that for the rest of my life, I'd come back only to visit. It was the land of limitations to me, the place where the big dreams of childhood were crushed under the weight of grown-up life. As in most small towns, many of the kids in my high school were afraid to leave. I was afraid not to.

From an early age, I knew that my parents once had their own dreams that died slow, agonizing deaths at the hands of their own fears. Their lives started out hard and never got easier. My mother, Janey, was the oldest of four. When she was eight, her parents divorced, and her mother was declared unfit and allowed to keep only her mentally retarded son. My mother's father cherry-picked the children he wanted, winning custody of my mother's two younger sisters. His mother, my great-grandmother, raised my mom. While my mother adored her grandmother, she spent the rest of her life believing she was a consolation prize.

My father, Chuck, was the eleventh of twelve children in a family that ended up so fractured that I knew only one aunt and one uncle and a tiny handful of my dozens of cousins. Dad's beloved mother died when I was only two. My mother, not Dad's many sisters, cared for her to the end, and I don't know what happened among the siblings during her illness, but my father never forgave them for per-

ceived wrongs. His father, by all accounts, was a demanding and bru-
tal man.

My parents met when they were thirteen, and Dad was the only
boyfriend my mother ever had. They graduated in 1955 from a tiny
high school in rural Ashtabula County, where Mom was a cheerleader
and homecoming queen and Dad was captain of the basketball team.
Decades later, both of them still said their senior year in high school
was the high point of their lives.

My mother wanted to be a nurse but was afraid she couldn't handle the science classes. My father, a superb athlete who was All-State
in basketball, wanted to keep playing the game for a college but was
afraid he wouldn't qualify for a scholarship. All they had was each
other. There was not a single person in their lives who placed a gentle
hand on their shoulders, pointed up, and said, "No, not down there.
Look up, way over there. That's where you want to aim."

They were engaged soon after graduating, but Mom's dream wedding, the one with bridesmaids and a dress so fluffy it would lift her
like a float down the center aisle at Cherry Valley Methodist Church,
died the day she found out she was pregnant with me. They eloped at
age nineteen, and Dad got a union card a few weeks later, joining
Local 270 of the Utility Workers of America after he was hired by the
Cleveland Electric Illuminating Company. It was a factory job he
hated every day of his thirty-six years at work, but that never stopped
him from giving it his all. My daughter, now twenty, still remembers
the advice he gave her after she told him about her first job:

"I always left the house forty-five minutes early," he told her.
"That way, if I got a flat tire, I still wouldn't be late for work."

When I went to college, I was stunned to learn that not all kids
knew what day their parents got paid. We knew that timetable by
what was served for supper. Dad's payday was every other Thursday,
and there were a lot of Tuesdays and Wednesdays in that second week
when our main course was fried Spam, bread and gravy, or yet another round of Mom's goulash. By the middle of the second week, we
knew even the pennies had run out if Mom didn't send me down the

street to buy a Hostess pie for Dad's lunch pail. We also knew chances were good our parents would end up in another one of their fights that left us all exhausted. Sometimes the stress of too little was just too much.

Throughout my childhood, my dad vowed that none of us four kids would ever carry a lunch pail to work. We were going to have careers, not jobs.

I was the oldest, and by the time I was in high school it had become clear that even with all of Dad's overtime pay, my parents were never going to be able to send their kids to college or own a house unless Mom worked outside the home, too. So she took a job as a nurse's aide at Ashtabula General Hospital. I was a junior in high school when she started getting paid an hourly wage for all her hard work, and her meager salary allowed my parents to buy the first, and only, home they ever owned. We moved from a cramped three-bedroom rental house on busy U.S. 20 to a five-bedroom colonial on a tidy little side street off Main Avenue. It was the first time we had a house with wallpaper, two bathrooms, and a working doorbell, one that chimed "just like Big Ben in London," my mom liked to say whenever her friends from the old neighborhood stopped by.

I was sixteen, and for the first time I had my own bedroom. My dad took me to Sears to pick out new furniture. I couldn't believe I could have a headboard that held a whole shelf of books, a chest of drawers, and a dresser with its own mirror—and all of it in real maple. I'd always had to stand on my parents' bed across from their dresser to get a good look at myself in the mirror, and that was a fussy undertaking because I had to take off my shoes first and then smooth the bedcovers after I hopped off. Now I had my own mirror and a nicer bedroom set than my parents'. After it was delivered, my mother ran her hand across the top of my dresser and said, "Well, a lot of responsibility comes with something as nice as this."

My face burned. I wanted to apologize to her for this lapse in my father's judgment that put me first, but the words wouldn't come. Their dresser was a gray hand-me-down of something meant to resemble wood, and until that moment I never thought she had wanted anything else. But everything I had had up to then, I'd had to share with my siblings. This was the first thing I'd ever been able to call mine, all mine, and I didn't want to give it up. Instead, I promised Mom I'd polish it every week with Lemon Pledge, and every week that's exactly what I did, trying to earn the right to own the first real wood dresser in the house.

Life changed in other ways, too, after we moved. Dad built his own garage, and he took up gardening, which he never wanted to do when he had rented. "Nah, why should I make a place look better for somebody else?" he said whenever Mom suggested any home improvements. "I want to work on my *own* home."

Some things, though, didn't change. I could still hear outside my window the whistles and groans of the trains winding their way toward Cleveland or Pittsburgh late at night. And we still had the portraits of Jesus and Jack Kennedy hanging in the living room. Dad called it "the Jack-and-Jesus wall," but only many years after the president was killed.

The Kennedys were the model for all things Schultz in our home, on a smaller scale, of course, starting with my mother. Imagine the tall, sophisticated Jackie squished down to four feet eleven with a beehive, and you had my mother's version of the First Lady. Mom wore white gloves to church because Jackie did, and strung pearls around her neck for an evening out because Jackie did that, too. She also raised all of us as if we were just an invitation away from visiting the White House. It was always "Thank you" this and "Yes, please" that, and she even tried to get us to say, "Oh, that would be so delightful," but none of us could manage to say it without elevating our voices to Eleanor Roosevelt heights and then collapsing with laughter.

Sometimes, Mom would talk about Jackie as if they'd just spent the afternoon over finger sandwiches and photos of their kids. "You're just a few months older than Caroline," my mother would say, as if she were trying to talk me into playing with a girl down the street. She also liked to say that had Jackie already been in the White House when I was born, she would have named me Jacqueline. Instead, I was named after Constance McKenzie of *Peyton Place*, and it always irritated my mother when I pointed out that I was the namesake of a woman who bore a child out of wedlock.

"Lana Turner played Constance McKenzie, and she was nothing but class in that role," my mother would say with her hand on her hip.

I was in first grade when JFK was shot, and it was the first time I ever saw my father cry. My parents had little money for books when I was growing up, but we had our own copy of the Warren Commission's final report on the Kennedy assassination, as well as numerous biographies of both John and Robert Kennedy. When my dad gave me an old trunk in 2002, I opened it to find stacks of newspapers and magazines from November and December 1963—all of them chronicling the Kennedy assassination.

For Dad, the Kennedys were a promise that even his life could get better. We weren't Catholic, and we weren't rich or famous, but just like the Kennedys, we were descended from immigrants and we were Democrats, and that was enough for my father. He raised us to believe that the workers' right to organize was our family's only route to power, and I used to joke that we knew Woody Guthrie and Pete Seeger songs before we learned any lullabies. He also raised us never to date bankers or Republicans, which we quickly learned were the same thing.

You'd think that, having steeped me up to my eyeballs in all this left-of-center activism, my dad would not have been at all surprised to learn he'd raised a budding feminist, too, but I thought his red hair was about to catch fire the first time I stood in the driveway and announced I would keep my name and discard my bra for the rest of time. When I was in college I sent my mother Marilyn French's feminist novel *The Women's Room*, and my father wouldn't speak to me for weeks.

"She threw the book at me," he roared in a rare phone call to my dorm room. As I quickly discovered, he wasn't tossing out a metaphor, either. Apparently, my mother had just read the now infamous passage where the character Val declared that all men "rape us with their eyes, their laws, and their codes." In an unprecedented moment of courage, Mom looked over at Dad, who was sitting in the recliner watching a basketball game, and hurled the paperback at his head.

Over time, Mom changed more than the rest of us. She was full of stories about her new job that she tried to make funny, but she was usually too tired anymore to cook a family supper every night. Family dinners around the table grew rarer and rarer until they just stopped. She always hated the heat of summer, but she started wearing sweaters on even the hottest days to hide the bruises on her arms she got from working on the "mental floor" of the hospital.

Later, she worked as a hospice home care provider, and her colleagues joked that people lived longer when Janey showed up. She loved listening to other people's stories, and they loved telling them to her. She would describe wondrous moments at the end of life, sad that she had to say good-bye but certain that she had cleared their path a bit. Dad would leave the room when she talked about it, but I hung on her every word.

Throughout it all, there was the unspoken message that Mom and Dad's lives would never be what they had wanted, but they had big hopes for us kids. And, as I later said on the campaign trail in so many speeches, they wore their bodies out so that we would never have to.

In 1998, my mother was diagnosed with a lung disease called idiopathic pulmonary fibrosis. She had never smoked, not ever, and this diagnosis stunned us. My mother, always quick to dive into her medical books, almost immediately realized that her disease would kill her. Her condition steadily worsened, and we were sitting on my front porch in early September 1999 when I asked her if she was afraid to die. She smiled at me and shook her head. "Oh, I'd hoped to see my grandchildren graduate from college, and I wanted to celebrate our fiftieth wedding anniversary. But it's not meant to be, and I'm okay with that."

She saw me wipe my eyes, smiled again, and then told me not to be so sad. "Listen, it's not your time yet. It's my time, and I know things you can't know."

She died two weeks later. She was sixty-two.

My father struggled mightily with her death, and for a while I wasn't sure he would live much longer. He was only sixty-three, but his body had the track record of a far older man. Bursitis had started attacking his shoulder when he was forty, and he underwent quadruple heart bypass surgery when he was only forty-eight. He later had heart stents put in, one time after a helicopter rushed him into Cleveland, and he had back surgery, too. He had high blood pressure and suffered repeated bouts of gout, and all of us worried about his affection for alcohol, which threatened to become the new love of his life.

Even longer than his list of physical ailments was his litany of regrets about my mother. He was haunted by what he felt should have been. Their life together was hard too much of the time, but my mother never stopped loving him. Two days before she died, she told me she still got butterflies when Dad walked into the room.

Just when I thought we would lose my father to heartbreak, he met a strong, kind woman named Theresa Congdon. She brought Dad back to life. I knew this woman was good for him when she declined an invitation to our wedding because she had already committed to volunteer at Mass. I knew he was crazy about her when I learned from my youngest sister, Toni—once a tattler, always a tattler—that he had called Theresa later that night from his cell phone to read her the menu from our dinner.

In recent weeks, Dad had undergone the first of two scheduled surgeries to clear his blocked carotid arteries. "I want to live," he told Theresa and Toni. "I've got things I want to do."

One of those things turned out to be campaigning for Sherrod— in his own way. My dad had once been a precinct captain for the Democratic Party. He didn't wear buttons, though, and nobody merited a bumper sticker on any of his precious made-in-America cars. Nobody, that is, until his son-in-law decided to run for the Senate.

"You aren't going to believe this," my sister Toni said in a phone call in March. She lived next door to my dad, so there was no refuting her claim when she said, "Dad has Sherrod's bumper sticker on his car."

"You're kidding."

"Nope. But don't make a big deal about it 'cuz then he'll get embarrassed."

"Got it."

When we showed up in Ashtabula for the April 1 rally at the Good People's Baptist Church, my father and Toni were already seated in the second row of folding chairs, right in front of the stage. Dad had a Sherrod Brown sticker on his favorite suede jacket.

"You won't believe how early we got here," Toni whispered. She always starts news like this, as if I'm forever doubting what she is about to say.

"How early?"

"We've been here for a whole hour already," she said, shaking her head as she gestured to dozens of empty chairs. "He wanted to make sure he got a good seat."

By the time I introduced Sherrod, we had a good crowd, and this local-girl-made-good took full advantage of the microphone to introduce the man who raised her to speak her mind. Twice I got to do that in April, and twice my father's eyes welled up as his fellow workers cheered for him.

That rally was an eye-opening morning for my father as he listened to one neighbor after another describe difficult lives that were only getting harder. His own eyes filled with tears when a man in his late seventies started to talk about how his wife's pension had been cut, but then broke down and handed the microphone to her. "If we had to rely on my husband's benefits alone, we wouldn't be able to afford dog food to eat," she said. Her husband, ashamed and scared, sobbed.

"Sherrod's got his work cut out for him," Dad said as we walked out into the parking lot. "We've got a real mess on our hands."

Dad watched Sherrod work the crowd, shaking hands and laughing with many people my father had known for more than thirty years. "He's one of us, Connie," he said. "He's going to win. I know a lot of people think he can't pull it off, but look at those people. I haven't seen some of them smile like that in twenty years." I looked at my father's smile and thought, *Ditto, Dad.*

Too soon, our driver, Walter, tapped on his watch and whispered, "We gotta go."

I turned to my father and whipped my camera out of my purse. "Let me take your picture, Dad." I was prepared for his usual lecture that he's the same man who raised me and he can't help it if I keep forgetting what he looks like, but instead, he just straightened up and grinned. "Well, then, take it," he said. "I don't have all day."

I saw him about two weeks later, this time with my sister Leslie, at an AFL-CIO dinner in Ashtabula. It was the same day my book hit the stores, and several people showed up with a copy for me to sign. I'd already sent Dad a copy, with this inscription: "Thank you for sacrificing so much of you to make so much of me."

An old family friend, long familiar with my father's cranky stoicism, pulled me aside. "Your dad's showing your book to everybody," she said. "Don't let him fool you for a minute. He takes it with him everywhere, and it's all he talks about."

This time one of our field organizers, Steve Lieber, drove me, and as we were leaving, my father tugged on my jacket.

"When are you going on the *Today* show?" he asked, loud enough for anyone within five hundred feet to hear. When I told him, he grinned again.

"I'll be watching," he said, and then he gave a wave.

Ten days later, Dad was gone.

seven

Name Game

From May through the rest of the campaign, I wore the one and only campaign button that read "Connie Schultz Supports Sherrod Brown." In case anyone wondered who I was planning to vote for, I guess.

Some days, though, if I was honest with at least myself, the button I wore should have read, "Connie Schultz Has Really Had It with Sherrod Brown."

Not Sherrod Brown the husband. He was still cute and cuddly, with enough passion for justice to give Moses a run for his shekels. What I was sick of was Sherrod Brown the product.

A big part of a campaign's fieldwork involves branding and marketing the candidate as if he were a new can of Pringles. Supporters could order Sherrod mugs, Sherrod key rings, Sherrod tote bags, Sherrod yard signs, Sherrod pins, even their very own Sherrod mouse pad, simply by clicking on SherrodStuff.com. After more than thirty years in elected office, this struck Sherrod as a perfectly normal thing to happen with one's name. I, on the other hand, began to feel as if I were married to Cher.

And then there were the Sherrod Brown T-shirts. Political activists and groupies love T-shirts, and it was a bit disorienting the first time I watched young women with Sherrod's name stretched across their bosoms wave their pens and yell, "Sign my T-shirt! Sign my T-shirt!" It's not that they were a threat—the sight of Sherrod attempting to sign their backs without touching any part of them bordered on a Monty Python skit—but the whole notion of Sherrod-mania was so far removed from the down-to-earth guy I knew, the one who saved airplane napkins because he hated to waste and pinned his socks together before throwing them in the laundry so they'd remain wedded right through the tumble dry.

I have to admit that I was initially excited when a staff person handed me my personalized Sherrod pin. Oh, my. My very own one-of-a-kind button singling me out as Queen Groupie. I imagined the staff brainstorming over pizza and beer late at night, wondering what they could do to recognize the tireless devotion of the tiresome wife. Maybe they were even thinking, *Hey, you know? The least we could do is give her a special pin.*

That's what I imagined, but the bubbles of my initial effervescence started popping as soon as I realized everyone on staff had his or her own one-of-a-kind button, courtesy of the marketing company hoping for a contract. Jeanne Wilson supported Sherrod Brown. So did Melissa Wideman, and John Hagner, and dozens of other staffers who now had their very own one-of-a-kind Sherrod pin.

"Everyone has this button," I whined to Sherrod late one night as he rummaged through the fridge for a snack.

"Everyone is wearing a button saying 'Connie Schultz Supports Sherrod Brown'?"

I stared at him, drumming my fingers on the counter.

He turned around and grinned. "Well, there's only one Connie Schultz."

"Actually, there are dozens of us," I said. "Google me. You'll find out."

"You Googled your name?"

"We all did, one day in the newsroom. Someone said it was a great way to show how utterly un-unique we are."

"You journalists really know how to have a good time."

I frowned.

"But," he said, wrapping his arms around my neck, "there's only one Connie Schultz like you."

"You aren't going to start singing 'Free to Be You and Me,' are you?"

"Only if you'll hum the chorus."

Okay, so my button wasn't so special. But for a whole five minutes or so, I did feel unique. That sheen dimmed after a man in Lucas County pointed to the button and said, "Who's Connie Schultz?"

"That's me," I said, smiling as the creases in his brow deepened to ravines.

"Should I know you?" he said.

"I'm Sherrod's wife."

He stared at the button for a moment. "You don't have the same name."

"Well. Right. We married only two years ago."

He chewed that one over for a second. "Well, what are you waiting for?"

Ah, the name game. Once I started appearing alone on the campaign trail I had to figure out a way to introduce myself. That was harder than it sounds, particularly in other parts of the state where most people hadn't even heard of Sherrod.

This realization scared me, even though Sherrod had tried to prepare me. "Most of those people won't even know who I am," he said.

"How can that be? You were secretary of state for two terms."

"In the eighties," he said. "And nobody knew who the secretary of state was before Ken Blackwell."

It turned out I had my work cut out for me.

At first, I'd thrust out my hand and chirp, "Hi, I'm Connie Schultz, I'm Sherrod Brown's wife," but too many people thought I'd just said "Sherrod Schultz." The power of alliteration. Even if they heard it right, older men tended to wrinkle their noses and say, "If you're his wife, why isn't your name Brown?"

So then I tried saying, "I'm Sherrod Brown's wife, Connie." People were friendly enough, but too often they smiled and said, "Well, hi, there Sharon, it's nice to meet you."

"No, I'm Connie. His name is Sherrod."

"Sharon?"

"No, Sherrod."

"What kind of name is that?"

I tried just once explaining that. "It's a family name. His mother's from Georgia."

"Georgia? Then why's he running here?"

I kept trying.

"Hi, I'm Connie, and my husband is Sherrod Brown."

"Who?"

"Sherrod. Sherrod Brown."

I'd point to my campaign pin. "That's him, and he's running for the Senate." I had to tinker with that, too, adding "United States" before "Senate" because too many thought I meant the Ohio senate. But at least they were willing to take a brochure.

And you thought all I had to worry about was my weight, my hair, my makeup, my identity, and my clothes.

Most days, I wore my special button whenever I stumped for Sherrod and usually forgot to take it off when I ran errands, which elicited reactions ranging from disgust to glee in the faces of fellow customers. The whole thing took some getting used to because I hadn't worn a political button since the day I started working for my college newspaper in 1976. It was a new concept for me, this stamping myself with the name of my husband.

Not wearing something identifying my support for Sherrod had its downside, too. I showed up at one fundraiser where two young girls were handing out Sherrod stickers. The hosts' daughter raised her ten-year-old eyebrows at my empty lapel and peeled off a sticker. "Here," she said. "You need to put this on."

I shot her my best mother's smile and waved her off. "Actually, I'm married to the candidate."

She rolled her eyes, turned to her equally appalled friend, and said, "As if *that's* an excuse."

At a rally in southwest Ohio, a woman who had designed her own Sherrod T-shirt came up to me loaded with pins.

"You need to put one of these on," she said, not bothering to introduce herself.

"I'm wearing knits," I said. "Pins tend to snag."

She frowned and shook her head.

"Look," I said, "do you really think anyone doubts I support my husband?"

She wrinkled her nose and leaned in. "You look hostile."

"Hostile?"

"Yeah, hostile to your husband. People are looking at you right now and thinking, 'What kind of wife won't wear her husband's pin?' "

I looked around the room at all the people smiling in my direction and thought, *Wow, they sure hide it well.*

Sherrod never really cared if I wore a campaign button, but he loved it whenever I clipped on the tiny pin that had become his trademark over the last five years.

Members of Congress typically wear one of two pins on their lapel: an American flag, or the official pin that identifies them as an elected official in the House or Senate.

Sherrod didn't wear either of those. This had nothing to do with his regard for the flag. To the disappointment of his friends in the American Civil Liberties Union, not to mention his wife, Sherrod had repeatedly voted for the flag amendment, which would criminalize acts of desecration of the flag. I opposed the amendment on First Amendment grounds, which made me just a tad more popular than Sherrod at ACLU brunches.

Sherrod also meant no disrespect toward his fellow congressmen who felt the need to be identified at all times as members of that elected body. He just wanted the symbol on his lapel to reflect the passion in his heart. So he wore a pin depicting a canary in a birdcage.

The canary pin first found its way to Sherrod in 2000, at a Workers' Memorial Day rally in Lorain to recognize workers who have been killed or injured on the job. The AFL-CIO started the annual observance in 1989, choosing April 28 because it is the anniversary of the Occupational Safety and Health Act. Sherrod was waiting to speak at the rally when Dominic Cataldo, a member of Local 1104 of the United Steelworkers of America, walked up to him and handed him a canary pin.

Cataldo reminded Sherrod that coal miners used to carry canaries down into the mines to alert them to the presence of dangerous gases. "It was the only gas meter they had," he told Sherrod. "They didn't have a union or anyone else looking out for them."

Sherrod immediately pinned the canary to his blazer, to the delight of the steelworkers. From that day on, he wore it on whatever jacket he pulled out of the closet. So many people pointed to it and asked for an explanation that he designed a four-by-nine-inch card telling the story of the canary and what it represented for American workers. Whenever someone asked why he wore the canary pin, he handed them this card:

> The canary represents the struggle for economic and social justice in our nation.
>
> In the early days of the 20th century, more than 2,000 American workers were killed in coal mines every year. Miners took a canary into the mines to warn them of toxic gases; if the canary died, they knew they had to escape quickly. Miners were forced to provide for their own protection. No mine safety laws. No trade unions able to help. No real support from their government.
>
> A baby born in 1900 had a life expectancy of 47 years. Today, thanks to progressive government and an aggressive labor movement, Americans can expect to live three decades longer. It has been a 100-year battle between the privileged and the rest of us.

We took on the oil and chemical companies to enact clean air and safe drinking water laws.

We overcame industry opposition to pass auto safety rules.

We beat back insurance and medical interests to establish Medicare and Medicaid for senior citizens and poor children.

We fought off Wall Street bankers to create Social Security.

We battled entrenched business interests to enact women's and civil rights, protections for the disabled, and prohibitions on child labor.

We fought for all of it. Every bit of progress made in the struggle for economic and social justice came over the opposition of society's most privileged and most powerful. Remarkably, it was ordinary working families who won so many of these battles against the most entrenched, well-heeled interests.

The canary signifies that the struggle continues today, and that all of us must be ever vigilant against the powerful interest groups which too often control our government.

After he declared his candidacy for the Senate, it didn't take long before the canary pin turned into a symbol for Sherrod's campaign. We bought thousands of the pins from the Steelworkers. Sherrod and I made a practice of removing the pins from our lapels and giving them to people whenever they asked how to get a canary pin of their own. So often, they would try to dissuade us at first, insisting that they didn't mean for us to give up our own pin, but inevitably they were touched when we assured them that we wanted them to have it. One retired railroad worker in Medina started to cry when I gave him mine. "My father was a coal miner in the hills of West Virginia," he said, tears streaming down his face as his wife held tight to his arm. "You don't know what this means to me."

Sherrod told the story of the pin so often on the campaign trail that by summer most of us had perfected our own imitations of him talking about the canary in the coal mine. We'd mess up our hair, tug at our imaginary lapels, lean into phantom microphones, and in our own versions of Sherrod's sandy voice, say, "You can't really see it from here, but I wear a canary on my lapel. . . ." Sometimes, four or five of us would perform our canary routine at the same time for Sherrod, and the sight of so many of us talking in raspy voices and tugging at our collars always cracked him up.

"All right, all right, I get it," he'd say, waving his hands as his cheeks flushed to high red. "You're tired of the canary story." That never stopped him from telling it, of course, and I never tired of hearing him tell it. Every time he talked about that canary pin, he was making it clear who he was fighting for.

Predictably, some of the bloggers took aim at the canary pin. One of them ran a contest to replace the slogan on Sherrod's bumper sticker: "We're In This Together." Their suggested slogans ranged from the profane to the pathetic, but Sherrod and I had to admit this one was funny: "Vote for me and you'll never have to hear the canary story again."

In June, we met a man at the Hog Heaven restaurant in New Philadelphia who reminded us why the canary story mattered.

Jeff Spradling was a sheet metal worker from Bellaire, but before that he had worked eight years in the coal mines. He was in his late forties, with blond hair tied in a ponytail and steel-blue eyes that wouldn't let go of you. He came up to Sherrod shortly after we arrived for a political gathering of about a hundred activist Democrats at the Hog Heaven.

"I don't usually care about politicians, but I have a friend who keeps talking about you," he said, his arms crossed against his chest. "I looked up your website, and read about the canary pin."

Sherrod nodded. "I'm glad you're here."

"Well, don't be too glad yet," he said. "I'm going to look you in the eye when you speak here. I'm going to see if you mean what you say."

Sherrod nodded again. "Thank you for that chance," he said.

There were a lot of working-class people there, so Sherrod talked about how selfless so many of them were when it came to caring about their communities. We'd seen this time and again on the trail.

Often, the more educated and privileged the audience, the more their questions and concerns reflected their own self-interest. Wealthy businessmen complained about the estate tax, which affected fewer than one percent of the most affluent Americans, and railed against raising the minimum wage, which was still only $5.15 in Ohio. Private sector doctors wanted Sherrod to raise their reimbursement payments for treating Medicare and Medicaid patients. One physician wanted to know what Sherrod was going to do to ease the restrictions on work visas for doctors from foreign countries visiting his hospital. I'm not saying these weren't important issues, but they didn't address the concerns of most working men and women in Ohio.

Meetings in working-class communities, however, were full of people asking what could be done to help their neighbors. They grieved when the town's only public pool or bowling alley closed, because the children—everyone's children—had nowhere to play. They worried about Medicare Part D because they had stood behind senior citizens and watched them negotiate with pharmacists over which doses they could skip, which pills they could cut in half. Their hearts ached for people in Appalachia who had to choose between bathing their children and watering their cattle because they couldn't afford the high cost of private water lines into their homes. These Americans weren't as educated as those doctors and businessmen, but they sure knew what was wrong with their country.

Sherrod talked about why it mattered that so many of them were willing to take time off on a sunny Saturday afternoon to show up at Hog Heaven to hear him speak. He started with the story about the canary pin, and then cast a wide net across the room.

"We need change in this country, and you can make that happen," he told them. "I know we don't all agree on some of those 'social issues,' but do you really care who lives together down the street, or are you more worried about keeping your pension, sending your kids to decent schools and affordable college, and having decent health care?" Heads slowly nodded all around the room.

It was a short talk, and as soon as Sherrod finished, Spradling walked up to me. "I have something for the congressman in my car," he said. "Could you come with me to the parking lot?"

Our ever-hovering driver, Walter O'Malley, walked out with me. Spradling leaned into his car and pulled out a dusty metal cylinder about seven inches long and full of dents. Holding it up by its thick S-hook at the top, Spradling gave a quick smile as I narrowed my eyes and tried to figure out what on earth he had in his hand.

"It's called a bug light," he said. "It replaced the canary in the coal mine. If its flame went out, you knew you had to get out of there. This is the one I carried down in the coal mines. I used it until I left the mines in 1985."

Immediately, I thought of my father's lunch pail, the one he tossed as soon as he left the factory. "You kept it," I said. "It must matter an awful lot to you."

He nodded, then handed it to me.

"I want the congressman to have it," he said.

"Oh, Jeff," I said, resting my free hand on his shoulder. "Are you sure?"

"Hey!" Sherrod yelled as he bolted out the front door. I motioned him over and passed the bug light to him. He listened wide-eyed as Spradling explained what it was, holding it high in the air to get a better look.

"I want you to have this," Spradling told him. "I want you to keep it as a reminder of who you're fighting for."

Sherrod thanked him, and made a promise. "I'm going to hang this in my Senate office in Washington."

"Let's get you elected first," Spradling said, flashing another quick smile.

For the rest of the campaign, the bug light held a place of honor in the center hallway of our home. A few times, I took it with me on the campaign trail and held it up as I told the story of a coal miner named Jeff who hoped that change was on the way.

eight

An Early Loss

I USED TO HATE TO FLY. AS SOON AS THE PLANE PUSHED AWAY FROM the gate, the hairs on the back of my neck snapped to attention and saluted until we landed.

Sherrod, who flew back and forth to Washington virtually every week, was less than understanding about all this. In fact, he thought it was hilarious, as if my fear of plummeting thousands of feet to an incendiary death made for one hoot of a punch line. In 2004, Bill Moyers stood right behind us as we boarded a flight from Madison, Wisconsin, to Cleveland. We were big fans of Moyers, and talking to him actually took my mind off the cylinder of steel and plastic we were about to trust with our lives. Once we were strapped in and the plane's engines began their usual roar, Sherrod turned to me, motioned toward Moyers three rows back, and said, "Well, baby, if this plane goes down, we ain't the headline."

The combination of a book tour and a Senate race cured me of just about all flight anxiety. Not right away, of course. In April, I was still Continental Airlines' frequent fretter. I was on my way to Norfolk to speak at a journalism seminar when our plane started jiggling like loose change in a dryer. Immediately, I pulled out one of my notebooks and started scribbling away, as if putting pen to paper would somehow distract God enough to keep us in the air.

"Dear God," I wrote, "are we not on the same page this year? Do you not understand that I must stay alive until Election Night?"

Hearing no response, I decided to bargain, but only after the pilot made the incredibly obvious if somewhat garbled announcement that we had "encountered some turbulence" and the seat-belt light would remain on for the duration of the flight. Far more alarming, he said the flight attendant had suspended her rounds with the refreshment cart, which I always interpret to mean we're all going to die but at least it won't be from flying cans of Pepsi.

"If I land safely," I wrote to God, "I will not utter so much as a peep of complaint about having to clean the house before our Friday fundraiser, and—*and*—I will appreciate the cramped quarters of the campaign car's backseat, which I only now realized is always safely on the ground."

The flight didn't smooth out until we landed forty-five minutes later. Immediately, my cell phone started beeping. Six new voice mail messages called for my attention. Three were speaking requests, two wanted my prompt attention to proposed changes to Sherrod's schedule, and the last one was from our Ohio fundraising director, Kimberly Wood.

"We'd like to put your leather sofas in your garage for the fundraiser. Do you have any problem with that?"

Why, I wondered, was I always in such a hurry to land?

Campaign fatigue, I soon discovered, is a wonderful sedative. A few weeks later on the trail, and short of someone screaming "We're all going to die!" I just couldn't work up any adrenaline over a few bumps in the sky. During one very long week in May, I was on my eighth flight in seven days when our plane hit the kind of wind power that drove little Dorothy to shriek "Auntie Em! Auntie Em!" Even the attendants strapped themselves into their seats, and the man sitting next to me suddenly said to no one in particular, "Sure wish I'd called my wife before we took off."

I leaned my head against the window with a thud, closed my eyes, and had a whole different conversation with God. "Oh, fine," I said with a sigh. "Go ahead. Take me down. At least I'll get some rest."

A few weeks later, one of my friends who hated to fly called me in the hope that I would support her decision to stay home from a once-in-a-lifetime trip to Europe. Instead of commiserating, I assured her that she was more likely to die in the embrace of a boa constrictor than to crash in a plane. "It's the rare human being who dies that way," I told her, "and you're not that special."

She sounded rather horrified, but I think my psychology worked. She went to Europe and had a wonderful time.

APRIL WAS FULL OF OPPORTUNITIES FOR ME TO FEEL LIKE THE journalist I was, rather than the political prop old-time party chairs wanted me to be. On the fifteenth, I went to Ohio University's journalism school for a panel discussion about opinion writing with my former colleague Tom Suddes, who was now a graduate student, and Leonard Pitts, a Pulitzer Prize–winning columnist for *The Miami Herald* and visiting faculty member who had become a friend over time.

During the Q-and-A, one of the professors in attendance asked what we thought about Jon Stewart's *Daily Show,* whose political satire was such a favorite among young viewers.

I said I had a lot of respect for Stewart's wit and pithy insights into what masquerades as the "real world" of politics, but I worried about a recent poll showing that many young people identified it as their only source of "news."

Leonard took a totally different tack, focusing on Stewart's wonderful sense of humor. As he offered examples of Stewart's trademark wit, I realized how much the campaign trail had already changed me.

A year earlier, I had thought Stewart was hilarious—and harmless. Now, I worried that he was stoking a particularly potent brand of cynicism that gave too many Americans a ready excuse to write off politics altogether. If all we had were buffoons running the country, why bother participating in this thing we call democracy? Why even vote?

After Leonard spoke, I described some of the people I had met so far while campaigning. I talked about the woman with two jobs and no health insurance, whose breast cancer was diagnosed and treated only because a friend sent her to a community clinic lucky enough to have grant money. I told them about the man in his fifties I met at the same clinic who lost his pension and almost "threw in the towel" and resigned himself to an eventual death from diabetes because he couldn't afford insulin. When I asked him why he decided to seek help, his blue eyes teared up and he said, "My daughter. I have a daughter, and she wanted me to live."

"Lucky daughter," I said to him, grabbing his hand. He nodded, unable to speak.

And then I told the audience about meeting rooms full of people just as nearsighted as I but without my money that allowed me to pay for contact lenses and thinner glasses. They had to buy the cheaper glasses, and so their eyes looked bigger than clamshells behind the thick lenses as they filled labor halls and banquet rooms in local restaurants for the chance to talk to Sherrod.

"I'm afraid I'm losing my sense of humor," I told the silent room. "I'm seeing the real-life problems of so many decent people in this state, and it's turning me into one somber woman. I can't laugh about those eyeglasses, or that man who almost let himself die because he was so ashamed he had no health care. I can't find the humor in that woman's breast cancer."

Leonard turned to me, put his hand on my back, and smiled. "Wow. That's a column. You just wrote yourself a column."

On the drive home that day, I realized I was starting to feel more certain about my decision to take a leave from writing my column to work in the campaign, in part because I was still doing what I did best:

listening to other people's stories, and then sharing them with the world at large. Instead of writing about them, I was giving speeches, but the goal was the same. I wanted to reach that place in people that makes them shake their head and say, "This has got to change."

I had meant it when I said Sherrod and I had gotten into this race because we wanted to have the right answer for our grandchildren who hadn't been born yet when they asked, "What did you do to help?" Doing this meant I had to sacrifice my column, perhaps, but not my writing. Every day, I wrote down pages of observations and conversations, so many of them with people used to being ignored and looking to Sherrod for hope. I'm a writer, and writing is the way I make sense of what's happening to me.

Two days later, I had a humorous reminder never to get too full of my writerly self. Sherrod and I drove to a labor event in southwest Ohio, where I was supposed to introduce him to a roomful of millwrights and their wives. I'm sure that, hours earlier, it sounded like a fine idea to have this daughter of a union activist introduce her husband, but by the time we got there we were competing with hours of revelry. The only thing missing was hurled tomatoes splattering against chicken wire when I took the stage and tried to compete with too many men who'd had too many beers.

The man who introduced me gave it his best. "Folks, listen up. This is Sherrod Brown's wife, and she won the Pulitzer Prize. I don't know what that is, but it sure sounds important."

I looked at Sherrod and we broke up laughing. I can't remember a word I said, only that I kept shouting into the microphone and at one point I was standing with my hands on my hips. Sherrod tried talking but ended fast after one of the guys yelled for him to sing.

I will never forget, though, the conversation that took place after Sherrod left the stage. A millwright in his forties came up to Sherrod and said, "You're a congressman, right?"

"Yes."

The man shoved up his shirtsleeves and pointed to more than a dozen scars on his arm. "These are the burns I get from the job. I've got them on both my arms. I've got them here on my head, too." He leaned over to give us a view of his scalded scalp. Then he smiled at Sherrod.

"Take care of us, okay?"

Sherrod nodded slowly. "I'll do my best."

Watching him walk away, we were silenced by the weight of it all.

JUST AS SHERROD'S CAMPAIGN WAS REALLY GAINING MOMENTUM, I had a book to sell. Even a local blogger's snarky suggestion that my jacket photo was retouched—"I guess a Pulitzer gets you a new face, too"—could not diminish my excitement.

We launched the book tour on April 19 at Joseph-Beth Booksellers on Cleveland's east side. Two months had already passed since my last column had run in *The Plain Dealer*, so I wasn't sure the turnout would number beyond family members and close friends who had promised to show up. By the time I walked onto the main floor, though, several hundred people were crowded into the store. I knew only about a fourth of them, which I could interpret in two ways: I didn't have nearly as many friends as I thought, or I had far more readers than I dared hope.

There was a third explanation for at least some of the turnout, but that didn't occur to me until after I gave my talk and started signing books. I had been signing for only ten minutes or so when I spotted the first bumper sticker. I shrugged it off as an ardent supporter hoping to meet my husband.

A few minutes later, though, it seemed that everywhere I looked I saw hands clutching shiny "Sherrod Brown for Senate" bumper stickers. I looked around the room and spotted several campaign staffers handing them out.

It was an awful feeling to realize the campaign had shifted into gear at my book signing; it felt even worse to realize how much it bothered me. I didn't write a book to promote my husband's candidacy. Worse, I could immediately imagine the newspaper headline on the six-inch snipe of a blurb:

Brown Profits in More Ways Than One
from Wife's Book Debut in Ohio

I wanted to get up from the table, march the staff into a corner, and say, "Look, I don't hand out my books at Sherrod's events, and I don't want you handing out his bumper stickers at mine." Talk about a bad headline. Instead, I asked them to stop immediately, even after one of the staff members insisted he only brought them into the store after several people asked for them, including a bookstore employee who requested fifty.

I lost count of how many people told me, as I wrote in their books, that they hoped Sherrod won. That was nice. The ones who told me I needed to start stumping on the campaign trail as soon as possible? Not so nice. Clearly, in the eyes of many Ohioans, I had already morphed from a newspaper columnist into a political wife.

During the Q-and-A after my talk, someone had asked me what it was like to be on the campaign trail. I responded the way I would countless times in the months ahead: This is such an important race, to Ohio and to the country, and I believe in Sherrod. We share so many of the same values. It's time for change.

What I wanted to say was "You don't know the half of it." Just as I didn't want to be reduced to the stand-by-her-man spouse, I didn't want Sherrod downgraded to just a candidate. There was so much more to the man, and to the marriage we had forged in such a short period of time. I wanted to tell them my stomach starts somersaulting every time I know he's on his way home, and how his face lights up whenever he first sees me walk in. I wanted to talk about how the energy swirls around a room as soon as he crosses the threshold, and how his default button is set to joy. I wanted them to know that every so often he leaves on my pillow love notes he writes on recycled stationery from his secretary of state days, and that sometimes he wakes me up in the middle of the night just to whisper, "I love my wife."

That's what I wanted to say, but I could imagine that headline, too:

Brown's Wife Loses It at Book Event;
"She's in Our Prayers," Says DeWine

I kept my mouth shut. Surely, I told myself, an entire book tour couldn't be about Sherrod's race.

Just as surely, I was wrong.

LESS THAN A WEEK LATER, ON A MONDAY EVENING, MY FRIEND Jackie and I were on the road to Dayton. This would be the only time during the book tour that I didn't have a professional driver provided by the publisher. Instead, I had jumped at Jackie's offer to spend some rare time together before I headed to New York and California. I was scheduled the following morning for an interview with a local TV station, followed by lunch with the *Dayton Daily News* columnist Mary McCarty and then a book signing that evening.

Jackie drove, and during the four-hour trip I called my dad. He was on the mend at home after a second surgery to clear out his other carotid artery, and I promised when I said good-bye to him in post-op at the hospital that I would read a fourteen-page letter he sent me that had been written by his mother, my grandmother, in 1946. I kept my word, and then called to talk to him about the letter.

Dad's mother, Regie, had sent the letter to Dad's oldest sister, my aunt Lillian, shortly after she had buried both her father-in-law, whom everyone called Pa, and her seventeen-year-old son, Dad's brother Harry. To enlist in the army, Harry had lied about his age. Recently, Lillian had sent a copy of the letter to my father. It outlined a series of events so tragic that my father choked up reading it sixty years later. For some reason, he wanted me to read it, too.

"I just can't write much of a letter now," my grandmother wrote in small, tidy script. "I am so crushed with grief I can't think clearly at all. Never, never did I ever think that such a terrible shock would ever come to me."

She began the letter on April 19, 1946, but was unable to finish it until May 8. Her father-in-law, Pa, had died just after dinner one night.

"He died in his chair," my father stressed when we talked. "Had a heart attack."

My grandmother immediately sent word via the Red Cross to her teenage son, Harry Junior, who was in the Navy and due to ship out soon, that his beloved grandfather, Pa, had died. "I only wish to God that I had never sent for him to come home," she wrote. "But it was the last thing he said when he left for California last November, 'If anything ever happens to Pa let me know so I can come.' "

The Red Cross confirmed that Harry Junior was on his way to Ohio and would probably be there in time for his grandfather's wake. He never showed up, and a telegram delivered the following morning told my grandmother that Harry had died in a plane crash.

A train carried Harry's body from Albuquerque. My grandparents met his body at the train station in Cleveland. Her description of her son's return home made me think about all the families who have lost loved ones in the Iraq War. It's a different era, a different war, but my grandmother's anguish sounded so similar to that of the surviving parents I've met or interviewed since the war began.

"It was an awful feeling to see that shipping case removed from the train," Dad's mother wrote. "I just couldn't believe my boy was in it, for it was a little less than eight months when I had stood at the same place and saw him off to Rhode Island after he had been home last August. I could still see him standing on the platform and waving good-bye."

Until my father sent me a copy of the letter, the only thing I knew about Harry's death was that the telegram had misspelled his name and that my father was only nine when his brother died. Dad and I talked for nearly an hour that day on the way to Dayton, and throughout the conversation, he kept pausing, clearing his throat, and taking deep breaths. "This letter was really hard to read," he said. "My mother was never the same after Harry died. I remember when she was dying, she kept calling out his name, and she kept saying he was in the room with her."

My dad had mentioned that to me only once before, when my mother was in her last days and started talking about seeing her beloved grandmother and father in her hospital room. My dad shot out of the room, and I found him sobbing in the hallway. "That's what my mother did just before she died," he had said, finally acknowledging what he had refused for so long to believe.

I don't know why Dad wanted me to read the letter then. He knew I felt a tie to my grandmother even though I had no memory of her. She had died when I was only two, but she had wanted to be a writer, and my father had given me a scrapbook I cherish, full of the tiny stories she had written about her community for a local newspaper.

"Pa died in his chair," he said that night. "Isn't that something? You can have dinner, sit down in your favorite chair, and just die."

THE FOLLOWING AFTERNOON, WE HAD JUST FINISHED HAVING lunch with the columnist Mary McCarty when I checked my voice mail messages. It had been such a fun lunch, full of laughter and the stories journalists inevitably share. My face was still warm from whooping it up when I listened to my sister Leslie's frantic voice: "Con, I'm sorry to leave this message, but I'm at Dad's house and the paramedics are working on him. He had a heart attack. I swore I felt a heartbeat when I found him, so I started pounding on his chest while Theresa called EMS." She started to cry. "He was gray when I found him. He was gray, just sitting in his chair."

Jackie turned the car toward Cleveland in the time it took me to say "Dad's had a heart attack." As we sped north, Jackie mined the news for hope.

"Maybe it's not as bad as it sounds, Con," she said. "She said the paramedics were there. Maybe he's going to be all right."

"No," I said, shaking my head. "The air's already different. He's gone."

Isn't that something, I thought. *You can talk to your dad for a whole hour the night before, but then, just like that, he sits down in his favorite chair and dies.*

By the time I got to University Hospitals of Cleveland, Dad was in intensive care, tethered to every machine he'd always sworn he never wanted. There was no one to blame. You call paramedics to save a life, that's what they try to do. My sisters and my brother were all there, and one look at their ashen faces told me all I needed to know about Dad's chances.

For two days, he lingered, never regaining consciousness. I had called Sherrod in D.C. on the way from Dayton, and he called repeatedly for updates. At one point, he asked if I wanted him to come home.

I did, more than I wanted anything, except for Dad to come back to life, but Sherrod would have to miss important votes in Congress on national security. They would not be close votes, but they were votes nonetheless, and it was his job to weigh in. And if he didn't . . . I said what he didn't dare:

"If you miss these votes, you'll be attacked, probably in an ad, for not caring about Americans' safety."

"I don't care what the Republicans say."

But we both knew he did, and there was no point in pretending we were a normal couple allowed to make normal decisions in a time of crisis.

"I won't be able to bear it," I told him, already imagining the attack ad. "I don't want to hear you explaining over and over for the rest of the campaign why you had to miss the votes." I could imagine how he'd start every response. "My father-in-law was dying," "Connie's father was dying," "My wife needed me because her dad was dying. . . ."

I joined my siblings in a two-day vigil by my father's bed as the medical staff tried everything they could to prove there was something still going on behind my father's frozen face. His pupils did not respond to light or touch. He never moved so much as a finger.

Sometimes, I was by myself, holding on to Dad's swollen hand, and I would look toward the doorway thinking, maybe, just maybe, Sherrod had found a way to come home. But he couldn't, and I knew that. I was angry at him, angry at the Republicans, angry at the campaign, but I was angriest with myself for feeling so needy. Sherrod called constantly, his voice full of pain for me. "I'm sorry I'm not there," he said, over and over.

Finally, I reminded myself that what I was doing was no different from what I had done as a single mother for so many years. Nobody ever said marriage to a member of Congress meant never being alone. Time for me to snap out of it.

Late into the second night, I traded places with Leslie, who would spend the night with Dad while I went home and got some sleep. I left around 2 A.M. and collapsed into bed a half-hour later. Shortly after falling asleep, I started to dream about my father. For some reason I can't explain, in the dream I am wearing a ridiculous denim jumper with a Superman emblem on my chest, running from room to room, down one hallway after another in the hospital, searching for my father. Finally, I find him as he is about to leave the hospital. He looks younger, and happy, and he turns to me and gives his trademark little wave.

Immediately after this, the phone rang. The woman's voice was soft and urgent.

"Ms. Schultz, we need you to the hospital."

"Okay."

"Please drive safely," she said. "But please come right away."

I pulled on the clothes I had removed only two hours before and shaved ten minutes off the usual drive to the hospital. Leslie was standing beside Dad, sobbing as she smoothed his hair from his freckled forehead.

"He had another heart attack," she said. "They resuscitated him again, but they said there's no hope."

The attending physician came in and kindly, but firmly, echoed the news. Dad's heart could not survive, he said. It wasn't pumping on its own, he wasn't breathing on his own, his whole body was shutting down.

I reached across Dad's chest and grabbed Leslie's hand. I told her about my dream, and then we talked about what Dad would—and would not—want.

"He would not want to live like this," I said.

"I know," she said, tears streaming down her face.

A few minutes later, Dad was gone.

THE FOLLOWING MORNING, MY EDITOR AT *THE PLAIN DEALER*, Stuart Warner, sent me an e-mail. He had called me as soon as he found out about my father's heart attack, and we had talked several times in the last two days. At one point, I had recounted to him a recent conversation with my dad.

"Do you want to write about it?" he wrote. "It really touched me, the stories you were telling about how he realized all his work meant something, and I think it would touch parents everywhere."

I called Stuart back to double-check, assuming that it would suddenly dawn on somebody at the paper that they would be giving prime real estate to a candidate's wife. But Stuart had cleared it with managing editor Tom O'Hara.

"If you want to write it, *The Plain Dealer* wants to run it," Stuart said. "You've written a lot about your father, and his story is the story of so many in Cleveland. They'll want to know what happened. And it will be good for you to write it."

I pounded out my father's obituary for the Ashtabula paper, the *Star Beacon*, then wrote what I really wanted to say about him in the column.

When my mother died, we stood for six hours to receive more than eight hundred mourners at her wake. My father said he never wanted to put his own family through that, but I think a part of him was afraid not nearly so many people would show up when he died. He always insisted on no wake, no funeral, and so Jackie's partner and our dear friend, the Reverend Kate Huey, held a short private grave-side service two days after Dad died. I was perfectly composed right up to the moment I saw my husband help carry my father's casket to his grave.

That same day, my column ran in my usual place in *The Plain Dealer.* Stuart was right: It helped to tell one more story about my dad. And it was the only chance I'd have during the campaign to really think about Dad and what it meant to lose him now.

This is what I wrote:

A few days after my mother died in 1999, I found my father bent over his garden, digging, digging, digging.

He had spent all of his adult life working with his hands, and so it was with his hands that he tried to excavate a patch of peace for his broken heart.

On Tuesday, a few minutes after learning that my father had suffered a heart attack, my own hands did what they've done all my adult life because of the work my father did with his.

Sitting in the passenger seat of a car speeding toward Cleveland, I pulled out a pen and started to write. I wrote what my sister told me over the phone, that she and Dad's dear friend, Theresa, found him unconscious and not breathing. I wrote that the medics had an awful time bringing him back. I wrote what my brother said, that it didn't look good and I'd better come home right away.

"I know what I'm doing right now," I wrote, acknowledging my game of make-believe as we raced over mile after mile of freeway. "I'm still far enough away that I can tell myself Dad is going to be OK. I haven't seen him yet, haven't seen the scared and weary faces of my siblings and Theresa. I can't see any of them, and so I will myself to see nothing at all."

I was digging, digging, digging for the root of hope.

My first column for this paper was about my dad's lunch pail, how I wanted it but he couldn't find it after retiring from 36 years in a job he hated. We shared opposing forces of the same passion for that pail. He wanted to forget what I must always remember, that he wore his body out so that his four kids could live a life he never knew.

There were moments during the vigil by my father's bed when I felt I was watching a whole way of life coming to an end. He was a working stiff, a manual laborer who always thought he was a no-body but believed he could raise his kids to be somebodies.

With a union job and too many nights of time-and-a-half, he pulled it off. There we were, his somebodies, four college graduates with far easier lives, tending to his every final need.

During the two weeks before my father fell silent, I had my best shot ever to shout out my thanks. My first book had just been published, and its pages are full of stories about him. Twice, I had the chance to introduce him to a cheering crowd in Ashtabula, where I grew up and he still lived.

"Now, I don't want any attention," he told me before both events, but if ever there was a time when I could ignore his orders, it was now. Both times, his eyes grew shiny in his stunned, freckled face as folks hooted and hollered when I described how his hard life had made so much of mine easier.

Last week, I told my dad that so many people were coming up to me at book signings to talk about him. It helped them, they said, to read the stories about his life. It made them feel center-stage proud to come from the working class, instead of squinting into someone else's bright light.

I told my dad about these conversations, and asked how he felt about it all. I'd been a little nervous writing so honestly about his life, about how he was a giant to me but invisible to much of the world.

"Well, I've been thinking about that," he said. "If it helps others to know they aren't alone, that they aren't the only ones who felt like I did, then maybe what I've done did matter." He shrugged his shoulders, but then he grinned. It was the first time I'd ever seen him proud of the work he did.

Dad had another heart attack in Thursday's early morning hours, and it was time to do what we knew he wanted. The machines that pumped his heart and filled his lungs with air were turned off, and I held on to one of his big, gnarly hands for the few minutes it took him to leave.

At 69, Chuck Schultz finally started to believe he was somebody.

Now, he's gone.

And here I am, left behind, my hands at the keyboard, digging, digging, digging for the reason why.

Hundreds of readers sent cards, letters, and e-mails over the next few weeks. I saved every one of them.

I saved something else, too.

A few hours after we buried my father, somebody sneaked into our driveway and pasted a Bush bumper sticker on the back of my car.

I kept that, too, as a reminder that there is no respite, not ever, from a campaign.

nine

Grounding the Candidate

As soon as I heard the hesitation in Joanna Kuebler's voice on the other end of the phone I knew something was up.

Joanna was the campaign communications director, but she had become my friend, too, after Sherrod hired her in 2004 as the press secretary in his congressional office. In addition to being very good at her job, she was intuitive and funny—and almost always knew when she was about to deliver news that would set my teeth to grinding.

"Okay, first of all," she said, "I just want to say this wasn't my idea."

"What wasn't your idea?"

"What I'm going to tell you."

"What might that be?"

"Well, I'm going to tell you."

"When might that be?"

"Well, now."

Silence.

"Joanna?"

"Right."

Big sigh.

"Well, a few days ago a Knight Ridder reporter was hanging out with Sherrod when he was leaving an event very late. So, he asked somebody, 'Where is the congressman going to catch his plane?' "

"His plane?"

"Right. He thought Sherrod would be taking one of those small planes, but we told him that, no, Sherrod always rides in a car, that he never uses those small prop planes."

"Does he know why?"

She hesitated. "Well, yeah, because I didn't think it was a big deal and, anyway, I agree with you."

"And?"

"He thinks it's a big deal."

"You're kidding."

"*So* not."

When Sherrod asked me to marry him on Thanksgiving Day 2003, I told him I would marry him on one condition: "If you ever run for statewide office, I don't want you flying on any of those little planes."

"Never?"

"Not ever."

Three months before I met Sherrod, Senator Paul Wellstone had died, along with his wife and daughter and three staff members, when their small airplane crashed in his home state of Minnesota. He was the fourth sitting United States senator to die in a plane crash, and I could still recite the others listed in the *New York Times* story by Katharine Q. Seelye: Bronson M. Cutting of New Mexico, Ernest Lundeen of Minnesota, and John Heinz of Pennsylvania.

Seelye went on to name other prominent politicians who had died in small plane crashes, including former senator John G. Tower, commerce secretary Ronald H. Brown, and representatives Mickey Leland, Hale Boggs, and Nicholas J. Begich. Senate candidate Mel Carnahan of Missouri also died in a small plane crash in 2000.

It didn't take a mind of any particular brilliance to see that candidates and their staffs can lose hold of their common sense when campaigns heat up. Money, and votes, can be won or lost by how many events you make or miss, and I had absolutely no faith that a candidate and his staff, blinded by fatigue and ambition, would make the right choice when it came to whisking him off to the next appearance. I imagined an exhausted Sherrod surrounded by eager young staffers looking up at the tortured skies and declaring, "What's a little lightning when you've got five hundred donors waiting for you in Cincinnati?"

Senator Harry Reid of Nevada was quoted in Seelye's story as saying that Wellstone's death "engendered a feeling of helplessness."

"I can control what I speak about or what others speak about on the floor, I can campaign for people, I can raise money," he told her. "But I can't control what airplanes do."

I liked former senator Timothy E. Wirth's perspective a lot more. He told Seelye, "You surround yourself [with] a set of rules so that you don't get victimized, and in weather, you shut down. . . . We always had a senior person, a close friend, not a campaign person, who would be able to tell me to go jump in the lake if I got carried away."

Way to go, Wirth.

I recited the *New York Times* story line and verse to Sherrod on the night he proposed, and repeated my one demand. "I'm not going to change my entire life for you and love you with all my heart and all my soul and have it all end because you were in a hurry to get to a fish fry."

"I'll never ride in those planes," he said.

"Never?"

"Not ever."

Apparently Steven Thomma, a reporter based in Washington with Knight Ridder Newspapers, found this fascinating.

"He wants to talk to you," Joanna said.

"About *this*?"

"Yeah."

Now it was my time to be silent.

"I'd never try to tell you what to do," she said. "Not that I could, and not that I would want to . . ."

"Joanna."

"Can he call you? He says it won't take long."

"You bet it won't."

"You know, it *does* say something wonderful about the two of you."

"Which part? That I love my husband or the part where I don't want him to die?"

"You know what I mean."

"I guess that does distinguish me from all those wives who don't love their husbands and do want them to die."

Long sigh from Joanna.

"Please?"

"For you, Joanna. Just for you. Go ahead and give him my numbers."

Hours later, Thomma was on the phone.

"I find it interesting that your husband would agree to this," he said.

"Really?"

"Well, you have to admit, it's a weird request."

"Oh, really," I said. "Are you married?"

He cleared his throat. "Yes."

"Go ask your wife if she thinks it's a weird request."

"Okay. Good point."

"I have several good points, Steve. Would you like to hear them? I can talk to you about health care, or how we're going to raise the minimum wage, or maybe you'd like to chat about the war."

"Actually, I want to write about how your husband never takes small planes."

"This is a story?"

"I think it is. I think readers will care."

And so for the next half-hour or so, we talked about why Sherrod doesn't fly on small planes and why this was a good thing for our marriage. I referred him to Seelye's sidebar in *The New York Times,* too, in an attempt to illustrate further the soundness of my mind.

His story ran in newspapers across the country. All 604 words of it, and only Alix Felsing, the national editor at *The Charlotte Observer,* added a phrase identifying me as someone other than Sherrod's wife.

"Would it be accurate," she wrote in an e-mail to me, "if we said you won a Pulitzer as a Cleveland *Plain Dealer* columnist and that you're taking a year off to help campaigning . . . ?"

She had the inside track on how I might be feeling about the identity theft of campaigning because she is the proud, but often invisible, wife of the *Observer*'s popular columnist Tommy Tomlinson, who was a Pulitzer finalist for commentary in 2005. Tommy and I had exchanged friendly e-mails for a while, and met during the campaign after we both agreed to help judge the Cox Newspapers' annual journalism contests.

When I wrote her a gushing thank you, she responded: "I wondered if you might be experiencing some of the career erasure that I did when I married Tommy. He is my favorite husband of all time, of course, but when I solve the newspaper crisis and create world peace and cure cancer, my obit in this town will read: wife of Tommy."

Sistah!

I do, however, give Thomma credit. He didn't make me look like a loon. In fact, by the time he filed his story he seemed persuaded that perhaps my request wasn't as bizarre as he first thought. He even cited this little statistic from the National Transportation Safety Board: Small planes are "40 times more likely to be in accidents than commercial jetliners."

Then he added this description of a small plane flight by former senator Lauch Faircloth, a Republican from North Carolina, when he was running for governor in 1983. The plane took off from "a poorly lighted airstrip riddled with puddles." This is what happened next, according to Faircloth:

"We were at liftoff. The plane hit a mud hole. It skewed the plane off to the right. We were knocking over trees like a bulldozer. It ripped the wings off. The plane was on fire from one end to the other. Fortunately there was a lake off to the side."

A lake? As in body of water? Did I mention I can't swim? I reached for my inhaler and kept reading.

"We hit the lake and it momentarily put the fire out," Faircloth continued. "But only momentarily. We got out and got away. . . . I was underwater when I saw the light above us and I knew what that was. I swam underwater maybe 20 to 30 feet. By that time the flames from aviation fuel were 100 feet in the air. The fortunate thing was they lit up the area. I could see the shore, and got there."

Am I a genius or what?

Thomma ended his story with our campaign aides insisting that Sherrod meets more voters by riding in a car, what with all those bathroom and hamburger stops. His walk-off was a quote from me:

"It's also a reality check . . . nothing is so important that we have to put ourselves or staffs at risk. I don't care what people think, I get my husband home at night. . . . I'm his wife, and I love him."

The next day, a Republican blogger posted the story and added this comment: "Oh, sure, she loves her husband. Then why did she keep her own name?"

ten

The Hair Apparent

MEN, MEN—EVERYWHERE MEN. ALL OF THEM WHITE, MOST OF them middle-aged.

It was obvious, from Sherrod's announcement tour in December 2005, which reporters would be covering Sherrod's race. Back then, we were standing with our kids and several staffers in a crowded conference room in the Ohio state capitol building, cameras flashing like fireflies. I looked out at the journalists filling the oblong table in front of us, running the TV cameras on the periphery, and I couldn't help but detect a theme.

Now, I have nothing against white men. My dad was a white man. My husband is one, too. So is my son. Not to mention many good friends, most of my newsroom colleagues, and, with occasional exceptions during my career, all of my bosses. I do think, however, if only white men are weighing in, you lose certain perspectives, such as those coming from entire groups of people who don't enjoy the same political, economic, and social advantages that come automatically to a lot of white men. Women, and people of all colors, come to mind.

Some Ohio political reporters, such as *The Plain Dealer*'s Mark Naymik, the Toledo *Blade*'s Jim Tankersley, and the *Dayton Daily News*'s Jessica Wehrman (a woman!), maintained a refreshing focus on issues throughout the campaign. They also challenged DeWine on his increasingly ugly allegations and tactics as the campaign progressed. Not coincidentally, they were younger than the average political reporter and columnist in Ohio.

Some of the other political journalists struck me as having covered politics for too long, which is however long it took them to become so cynical about the process of democracy that anyone who participated in it must be up to something that could not be good or real. They often seemed to focus less on issues than on polls and ad wars, which were easier to cover and kept the horse race galloping along.

One curious trend I noticed with longtime political writers in Ohio was their operating assumption that Sherrod was an angry man. For some reason, they apparently couldn't believe that fifty-three-year-old Sherrod Brown would risk a safe seat in the House and take on a two-term incumbent because he cared about the country. His longstanding commitment to social and economic justice just couldn't be what made him hit the road, day after day, week after week, to attack corporate greed and the government's betrayal of the middle class, or so the theory went.

He wasn't committed. He was just mad.

Columbus Dispatch reporters Jack Torry and Jonathan Riskind seemed wedded to this notion for a while when they set out to write a profile of Sherrod. We first discovered this when concerned friends started calling after Torry or Riskind interviewed them.

One of Sherrod's oldest friends, John Kleshinski, was really worked up about this.

"What's up with this anger theme they're pursuing?" he asked. John and Sherrod grew up in Mansfield, and had known each other for more than thirty years. "He kept pushing me, kept insisting that Sherrod was angry, and I kept telling him he had it wrong, that Sherrod is not angry, he's passionate, and he cares a lot about the state of the country. That has nothing to do with any kind of personal anger. Where are they getting this stuff?"

I, too, answered that question from Riskind, and then Torry, and I assured both of them that the last thing this middle-aged woman would have wanted to marry was an angry man. Unfortunately, I inadvertently fueled their theory by telling them about our Ping-Pong table.

We had celebrated our second wedding anniversary in April, and I decided to surprise Sherrod with something to help him work off the stress of the day. I bought him a Ping-Pong table, and I think I should get mega wife-points for agreeing to put it in our living room for the duration of the campaign. My theory was that after long drives in the car around the state of Ohio, we could unwind a bit with a few light-hearted volleys.

What I had not counted on was that no matter how tired or weary from the road, Sherrod was one competitive sportsman.

"Sports?" you say. "Living room Ping-Pong is a sport?"

In our family, you betcha.

Night after night, Sherrod whacked that little ball as if he were playing for the title in the international World Tennis Team Championships. Leaping and lunging, charging and diving, he was one hustling hunk of he-man as he Ping-Ponged his hapless wife into table tennis oblivion. Sometimes after he won, which was always, he would make me laugh by hopping on the side of the table as if he were jumping the net, and then imitate the roar of the crowd.

I may have mentioned this during my interviews with Riskind and Torry.

To my horror, their story began with this:

Late most evenings, you can find Sherrod Brown smacking a ping pong ball in his center-hall colonial home in the Cleveland suburbs, sometimes imitating the roar of a crowd after a particularly good shot. He thinks about the war in Iraq and—whack. He frets about the minimum-wage worker he met that day and—whack. He dwells on the guy he met without health insurance and—whack.

In a field dominated by driven Type A personalities, Sherrod Brown, a 53-year-old Democratic congressman from Avon, stands out for his political intensity, his religious enthusiasm and his passionate belief that he is one of the bulwarks standing between the guys with the black hats and the everyday worker. He is so determined to prevail and he employs such zinging rhetorical jabs that some critics wonder if he is more angry than intense.

Oops.

I don't know how they came up with Sherrod's supposed thoughts during our games, but I had nobody but myself to blame for the starring role of the Ping-Pong table, which quickly took on a life of its own for the rest of the campaign. It was a convenient metaphor for whatever reporters were looking to prove: Sherrod was always competitive; Sherrod was angry; Sherrod and Connie were an intense couple; Connie was a great wife. (Okay, no one wrote that in reference to my gift of the Ping-Pong table, and I consider that a major lapse in the coverage.) For weeks, everywhere I went, people asked or joked about the Ping-Pong table, and Border's in Westlake even gave me a bucket of balls at my book signing, after hearing me answer a question about Ping-Pong on a local public radio show.

As for the anger angle, Sherrod might have anticipated this had he considered how often he lectured these reporters about how to do their jobs. Sherrod is a true policy wonk. He loves the world of ideas, and that's what he wants to talk about. Too often, especially during a campaign, political writers focus on process. Inevitably, at least one of them called every time a new poll came out and asked the same old questions: Are you worried (or encouraged)? How do you explain the voters' change of heart (or resolve)? Does this change (or affirm) your campaign strategy?

There were so many public polls that after a while it felt as if voters were suffering one long mood swing punctuated with hot flashes, especially in the first few months of the campaign. By the last few weeks, Sherrod was so consistently ahead in polls that some political columnists became a source of entertainment for us. So many had predicted that Sherrod either couldn't win or would be in the fight of his political life. Now these same columnists were arguing that their earlier predictions were actually more nuanced and sophisticated than their one-note analyses had suggested.

And then there were the four debates. After every one, the overwhelming amount of coverage—including the photos that were published—depicted the demeanor of the candidates rather than the substance of their arguments. It seems to me that if you put two men in a room to pick each other apart, you're going to get some arguing. You also will be able to tell who stands for what, but that didn't seem to get nearly as much ink. This made Sherrod testy on occasion, and he wasn't shy about expressing his displeasure, like when the reporter in question was seated across from him or shuffling alongside him with a microphone in his face.

Reporters sometimes complained to me about Sherrod's reprimands, and I wasn't without sympathy for them. I'd been on the receiving end of Sherrod's tirades about the media, especially when we first started dating, and they ain't a lot of fun. He was right that political reporters often asked only the questions they thought would confirm their own assumptions, and that some of them did not educate themselves enough on complicated issues such as trade and the budget deficit. But most reporters I know work hard, and increasingly, they are waging battles in their own newsrooms, which are suffering from budget cuts and editors who've become consumed with profit margins and who fear complaints from the far right.

I don't know a human being who responds well to a diatribe, and

whenever a reporter pulled me aside to complain about an upbraid-
ing from Sherrod, I would have another talk with my beloved that
usually started, "So, I hear we had a little talk with. . . ."

Despite some frustrations with the Ohio reporters, overall they
did a better job of covering the campaign than the national reporters,
who parachuted in for a day or two, if that, and then filed their stories. Outside journalists also had a tendency to divert the discussion
from the issues that Sherrod had decided were central to his campaign: jobs, health care, and education.

We had to remind ourselves constantly that Sherrod, not the
press, was in charge of setting the agenda for his campaign. In June,
for example, a *Newsweek* reporter called Joanna to ask whether the
murder of al-Qaeda leader Abu Musab al-Zarqawi in Iraq would
change our campaign strategy. Sherrod and I were in the car when the
call came. At first, we started to speculate on how it would affect our
campaign, and then it hit us: Nobody in our campaign heard this
news and thought, "Oh, wow, Zarqawi's dead. We have to change
what we're saying."

Zarqawi's murder had nothing to do with our campaign strategy.
That same week, we had lost two more Ohioans in the war. The goal,
the ever-present concern, was how to end this war and bring our
troops home. Sherrod had voted against the war from the beginning,
and we had already attended too many funerals and wakes for fallen
troops. Just because a reporter perceived Zarqawi's murder as a political opportunity didn't make it one.

We encountered this continuously in the campaign: A reporter
would decide something was relevant or true, and Sherrod would
have to spend considerable time and energy trying to steer him or her
back to the issues he thought mattered. Granted, this can quickly
evolve into a game on both sides, and journalists are right to be skeptical whenever a politician begins a sentence with "The real issue
is . . ." But sometimes reporters start with an assumption and then
cling to it for dear life no matter how much irrefutable evidence is offered.

As a journalist, I could certainly see both sides. Journalists and politicians are mighty suspicious of one another. Much energy in a campaign is spent trying to manipulate the media, and just as much effort in the media is invested in trying to capture a "gotcha" moment that can make instant news and derail a candidate. It can lead to testy exchanges, particularly as fatigue takes its toll in the final weeks of a long campaign. There were many days when I thought everyone involved could have benefited from a good nap.

There were exceptions in the national media. Peter Slevin of *The Washington Post* stood out as someone who researched every story as if it were a master's thesis. He was tough, but he was always fair. He also managed to coax from Sherrod the most amusing—or mortifying, depending on whom you asked—quote regarding our relationship.

Peter had tagged along with me for a few events and couldn't help but notice that some women asked if I would be moving to Washington if Sherrod won, their voices always laden with concern. The not-so-subtle message seemed to be that the only thing keeping my charming husband faithful to our marriage was my proximity.

Peter bounced this theory off Sherrod at some point in the campaign, and in the course of a follow-up call to my cell phone he gave me a heads-up on Sherrod's response, only days before his profile of me ran on page one of the *Post*'s Style section.

"*What?*" I said, asking him to repeat what Sherrod had said.

Peter cleared his throat. "Sherrod said, 'If I ever did anything, she wouldn't just cut my balls off. She'd write about it.'"

I gasped.

"You aren't running that, are you?"

"No, we don't use the word 'balls.'"

Oh, good, I thought.

What Peter didn't tell me, probably because he thought all my years in journalism had prepared me for this little sleight of hand, was that the *Post* would run Sherrod's quote, only substituting the word "testicles" in brackets.

Oh, great. Thousands of readers now thought that it was *fear* driving my husband to profound levels of loyalty. Fear of the lovely wife. I'm still hearing about that one.

THEN THERE WAS THE ISSUE OF MY HUSBAND'S APPEARANCE. Specifically, the longtime practice in the media of describing him as "rumpled" and "disheveled," not to mention all the commentary on his delightfully unruly hair.

I'm not saying I married Sherrod because he was cute, but I'd be lying if I said that his curly hair didn't help him through many an argument. And I loved that he didn't really care about how he dressed. As he always told me, he was clean. What more could a woman demand?

Still, I did try to work a woman's magic. His old friend Dennis Eckart, a former congressman, liked to say there was Sherrod B.C. and Sherrod A.C.: Sherrod Before Connie, and Sherrod After Connie.

Unfortunately, most reporters never took note of this crucial transformation in the Life of Sherrod when it came to describing how he looked.

When I met Sherrod, he always wore T-shirts under his dress shirts, but none of them were white. He refused even to open the pack of white undershirts I bought him shortly after we started dating. He had plenty of T-shirts, he insisted, referring to the booty typical of any longtime elected official: dozens upon dozens of T-shirts from a wide range of constituents. Hospital presidents, small-business owners, union members, cause-of-the-week activists—you name 'em, they've got 'em, all in size XL and emblazoned with slogans in big, bold letters.

"Why waste money on undershirts when I have all of these?" Sherrod would say, pointing to the colorful mountains of cotton ranging from dingy white to neon green. Why, indeed.

So, during the campaign, my daily checklist included eyeballing his dress shirt every morning to make sure no logo or slogan was bleeding through. "Locked out at AK Steel—WHY?" read one that got him stopped at the door. Another shirt banned for the duration of the campaign blasted front-and-back protests: "STOP Fast Track Authority Running Over the American Dream," read the front. The back, which I noticed as he was leaving for the car, shouted a new translation of NAFTA: "North America's Future Traded Away."

Whenever Sherrod was in Washington, he had the habit of washing out his shirts in the shower rather than taking the time to run them to the laundry down the street. Clean is clean, was his theory, and he didn't much care that they were as wrinkled as used bedsheets. He figured, once his suit jacket was on, only the front of his shirt would show, and most of that was covered by a tie.

I received rounds of unmerited praise from friends and strangers when I started ironing Sherrod's shirts. When he decided to run for the Senate, I bought more than a dozen no-wrinkle dress shirts, two "travel suits" meant to hold up to the most rugged of rumple, and several "TV ties" from salesman Allen Roy at a local Jos. A. Bank shop. Normally I don't mention brand names, but over time Allen Roy became a real Sherrod advocate, calling my cell phone to complain when reporters continued to describe Sherrod as "rumpled" and "wrinkled" when he was wearing clothing specifically designed to thwart such conspiracies of nature. I think Allen took some of this criticism personally.

"Have they even *looked* at him lately, or are they just using file photos?" he asked in one call. In another call, Allen reminded me to switch Sherrod's ties more often. "People notice these things," he said.

I realize all this hovering on my part suggests I was Sherrod's mother, not his wife, but I'd lost that battle months ago. Total strangers were forever advising me on Sherrod's appearance, as if how he looked was my full-time job. They also felt free to comment on how thin he looked, wondering aloud if I ever cooked for him.

Then there was the hair brouhaha. Sherrod kept telling people "Change is coming," but I had no warning on this one. It started out like any other day. I gave three speeches, then checked my cell phone for messages on my way home. That's when I heard the voice of Sherrod's colleague and dear friend, Congresswoman Stephanie Tubbs Jones.

"Girlfriend," she said, "all I'm going to say is, it'll grow back."

What was she talking about?

I learned three hours later, when Sherrod walked through our front door fresh from Washington and a trip to the House barber.

One look at him, and I screamed.

Every last curl was gone.

Oh, reporters and bloggers jumped on this one. The haircut was part of Sherrod's new "Senator image."

They were right that there was a strategy behind Sherrod's haircut, but they got his motive all wrong.

"I didn't want to have to go to the barber again for a while," he said, holding me close and patting my back as if he were putting out a campfire. "Besides, baby, it'll grow back."

When it came to Sherrod's wardrobe, we never knew when the next hit would come. At a press conference on a muggy August day in Toledo, a woman pulled us aside and said Sherrod should be dressed in cargo shorts.

"Cargo shorts?" Sherrod said, wrinkling his nose.

"Yes," she said. "Cargo shorts. They're more appropriate in this weather."

Sherrod had no idea what these were, so during the news conference I pulled out my digital camera, which I almost always carried in my purse, and photographed the three TV cameramen who showed up to cover his event. All of them were wearing versions of the saggy shorts.

I showed Sherrod the photo once we were back in the car. He took one look at those baggy rear ends and said, "I don't think so."

Novelist Dan Choan, who lives in Cleveland Heights and became an occasional writer about the race for the *New York Times* op-ed page, took a shot on August 6. After interviewing a neighbor, his wife, and someone at a bar, Choan concluded that no one in Ohio cared about the Senate race and that Sherrod "looks like the manager of the men's department of the new Macy's." Some guy at Macy's had to be real mad at that one.

Speaking of *The New York Times,* columnist David Brooks weighed in on Sherrod's appearance, too, writing that Sherrod wore "cheap suits." This really set off Allen Roy, of course, and I wasn't too happy about it either, having been the one who handed over the charge card. But then, Brooks also claimed in the same column that Sherrod found a seat in the middle of a crowded room to draw attention to himself, when in reality Sherrod was pulling up a chair to sit next to his mother.

Sherrod took all this coverage of his attire in stride. He was who he was, and no amount of hovering with a can of spray starch was going to change him. I was reminded of this one morning in June when I tried to persuade him to pack four ironed shirts instead of the three he'd already stuffed into his duffel bag for another week in Washington.

"I can always wash one out in the shower if I need a clean shirt," he said.

"Sherrod."

He grinned and gave me a kiss.

"Baby? You got me to eighty percent. The last twenty percent is going to be real hard."

eleven
Family Matters

MOTHER'S DAY WAS ON THE HORIZON, AND WE WERE TRYING TO figure out how to carve out time with Sherrod's mother.

That's when I started to see politics as a beast that was forever trying to set different rules for families and marriages.

Politics wanted us to believe that all the cherished rituals and traditions of family life—birthdays, anniversaries, graduations, even dinner at home—were but obstacles in the way of victory, and victory was the thing that mattered. Everyone in the candidate's family was expected to join in lockstep with the campaign.

But that beast was wrong—it was the rest of life that breathed oxygen into our lungs, and it was alarming to see how politics forced spouses and family members to become warriors in the fight for family.

Recently John Ryan and I had been on one of our rare trips together. He sometimes asked to drive me so that we could go over various aspects of the campaign, from staffing to issues, but also so that he could check on how I was doing.

About an hour into our drive, he turned to me and said, "I've never known a spouse to give so much to her husband's campaign."

I looked at him in horror. "You mean not all wives *do* this?"

"Oh, no. No way. They'll say, 'Okay, you go ahead and run, and I'll show up for the occasional event.' But most of them go on with their own lives. What you are doing is phenomenal."

"Don't nominate me for sainthood just yet," I said. "I'm a journalist, remember? It wasn't like I had a life I *could* go on with as long as Sherrod was running for the Senate. What was I going to do? Sit home and pout?"

"Okay, no saint status for you," he said. "But still, your level of involvement is rare, and I'm glad you're here."

I was surprised by how much John's words meant to me. As we drove through the night, I looked out the window and blinked back tears I couldn't explain. I started thinking about my daughter, Cait, who was the youngest of our four kids. She had felt the demands of the campaign perhaps a bit earlier than the others, which I didn't fully understand until a call from her sent up a flare.

Cait and I had been quite the duo for eleven years of single parenthood. It was Mom and Cait, all the time. Whenever she called, I dropped everything to talk. That's how it had always been before marriage to Sherrod, and I thought nothing had changed until that spring day when she called and must have sensed I was in the middle of something. I was in Los Angeles, waiting for a flight home.

"I know you're busy, Mom," she said almost immediately. "I'll talk to you later." And then she hung up.

I held the silent phone to my ear and realized this was the second time in as many days that she had done that. I called her right back.

"Hey, I'm never too busy for you—you know that, right?"

"Okay, Mom."

"Cait?"

"Ohh-*kaay,* Mom. I gotta go."

I felt sick to my stomach. The vertigo of campaign life was distorting my vision.

Days earlier, my son, Andy, and his fiancée, Kristina, had excitedly e-mailed the date of their engagement party in Long Island. I went from seeing the party as a celebration of their impending marriage to something that would derail my work for the campaign—all in the few minutes it took me to realize I was scheduled to give three speeches that day.

What a ludicrous response.

Sitting on the plane waiting for takeoff, my mind raced. Would Andy and Stina forgive me if I told them I could not spare the two days it would take me to fly there and spend time with his future in-laws? (They did, and our son-in-law, Michael Stanley, attended on our family's behalf.)

How would Sherrod do without me? Everyone on the campaign told me he did better when I was with him. What if, in a moment of frustration and exhaustion, he committed an error in judgment that ended up as a prime "gotcha" moment in the press? And what on earth made me think I could possibly have that much influence on him in the first place?

I thought about what my friend Michael Naidus had said to me at dinner the night before. Michael was a segment producer for Craig Ferguson's show, and we became instant friends after my first appearance on *The Late Late Show* in the fall of 2005. Michael was kind and smart, and I had come to value his dead-on observations about people and life in general. He was one of the first to send an encouraging e-mail after I took a leave from *The Plain Dealer,* urging me to continue writing columns and send them to him instead, until I returned to the paper. He had been worried about me then, and after listening to me describe the campaign, it was clear he was still concerned.

"You will have to work hard not to be cynical by the end of this campaign," he said. "I think you're up to it; in fact, I know you are. But I want you to be aware, so that it doesn't sneak up on you."

He was the second person to remind me to be ever vigilant when it came to focusing on what mattered. Two days earlier, the *Today* show's Ann Curry had kindly praised my composure during our segment when we discussed my book and my father's recent death. She said she was devoted to her father, and then she said she had already lost her mother and a brother.

"You know what I learned?" she said. "If you can focus on gratitude, you can't be sad." She smiled and nodded, her eyes misting. "If you're grateful, it's impossible to be sad at the same time."

On the five-hour flight home, I stopped thinking about what I had lost and tried to focus instead on my own gratitude list.

I was grateful that my father got to see my first book, and his starring role in it, before he died.

I was grateful that Sherrod had the chance, the privilege, of running for the U.S. Senate, and for the many decent, hardworking people willing to take a chance on him.

I was grateful, too, for our kids, Andy, Emily, Elizabeth, and Caitlin. All of them—and our son-in-law, Mike Stanley, and Stina, too—were already involved in the campaign and would dramatically increase their efforts, and their level of sacrifice, as Election Day neared. They believed in Sherrod with all their hearts, and they willingly disrupted their lives for an entire year because they also believed in what and who he was fighting for.

And I was mighty grateful that my mother-in-law was healthy and full of fight on behalf of her son. This was no surprise to anyone who knew Emily Campbell Brown. During the 2004 presidential race, she had been so frustrated by the lack of a voter registration drive in Mansfield's African American community that she set up a card table at a shopping center day after day and led the effort to register more than a thousand voters. Before Sherrod's campaign was over, she would commit to raising ten thousand dollars and then raised more than thirty thousand with a single fundraiser in Sherrod's hometown of Mansfield.

We would make time for her on Mother's Day, and I would start making more time for my daughter, too. She was a sophomore in college and the only one of our children still living near home.

I landed in Cleveland and headed for a fundraiser, where I would speak for Sherrod, who had votes in Washington. I called Caitlin on the way, but she didn't answer.

I left a message, spoke at the fundraiser, then headed for a labor event.

A half-hour later, I left another message for her. Gave another speech.

Two hours later, I called again. This time she answered.

"Hey. What's up with not returning my calls?"

She sighed. "I returned all of them, Mom."

"Did you leave messages?"

"Yup."

Walter O'Malley, our driver, looked over at me and shot a sympathetic smile. "You left your phone in the car, remember? You didn't want it to ring during your speeches."

At that moment, there weren't enough apologies in the world to convince my daughter that she mattered at all. I was going to have to wrestle that beast called politics on a regular basis.

An hour later, I was standing in my kitchen when my youngest sister, Toni, called.

"Hey, Con, can I ask you a question?"

"Shoot."

"You think it's okay that I've called Dad's house a few times to hear his voice on the answering machine?"

I grabbed a chair and sat down.

"It's fine," I said.

"You sure?"

"Yeah. Now, if you're doing that six months from now, we'll have to have a talk."

"Okay."

I was grateful that she trusted me enough to call.

MAY TURNED OUT TO BE A MONTH OF REVELATIONS FOR SHERROD and me. And in the process, he started whistling again, which I knew was a very good sign.

When you're running for elected office, people seldom ask, "How are you?" What they always want to know is, "How's it going?"

In the beginning of the campaign, Sherrod and I answered too honestly. We'd shake our heads and say, "This is so hard." Sometimes, we'd list the reasons why: the endless push to raise millions of dollars, introducing yourself to entire regions of people who had never heard of you, total strangers giving you unsolicited advice on everything from how you wear your hair to what colors you choose for your bumper stickers. And then there was all that wear and tear on our middle-aged bodies as we traveled hundreds of miles a day cooped up in a car.

It didn't take long, though, for us to realize that whenever we answered like that, their faces would fall. They weren't really asking out of any concern for us. They were asking "How's it going?" because they wanted reasons to be hopeful. It had been fourteen years since a Democrat had won statewide office in Ohio, and the last thing they wanted to hear was whining.

Fortunately, around the same time in May, an activist in Cincinnati named Michele Young came to a book signing and immediately adopted me as her project. We were the same age, both mothers, and where I saw the end of my identity, she saw the beginning of a whole new career.

"You need to read this new book about Franklin and Eleanor Roosevelt," she told me. "I'm going to send it to you. It's all about how they gave people hope. That's what you and Sherrod need to do, too. We need hope, Connie. Hope."

The book, *The Defining Moment,* by *Newsweek*'s Jonathan Alter, arrived at the campaign office a few days later. It focused on FDR's first hundred days in office, and I devoured it, reading sections aloud to Sherrod late at night.

"What FDR changed most in his first one hundred days was how Americans felt about their future," I said. "He gave them hope, and that's what we have to do."

After that, Sherrod and I started talking a lot about the concept of hope and how to bring it alive for the men and women of Ohio. We started by offering a very different answer to the question "How's it going?" We knew it was important to be upbeat no matter how bad a week we were having, and this helped us focus on what was actually going right.

"It's going better than we dared hope," I'd tell people. They often looked a little surprised at first, then relieved, even delighted. Our job was to stoke a hope in them that we were ready for whatever came our way and embolden them for the long days ahead.

Over time, I started to think that voters don't want you to be one of them when it comes to what you can endure. Oh, sure, they want to know you're a lot like them when it comes to where you shop for groceries and how much you love your kids, but they want to believe you have the kind of strength and courage that keeps you standing in the middle of a hurricane. We saw that question in their eyes every time they warned us about a Republican "October surprise," spun worst-case scenarios about voter fraud, or conjured up images of a diabolical Karl Rove who would do anything to keep Sherrod out of office. They'd lay out the threat, and then look at us as if to say, "Are you up for this?"

Our answer had to be, "You betcha."

And every time we said it, we meant it. That's the funny thing about focusing on what you can do rather than what isn't happening at the moment. I don't think it was coincidental that I started feeling better about the campaign as soon as I began reassuring others that we knew what we were doing and could handle any ugliness that came our way.

Good thing, too, because it wouldn't be long before we'd have the chance to prove it.

If Not Now—When?

twelve

By the end of May, Sherrod was getting nervous about his campaign's ad strategy. Immediately before the Ohio primary, Mike DeWine went on the air with two positive ads meant to depict him as a mild-mannered "independent" in the midst of rampant partisanship. It would be one of the few consistent themes of his campaign: Mike DeWine, unlike ardent liberal Sherrod Brown, could "get things done." Sherrod, just as consistently, kept pointing out that Mike DeWine voted with President George W. Bush 96 percent of the time but spent most of his campaign bragging about the other 4 percent.

Most political analysts say that positive ads do little to persuade voters, but candidates who can afford to do so usually start with feel-good ads praising themselves. DeWine, who had nearly double Sherrod's cash on hand by then, was no exception.

One of the constant pressures in such a high-stakes race is deciding when to go on the air with campaign ads. Television advertising devours more than two-thirds of fundraising dollars, and Ohio is one of the most expensive states in the country because it has so many separate television ad markets: Toledo, Cleveland, Columbus, Cincinnati, Dayton, Youngstown, Steubenville, Lima, and Zanesville, as well as the Wheeling and Huntington/Charleston markets in West Virginia, which reach into southern and eastern Ohio.

It was our estimated television budget that forced us to set a fundraising goal that started at $7 million, considered very low, and went as high as $17 million, which would put us in the ballpark with DeWine, or so we thought. Everything was speculation. We had no idea how much of that money, if any, would be raised or contributed by the Democratic Senatorial Campaign Committee.

On May 31, I had a lengthy conference call with our pollster, Diane Feldman, and two of our consultants, David Doak and Tom O'Donnell of DCO Media. John Ryan and various other staff members also joined the call. Sherrod had asked for the strategy session because DeWine had already spent nearly eight hundred thousand dollars on soft ads meant to lift his profile with Ohio voters.

We had spent nothing on TV ads so far, and, barring an attack ad from DeWine over the summer, we didn't plan to go on the air until after Labor Day. This strategy was starting to worry Sherrod. He wanted to discuss whether we should go up earlier on TV. He wanted to define Mike DeWine before DeWine had a chance to define Sherrod Brown. Sherrod was especially concerned about southern and western Ohio, where many people had never heard of Sherrod.

Diane Feldman was just as concerned that Mike DeWine benefited most when voters didn't know much about him, and that it was our job to get the word out about his special-interest money and his votes that betrayed the middle class.

Sherrod couldn't join the call because of scheduled speeches, so I took notes throughout the phone call. Rereading them months later, I realized the conversation illustrated a great deal about the how and why behind campaign ads. It also provided a glimpse into how we made decisions about when, and what, to air in our own campaign, and reflected a general anxiety over how much the DSCC would help Sherrod. I was noticeably silent in the following exchange because I had never been involved in a campaign, and all this back-and-forth about how and when to market my husband rendered me speechless, which is rare indeed.

Pollster Diane Feldman had worked for Sherrod for ten years, and she knew Sherrod better than any of the other consultants. Smart and direct, Feldman seldom drew attention to herself with self-promotion. We paid a lot of attention to her because she was virtually always right, and I listened with a heavy heart when she said it was up to us to define Mike DeWine, and then outlined how we should do it.

"We should be more pointed on our negative," she said. "It helps Mike DeWine in Ohio when voters don't know him. We need to connect him to [the political scandals in Ohio], to the pay-to-play culture. It puts the world on notice that we'll go after him. It also attacks the whole notion of DeWine as moderate."

She added that she had "enormous concerns" that waiting could hurt fundraising for later ads.

David Doak laid out what a "perfect world" would look like in a campaign: "We'd go up first and define Sherrod in positive terms but choose those traits we'll use to contrast him with DeWine. Then we'd hit hard on DeWine before he hits us. Then we'd hit hard in response after DeWine attacks Sherrod."

That perfect world was also an imaginary world for the Sherrod Brown campaign. "I think DeWine will have more money than we do," said Doak, "so we have to bypass the first stop and move right to the second."

Tom O'Donnell posed the crucial question: Do we want to start this war early? "DeWine's interest is to run us out of money early so they can overpower us in the fall," O'Donnell said. "Do we want to start this war earlier than later?"

O'Donnell was also wondering just how much the DSCC would

invest in Sherrod's race, which was one of about a dozen competitive Senate races. "One thing that worries me is that the DSCC doesn't think Ohio is special," O'Donnell said. "Their only interest is how to get the majority for their bosses. If you're in the hunt, you get the money. If not, you're cut off."

Doak agreed. "My experience is that at the end, whoever looks closest in the polls gets the money."

The bang for the buck mattered, too, said Feldman. "If we're two points ahead and Rhode Island is two points ahead, then they're going to give it to the smaller, cheaper state because Ohio sucks up the money," Feldman said.

"In the same way we strategize against the DSCC, they're strategizing against us regarding the decision to help us early versus later," Doak added.

Michael O'Neil, an Ohio native who worked for the DSCC, came over to our campaign to help with fundraising. He said our hunches were right. "Pretty much everything said here is true. The DSCC is going to give us a certain amount of money. After Labor Day, it may go up, but it won't go down."

Doak said that meant we needed to get aggressive—now: "That argues for doing what we need to do early to stay in the race. If we go soft, then DeWine will come back and cream us. Getting to DeWine early means we can paint the picture of DeWine."

Feldman cautioned against using a strategy meant to pump up Sherrod. Her polling and focus group research indicated that was a losing strategy. "Having listened to these swing voters, I can tell you they're not going to vote *for* anyone. As wonderful as Sherrod is, it is far harder to get them to believe in Sherrod Brown than it is to get them to vote against DeWine."

O'Donnell was growing impatient on the call. "We have no idea what DSCC is willing to spend. This conversation is premature until we have some kind of ballpark figure from DSCC."

And Feldman felt we were aiming too low in our fundraising goals.

"Our seven-million-dollar budget scares me," she said. "We won't be able to go up right after Labor Day."

There seemed to be so many variables: O'Donnell said the only thing that would raise money for Sherrod was good poll numbers. Doak said we should look at this as a chess game: We have to anticipate DeWine's moves. Then O'Donnell added that we had to be in a position to respond quickly, which meant having enough money to go up with ads.

Then we went back to the war analogy again.

"We can either start the war or wait for him to start the war," Doak said. "DeWine could be saying, 'What could the DSCC do with money if we start now?' Republicans will spend more money than we do. 'Early' is not defined in calendar terms. It's relative to the other person's race. If DeWine goes up on TV, we can't afford not to. If the DSCC won't help, we're going to have to gamble."

Then he added that going early was not "in our strategic interest" because we didn't have enough money.

In the alternative, we would have to rely on our press operation to get the word out, Feldman said. More news conferences, more radio calls, more interviews and press releases.

That conversation quickly returned to what the DSCC might, and might not, do to help Sherrod win.

"We can't look at the DSCC as a savior," Doak said, "but at some point we will have to be willing to gamble. The key question: We have to figure out what they *will* do for us. We don't know how much they *may* give us, but we have to try to rope them into making them help us."

O'Donnell wanted us to get aggressive on our own. "People aren't in the mood to be romanced," he said. "They want to see how the other guy's a schmuck. DeWine had a $750,000 buy and look what it got him: Nothing."

O'Donnell was right. Some public polls showed DeWine getting a slight bump, if any, from his puff ads, but our internal polling indicated that DeWine had just wasted a lot of money. Sherrod was pulling ahead.

Joanna raised the question Sherrod and I asked ourselves every day: "What if DeWine goes negative?"

"We have to go up," Doak said. "We can't worry about tomorrow. I trust Diane's poll. After three weeks of TV, we're ahead. We shouldn't worry about these crazy public polls."

Feldman recited her public poll primer that she would have to repeat many times to us during the campaign: "In some of these public polls, you're talking to a lot of nonvoters and people who are paying absolutely no attention. It's bad polling. I believe my poll is real and predictive." (She ended up being right.)

Joanna wanted to know, if polling drove fundraising, which polls the DSCC was paying attention to.

For now, they were tracking Diane Feldman's. That sharing of information, though, would end sometime in August because of the McCain-Feingold Campaign Finance Law, which forbids any communication between campaigns and independent groups. The DSCC was doing its own polling, too, and we would not be able to know their numbers, either.

There were a lot of sighs all the way around. Would the DSCC stay with us, or would we have to hold our own in the endgame?

As it turned out, the DSCC would help Sherrod more than any other Democratic Senate candidate in the country.

But on May 31, we didn't know that. All we knew was that Mike DeWine had a lot more money than Sherrod, and he had a history of waging ugly campaigns.

We were stuck in a waiting game, hoping that money wasn't the only thing that could defeat Mike DeWine.

thirteen

Coming Out

SOMETIMES I DIDN'T LIKE THE PEOPLE WHO SUPPOSEDLY WERE ON our side. Even worse, I didn't like who I was when I was with them.

In early June, Sherrod and I attended a dinner for hundreds of Democratic supporters around the state, many of them major donors to political campaigns. An affluent couple was seated at our table, and when one of the evening's speakers mentioned his Christian values from the stage, they started shaking their heads.

"I hate that Democrats are suddenly talking about their faith," he said. "I think born-agains are idiots, but I'll fight for their right to be idiots—just keep them away from our government."

I am an ardent advocate for separation of church and state, but his derision for born-again Christians wiped away any appetite I might have had for the dinner. I wanted to lean over and say, "My mother was a born-again Christian, and she was one of the kindest, most progressive people I've ever known."

My mother, Janey, was devout, and she raised us to believe that being a Christian meant fixing ourselves and helping others, not the other way around. Her faith was simple: God loves everybody, no exceptions, and that's the standard for the rest of us. While we did not agree on everything, my mother and I found common ground in the social justice issues driven by our faith. It stung to hear this man at the table lump my mother with the far-right fanatics who had co-opted our faith for their own political use.

This happened too often when I was in the company of fellow liberals. Many of them seemed to harbor a troubling disdain for other people's practice of religion, and it was counter to what liberals are supposed to stand for, which is tolerance at all levels.

Every poll on religion shows that the overwhelming majority of Americans believe in God, and Sherrod and I were meeting them every day on the campaign trail. We sat next to them in African American churches, where, without fail, someone always handed us their own Bible to follow along when the preacher recited scripture. They worked at homeless shelters and soup kitchens, and at family planning centers. They were accountants who worked after hours to help poor parents fill out forms for the Earned Income Tax Credit, well-paid union members fighting for an increase in the minimum wage, and lawyers volunteering to represent indigent defendants.

I didn't say any of this to my dinner companions. In their eyes, I wasn't Janey Schultz's daughter, and I wasn't a newspaper columnist. I was the wife of Senate candidate Sherrod Brown, and challenging them could hurt support for my husband. If I'd learned anything by June, it was that there was no such thing as a private conversation in politics. So, instead, I sat there and held my tongue, angrier at myself than at anything they had said.

Later that same evening, the husband of Jennifer Brunner, a long-time friend of Sherrod's who was running for secretary of state, helped soften the edges. Rick Brunner was a practicing lawyer who put his own career on hold for a year to work on his wife's campaign. No matter how exhausted, he always beamed whenever he ran into us. He was having the time of his life. When we joined other statewide candidates and their spouses onstage, Rick turned to me and gushed, "Isn't it great getting the chance to spend so much time together? I mean, I know it's hard leaving your job, but isn't it wonderful to travel so much together?"

I had to admit he was right. This was the most time Sherrod and I had spent together since we'd married two years before, and the rigors of campaign life were actually bringing us closer.

"You learn so much about someone when you spend this amount of time together," I shouted over the din of the music and applause. "Good things. You learn a lot of good stuff."

He grinned. "Yeah, you sure do."

I watched big burly Rick standing next to his wife, his hand resting gently on her back as she waved to the crowd. Every muscle in his face telegraphed what he was thinking: "Look at my wife. Ain't she something?"

"What are you smiling about?" Sherrod asked. He knew these staged events seldom brought out my cheerful side.

"Oh, nothing," I said, reaching for the curls that were no longer on his head. "Oy. This hair."

"It'll grow back, baby," he said, pulling me close in front of the hundreds of cheering people. "It'll all grow back."

IN RETROSPECT, I SEE THAT JUNE WAS MY "COMING OUT" MONTH in the campaign. Finally, I had found ways to use my journalist's skills to feel useful in my husband's race.

The first break came when Romi Lassally, features editor for Arianna Huffington's progressive blog, *The Huffington Post*, sent an e-mail asking me to write about Sherrod's campaign. Her father-in-law, Peter Lassally, had told her I was on a leave of absence but itching to write. Peter had produced Johnny Carson's show, and now did the same thing for Craig Ferguson. We had gotten to know each other over dinner one night with his remarkable wife, writer Alice Lassally, and my friend Michael Naidus, who set up the whole thing because he never stopped looking out for me. Now, apparently Peter had taken on that job, too.

Romi is forty-three, a married mother of three with boundless energy who almost single-handedly breathed new life into me as a writer. She didn't know that. In fact, she acted as if I were doing *her* the favor when she asked me to write dispatches from the road. Her timing could not have been better.

Romi's first e-mail came on the heels of a disappointing exchange I'd had with an editor from *Women's eNews,* a blog originating in New York. Its mission statement reads, "Women's eNews is the definitive source of substantive news—unavailable anywhere else—covering issues of particular concern to women and providing women's perspectives on public policy. It enhances women's ability to define their own lives and to participate fully in every sector of human endeavor."

A local freelance writer had pitched a profile of me to *Women's eNews,* but their senior editor dismissed the idea out of hand because I had taken a leave for my "hubby," as she put it.

The writer was stunned, and I was furious. I've been a feminist since my late teens, and the response of this editor, who was almost exactly my age, triggered old memories of my time as a stay-at-home mother, when I felt judged as pointless by some women who had full-time careers. The whole point of feminism was to provide a full palette of options for women, and then respect the choices they made for their own lives. We are not a monolithic group—wasn't that our point?

I wrote to that editor, assuring her that I was not trying to persuade her to change her mind about covering me, but I did hope she wouldn't write off the next feminist whose choices didn't meet her criteria for a meaningful life. I laid out my reasons for taking a leave of absence, and ended my letter with a plea:

> Please try harder in the future to cast a wider net when deciding which women merit your attention. I've been a feminist since adolescence, and at 48, I'm still meeting women who make me

stretch the boundaries of how we define the word and embrace the cause.

Instead of addressing the issue, she responded by asking me to write for their website. I declined, assuring her that I suspected no evil motives on her part but did hope we could pursue the discussion of how we define feminism. She wasn't interested in that. Instead, she accused me of overreacting to her original note. She did, however, apologize for calling Sherrod my "hubby."

See why I was so happy to hear from Romi Lassally?

I wrote only four pieces for *The Huffington Post,* including one on why Sherrod and I weren't afraid of Republican smear tactics, but my lack of contributions wasn't because Romi wasn't prodding me for more. She was always coming up with column ideas, and she was a wonderful sounding board for me whenever I needed to vent about life on the road.

"Oh, you should write about that!" she'd say. "Oh, that one, too, that would make a great column!"

Campaigning, I found, sucked up most of my energy, and I ended up not writing as much as I'd hoped after a daily regimen of note taking. But I am so grateful to Romi for believing that this wife, on a leave of absence from her own career, still had something worth saying.

THE OTHER BREAK FOR ME CAME AFTER I BOUNCED AN IDEA OFF Sherrod and John Ryan.

We knew Sherrod could not possibly visit every town and village in Ohio. So, what if we used me to focus on small towns, where so many working-class voters lived and worked? I was a small-town girl myself, having grown up in Ashtabula in a blue-collar life right out of a Bruce Springsteen song. I could talk to people and, more important, listen to them and take notes, with the promise that I would share their hopes and concerns with Sherrod.

John and Sherrod loved the idea, and John suggested calling it Connie's Hometown Tour. We scheduled five to seven stops in a single day across several counties, with Sherrod recording radio ads that would run a few days before each visit asking folks to welcome his wife, Connie, to their hometown. Joanna and her press team did advance work with the media to attract coverage in many of the smaller newspapers and local radio and TV stations. I soon learned that small-town reporters enjoyed chatting with a fellow journalist from Ohio's largest newspaper. I knew I was really succumbing to campaign fever when I celebrated any headline that called me "Sherrod Brown's Wife."

I had various drivers during that time, and they all felt like family after a while. If ever there is an unsung hero in a campaign—besides the scheduler—it is the driver. You count on him to stay awake when you're exhausted and to get you there on time no matter what obstacles roll out in front of you. He is forever on the lookout for the perfect parking space and tolerable bathroom stop, and his radar is always up for the other party's trackers, who hope to capture you on videotape in a clumsy or, God forbid, inappropriate moment. The driver makes sure you always have enough brochures, buttons, and stickers, keeps the car stocked with bottled water, and listens as you practice material for speeches.

One more thing: Our drivers had to keep to themselves everything they heard in the car. In that spirit, we nicknamed the campaign car "Vegas."

Three young men drove me: Chris Stelmarski, a newly minted high school graduate who doubled as our IT guy because he'd never met a computer problem he couldn't solve; Zach West, a recent college graduate who lived and breathed politics, having known Sherrod since the day he was born; and Ben Nyhan, another recent college graduate of unflappable resolve, who volunteered for us long before he was paid and never stopped thanking me for the adventure of a lifetime.

Field staff and volunteers, under the direction of John Hagner, "outperformed their résumés," as John Ryan always put it. They built events for Sherrod and me throughout the campaign.

None of the hometown tours would have worked without Wendy Leatherberry, a seasoned veteran activist at age thirty-one, who used up weeks of vacation from her social services job to volunteer as my ever-present traveling companion.

Wendy was raised to save the world. She is the only child of Bill Leatherberry and Diane Phillips-Leatherberry. They named her childhood cat Sam, after Sam Ervin of Watergate fame. When she was six, they took her to the swearing-in ceremonies for Ohio's new governor and newly elected secretary of state, Sherrod Brown. She was in second grade and was supposed to write a report about her experience as a trade-off for missing school, but the teachers in her school district ended up being on strike that week. Her mother took her to the picket line so that Wendy could give her report in person.

In 1986, writer Jimmy Breslin interviewed eleven-year-old Wendy after a confluence of circumstances alerted him to her desire to be president of the United States. When he asked her what her first act as president would be, the little squirt didn't hesitate. She told him she would withdraw William Rehnquist's nomination for Chief Justice of the Supreme Court.

In seventh grade, she was already donating babysitting money to a presidential campaign, insisting that her parents allow her to buy a money order so that Joe Biden would know the money came directly from her. When she was a freshman in college on a visit home to celebrate Passover, her mother insisted they have dinner at a shopping center in the black community where someone had recently been shot. The point of this impromptu excursion was to prove that white people weren't afraid.

By the time I met Wendy, she had already held significant roles in several campaigns and was the youngest member and only woman on the Cleveland Heights–University Heights school board. She was also board president, and I bragged about her constantly in speeches, especially when the room was full of women.

Wendy had been a steadfast reader of my column and a friend, so she already knew we had a lot in common. What she didn't know at first was how uncomfortable I was with campaigning.

I wasn't accustomed to approaching strangers without a reporter's notebook. It was one thing to be armed with a pen and pad and scribbling down the answers to questions I asked. It was another to thrust out my hand and try to convince someone visiting the cow barn at the county fair that they should care about my husband. I wince at how awkward I felt when I showed up at diners or festivals and interrupted someone's conversation to talk about a Senate race that hadn't even crossed their minds.

After one particularly hot and exhausting round of county fairs, I wanted to put a stop to those visits—and the tours. I was not convinced we were doing any good, and my asthma was acting up. I was tired of wheezing my way through dusty days. Wendy had the courage to sit down and write me a lengthy e-mail about why I needed to keep going.

"The whole point of the Hometown Tour is to show people in smaller communities that they matter," she wrote.

> It's a fact that county fairs are a huge focal point in many of these communities. I think that leaves us in the position of requesting that field staff structure our participation in fairs for the most positive experience it can be.... We all found [a previous tour] a useful exercise because you were able to meet and talk with "real voters" who aren't already engaged in some way....

I picked up the phone.

"Oh, okay, I'll go," I told her, "as long as you're with me."

"Deal."

Wendy was always at my side, taking notes, reminding me of names, spotting people I ought to meet. She was also good at whisking me off when it was time to go.

Everything, it seemed, came with a learning curve. I was used to giving speeches, but not the kind that began and ended with my husband's opinions, and I was as bored as the rooms full of people listening to me had to be as I rambled on about health care this and lost jobs that, constantly peppering my remarks with references to Sherrod.

I had been brainstorming with Wendy on how to pump up the talks, and she kept pushing me to tell stories from my own life. I wasn't convinced that anyone would care about that. Then one evening I stood within spitting distance of yet another man suggesting I didn't know my place because I wouldn't change my name.

We were in a working-class town in eastern Ohio, where almost 150 people, mostly older couples, had gathered for an annual Democratic dinner. I was scheduled to speak for Sherrod, and the man in his seventies who introduced me said, "Well, now we're going to hear from Sherrod Brown's wife. She's one of those women who won't change her name, but here she is."

I saw Wendy exchange glances with our driver, Chris, and then she shot me a weak smile. I returned the smile, and hers vanished. She knew I was up to something.

"Well, that's right," I said, standing in front of the room. "I didn't change my name. It's Connie Schultz, and let me tell you why."

I explained how Sherrod and I had been married less than two years, and how I was already entrenched in a career where my name was my currency. Then I shook my head.

"But you know what? That's not the only reason I kept this name. I want to tell you about my parents."

I told them the story of Janey and Chuck Schultz, how neither of them had gone to college but insisted on it for their four children.

"My mother was a nurse's aide and a hospice worker. My father was a union member and worked for the utility company in a job he hated every day of his life. My mother died at sixty-two. My dad just died of a heart attack at sixty-nine. My parents wore their bodies out so that we'd never have to, and one of the reasons I fell in love with Sherrod Brown was because he has spent his entire career fighting for the people I come from."

By the time I was finished, many in the room were wiping away tears, including the man who had refused to introduce me by name.

"I think Schultz is a wonderful name!" he announced from the front of the room. "I don't think you should ever drop your daddy's name."

He walked me all the way to the car, telling me he'd just had heart surgery himself and sometimes it clouded his thinking. I gave him a big hug and told him I hoped he felt better real soon.

"You need anything, Sherrod needs anything, you give us a call," he said through my open window. "We're going to make him the next senator from Ohio."

Wendy waited until we pulled away.

"Told you."

"Sorry?"

"Told you to start telling your own story."

"Yeah. Well. Some things you learn the hard way."

From then on, Mom and Dad were on the campaign trail with me, and the going got a lot easier.

One evening, after a long Hometown Tour day, my godson, Davis Filippell, rode home with us. Davis's parents, Mark and Buffy, had stood by me during the most difficult time in my life, when I was going through my divorce in the early 1990s. I have known Davis since the moment of his birth, and at age sixteen he was proving to be a devoted campaign volunteer, calling voters from headquarters, doing advance work for campaign stops, and stepping up wherever he was needed. This was his first time working for a political campaign, and our first time together on the campaign trail. On the ride home I asked him what he thought he had learned so far.

"This is so much more work than I had imagined," he said. "Everybody works so hard every day for months and months—and at the end of it all, you can still lose."

I looked at his face, and realized he was really worried that Sherrod would not win.

"You know what," I said, "Sherrod's going to be home when we get there. Why don't you talk to him about that?"

"Really?"

"Yeah. Really."

As soon as Davis and I walked through the door, Sherrod asked how our day had gone. I turned to Davis and said, "Go ahead. Tell Sherrod what you asked me in the car."

I watched my godson and my husband standing less than a foot apart in our kitchen as Davis laid out his concerns and Sherrod answered.

"Davis, politics can be cruel," Sherrod said. "In primaries, you can have a lot of losers, but always only one winner."

Sherrod looked at Davis's worried face and smiled.

"Nobody's working harder than we are, Davis. And there's no way Mike DeWine and his people are working as hard as we are. And that's why we're going to win."

Davis smiled, and Sherrod shook his hand.

"They also don't have you," Sherrod said. "No way are we going to lose."

WENDY INADVERTENTLY HELPED ME FEEL MORE COMFORTABLE IN my own skin, too. With a camera always in tow, she took photos everywhere we went, and she encouraged me to write stories for the campaign's website about the people we met and the places we visited. I did a little of this, but I was uncomfortable writing what amounted to a society column, and I cringed at the sight of so many bad photos of me posted on the Web.

I had expected others to scrutinize my appearance. I had followed the coverage of Theresa Heinz Kerry and Elizabeth Edwards, and I knew how cruel writers could be in the name of journalism. What I didn't expect was my own sudden obsession with how I looked on any given day.

There was something about the honesty of photos taken in broad daylight that forced me to come to terms with an essential truth I had managed to dodge when no one was constantly aiming a camera at me: I was no longer thirty. I wasn't even forty. I was one year from fifty, and the longer I campaigned, the more I looked it. Sherrod kept telling me I was beautiful, but fatigue dulls the hearing, I guess. I also knew my lifestyle had morphed into one of inertia, of an armchair quarterback. I went from exercising and walking on a regular basis to spending entire days plopped in a car. Healthful meals were rare, as was a full night's sleep. You have to be twelve for that not to take a toll.

It came to a head—my head, actually—one morning after Wendy e-mailed some recent shots from a Hometown Tour and I almost started to cry at the sight of me. I had to change the way I looked at myself, and I had to change now. I was spending more time worrying about how high I had to hold my chin to have just one than about how I could reach people with a message of hope. That was not the woman I knew, and I didn't like her much.

It hadn't helped that women I *didn't* know felt free to give unsolicited advice on everything about me, from the length of my hair to the cut of my coat to the way I looked at my husband whenever he spoke. I was no stranger to that kind of meddling, though. I'd been getting free criticism about my hair and the shape of my face from women readers ever since I started writing a column. I made matters worse by wearing stiff suits that made me feel sawed off at the waist by the end of the day. I'd never been one to wear a lot of business suits. Why on earth was I doing it now? Who said this had to be the uniform?

I changed my outfits, and my attitude, and the funny thing is, when I browse through campaign photos now, I look just fine in most of them. I do, however, lament the time and energy I wasted worrying about that, especially when I think of some of the women I met during those Hometown Tours.

There were whole rooms full of feisty women who decided to form their own activist groups because, as one woman in Knox County told me, "We got tired of the men at Democratic headquarters asking us to make coffee and do the Xeroxing." It was heartening to see so many women, most of them at least in their forties, and many of them a lot older, organizing to change the country. At an age when our culture wants us to believe women become invisible, these women were bigger than life. They were meeting in the smallest of villages and the largest of cities, and they loved hearing stories about women like them whenever I showed up.

Two women are lodged in my memory from the Hometown Tours. One of them, Mona Parsons, was a member of Military Families Speak Out. Her son had served in Iraq, and he made it home safely. He came home, though, to a different mother. She wanted to bring all the troops home, and she approached me before I spoke at a women's event in Knox County.

"Do you mind if I say a few words before you speak?"

"Of course not," I said. I'd lost count of how many women thought they needed permission to join the discussion.

She leaned in, and I could barely hear her. "I'm not a very good speaker," she said. "I get all nervous, and my voice trembles."

I reminded her of the advice of Maggie Kuhn, the founder of the Gray Panthers: "Speak your mind, even if your voice shakes."

She smiled at that, and nodded. "Okay, then."

The entire room grew silent as she spoke from her heart, asking them to pray for the safety of the troops and demand their safe return home.

Another woman, a mother in Appalachia, became one of my regular stories—and Sherrod's—on the road after she knocked the wind out of me at a potluck dinner.

She was in her mid-thirties, her four-year-old daughter at her side. She was wearing a cap on her bald head. She had just finished treatment for breast cancer, and all I could think about at first was how scared she must have been with cancer in her breast and a child so young.

We sat together for dinner before my speech, and she told me that I shouldn't worry about her. "I'm going to be fine," she said, smiling.

Then she gestured to the crowd of women in the room. "But these people here? These people need hope."

After my short talk, we headed out for the next stop on our long drive home. Before I climbed into the car, Wendy handed me a $200 check that the mother had written to Sherrod's campaign. Drawing a deep breath, Wendy told me what the woman had said as she handed her the check.

"I hope you don't mind, but I had to postdate it. I don't get paid until Friday."

fourteen
Karl Rove's Blunder

On the morning of Friday, July 14, Sherrod and I boarded exactly the sort of plane I had made him promise he would never, ever use.

I should have known something was up when we had to give our weight before we were allowed to board. It was an eight-seater, single-pilot flight from Boston to Nantucket, where we were headed for a series of fundraisers. I pulled out my digital camera, snapped a photo, and then fired off an e-mail from my BlackBerry to our scheduler, Shana Johnson:

> How is it that I can see the mole on the back of our pilot's neck? you ask. Because I was in the last seat on this plane, and it was only FOUR SEATS AWAY from the ONE man charged with keeping us from nose-diving into the sea. How did this happen????

It had been an eventful month so far. Two new public polls showed Sherrod leading DeWine by six to eight points. And after months of angry outbursts about Sherrod, his former Democratic primary opponent, Paul Hackett, had publicly apologized and declared his support. Paul's wife, Suzi, and their three young children circled him at the joint news conference. As I watched first Paul and then Sherrod address the crowd in the 95-degree Cincinnati heat, I felt as if we were witnessing a holy moment in an unholy profession. It generated a lot of press coverage, in Ohio and across the country.

Their truce was a personal victory for Dayton blogger Chris Baker, editor of *Ohio 2nd,* who originally had supported Hackett. Baker was a smart and dedicated progressive, and he had posted a lengthy interview with Sherrod and then lobbied Hackett to mend the hole in that fence. Baker made all the difference. Sherrod and Hackett's public embrace buoyed party activists in Ohio and boosted fundraising, particularly in California, where some liberal donors had refused to support Sherrod, despite his thirty-year record of progressive politics, because they believed the national Democratic party had forced Hackett out of the race.

I tried to focus on this, the good news of the campaign, rather than the realization that the pilot had just opened a window—a *window*—to let in some fresh air. I thought all planes had to be hermetically sealed to stay in the air, so this was a disconcerting development, to say the least.

Shana called me as soon as we landed. It should be noted that she was having a hard time stifling her giggles.

"Connie?"

"Shana."

"Seriously, Connie," she said, not sounding serious at all, "it was the only way to get you to the island, unless you wanted to take a really long boat ride."

"You know how I feel about these planes."

"Yeah, but I thought you only meant you didn't want Sherrod to go down *alone* on one of them. You know, because of how much you love each other and everything."

"You're joking."

"Well."

"Did Sherrod know we'd be on this plane?"

Silence.

"Shana?"

"I can't speak to what is in the candidate's head."

That was all I needed to know.

I bade Shana good-bye and turned to my husband.

"You knew."

"What?"

"You knew what kind of plane we'd be on."

He sighed. "You told me long ago to stop worrying about these kinds of details. I'm focused on winning a Senate race, just like you said."

Silence.

"You *did* say that," he said.

Then it hit me.

"What's wrong?" he said.

"How are we getting *back*?"

He wrapped his arm around me and led me off the tarmac.

"Try not to think about that, honey."

Only 115 more days. And counting.

We weren't on the island for more than a half-hour when Joanna called with news that would alter the course of the campaign.

"Well, the day we were waiting for has arrived," she said.

Mike DeWine had gone up with his first attack ad on TV. It included video of the burning Twin Towers, and it hit Sherrod hard on national security. DeWine started running the ad on a Friday, knowing we would not be able to answer with our own ad until Monday.

"It looks like a big buy, too," Joanna said. What she meant was that Ohioans all across the state would see it, and we couldn't respond until Monday because TV stations don't staff their advertising departments on weekends.

Joanna immediately began setting up a conference call to brainstorm our response. One of the first things Sherrod did was call his eighty-six-year-old mother. "I don't want you finding out about this on TV," he said.

Then we let our four children know, so that they wouldn't hear about it from someone else. Caitlin, our youngest and new to politics, was working at her summer job as a camp counselor for preschoolers when I reached her.

She greeted my news with silence.

"Cait?"

"Yeah."

"Did you hear what I said?"

"Yeah, Mom," she said softly. "I'm just letting it sink in."

Within the hour, we were on a conference call with the Triplets, our nickname for our consultants, David Doak, Tom O'Donnell, and Mattis Goldman. Our pollster, Diane Feldman; DSCC executive director J. B. Poersch; campaign manager John Ryan; and Joanna were also on the call.

"Apparently, we're the first Senate challenger to be attacked," Joanna said.

"We've got to respond and hit back," said O'Donnell. "This is going to be a lot of voters' first impression of Sherrod Brown. Women who are otherwise with us have concerns about national security."

"This ad is so unbelievable that if we refute it, voters will believe us," Doak said.

"And I'd prefer that the DSCC [Democratic Senatorial Campaign Committee] pay for the ad," added O'Donnell.

That was the big question: Who would pay for our response ad? Fundraising was picking up, but we still were far from where we needed to be before we felt comfortable spending the nearly $1 million we'd need to compete with DeWine's buy. We needed the DSCC's resources, and for a few more weeks, our campaign was allowed to communicate directly with them. In the last months of the campaign, new campaign finance laws would prevent cooperation between candidates, on the one hand, and special-interest groups and party committees on the other. In July, we were still allowed to know in advance if the DSCC would help us, which allowed us to save our money for the last weeks of the campaign. Soon, by law, that light would go dark, and the rest of the campaign would involve a lot of guessing on our part, never knowing when we would have help and when we'd have to go it alone.

By the end of our first conference call, we knew what our ad should say, but we had no idea who would pay for it.

Senator Chuck Schumer solved that riddle in the time it took him to beeline his way to me at our first, crowded event on Nantucket. He grabbed my hand as if he'd known me forever and said, "Connie, I know what you want to know, and I'm going to tell you right now: We're going to fight back, we're going to pay for the ad, and we'll be up on TV by Monday."

The wife in me wanted to hug him, but the journalist in me prevailed. I grabbed his hand with both of mine, and thanked him for believing in my husband.

Sherrod and I didn't actually see DeWine's ad until a few hours later, when Guy Cecil, political director with the DSCC, showed us on his laptop.

As much as I had tried to brace myself for the onslaught of ugly ads against Sherrod, I was still unprepared for the first time I watched his picture juxtaposed with the horrible images from September 11, 2001. It wasn't just that the ad lied about my husband's voting record on terrorism. That was bad enough, but I was stunned by DeWine's trafficking in national tragedy for political gain.

It's impossible to gauge how many Americans were hurt or offended by the ad, which was covered on blogs and in national broadcasts. There were all the families, of course, the ones who lost loved ones when the Twin Towers burst into flames. The ad began with DeWine insisting he approved it, and then turned to an image of the blazing towers.

I also wondered how many children saw the ad. There had to be so many children whose hearts still raced at the sight of those horrifying images. It was, after all, a day that changed all of us. We soon found out that the ad was the handiwork of the same firm that had produced the 2004 Swift Boat ads against John Kerry, which falsely accused him of lying about his military service in Vietnam.

DeWine's spokesman told *The Plain Dealer,* "This is chapter one."

Chapter two came sooner than DeWine expected. A few days after DeWine's attack ad went up, *U.S. News & World Report*'s Bret Schulte discovered that DeWine had used a doctored image of the Twin Towers. Apparently, the tragedy wasn't quite tragic enough, and an effort to depict more smoke after the first plane hit rendered the wrong tower on fire.

Minutes after Schulte's story hit the Web, reporters started calling our campaign. Journalists across the country weighed in. Some journalists described the deceit as simply politics as usual—a "misstep," or, as one reporter put it, a mere "hiccup." *Washington Post* columnist Al Kamen wrote, "This could be a very fun race."

Others, though, were not so willing to play into the tired old argument that nasty campaigns were as inevitable as Ohio sweet corn in August. As one reporter told us, "DeWine's nice-guy image is gone for good." Several journalists made it clear that they learned a hard lesson from the 2004 presidential race, when reporters waited too long to investigate the false allegations in the Swift Boat ads. This time, some reporters examined DeWine's claims point by point and exposed the distortions. They promised they would hold us to the same standard, which is what good journalists do.

At the time, DeWine attempted to dismiss the ad as a mistake by the consultants. He didn't fire them, though, and he continued to run the ad, complete with a new image of the smoldering Twin Towers.

Three weeks later, *The New York Times* confirmed that Karl Rove, the White House strategist behind so many ugly Republican campaign tactics, had pressured DeWine to run the ad. As it turned out, it set the tone for many of DeWine's later ads, and some political analysts now say his campaign never recovered from that initial blunder. It set up DeWine as a desperate and nasty candidate who would do anything to win, and Ohioans had had enough of that kind of politics.

It was also a turning point for us. Every campaign has its junctures, and the first DeWine ad presented two options for Sherrod, who had to decide how he would conduct himself in the face of the ugliness we had known was coming. A week after DeWine's ad first ran, Sherrod sat down at his computer and typed a letter explaining his decision to his entire campaign staff.

It was a rare afternoon at home for us, and I could hear the *click-click-click* of his keyboard as I folded laundry down the hall. It had been a long but exhilarating week for everyone, and he knew exactly what he wanted to say. I didn't read his letter until it popped up in my own e-mail box.

First, he praised his campaign field operation for recruiting hundreds of volunteers to march in more than a dozen parades over a single weekend in southeastern Ohio. Then Sherrod turned to what he knew was on everybody's minds.

He assured our young and devoted staff that DeWine's sleaze tactics were wheezing gasps in a lifeless campaign. Then he reminded them why our campaign was so different:

> On our side, there is a palpable passion for change, an enthusiasm the state hasn't seen since 1982 (before most of you were born), and a belief that our country can do a lot better. And we will continue to run an aggressive, always honest and honorable campaign to get there.

Long before a single vote had been counted, we'd already won.

fifteen

Dream On

IN A MESSAGE DATED AUGUST 1, 2006, A STAFF MEMBER FORWARDED an e-mail from the man hired to direct Sherrod's TV commercials, who instructed me to provide the following:

THURSDAY'S WARDROBE

Business-Professional Wear:
Three suits

Three blue dress shirts, could have slight color/style variations

Three white or off-white dress shirts

One of another shade or color if he has it and it works with whatever suit he brings

Eight ties, including two power red ties

Business Casual Wear, as if walking in a parade or going to the county fair:
Two pairs of tan/brown-tone khakis

One pair of khakis in dark color, navy, black, deep green

Six casual button-down shirts, try to bring a mix of colors that will work with the above khakis

Miscellaneous:

Handful of T-shirts for underneath

Comfortable shoes, since we won't really see his feet

FRIDAY'S WARDROBE:

Business-Professional Wear:

Three suits—two should be different than the day before, and one of them should be his ultimate power suit

Another three blue dress shirts, could have slight color/style variations

Another three white or off-white dress shirts

One of another shade or color if he has it and it works with the suits

Eight ties including 2 power red ties . . . at least 4 different than what was brought on Thursday

Business Casual Wear, as if walking in a parade or going to the county fair:

Two pairs of tan/brown-tone khakis, can be the same as Thursday

One pair khakis in dark color, navy, black, deep green—can be same as Thursday

Six casual button-down shirts, try to bring a mix of colors that will work with the above khakis—hopefully half are different than Thursday's

Miscellaneous:

Handful of T-shirts for underneath

Comfortable shoes, since we won't really see his feet

In a message also dated August 1, 2006, I sent this response:

I just read the wardrobe list and you can tell the director to dream on. We'll have a mix, but not nearly the number he wants, especially on such short notice. Sherrod will look fine.

Sherrod doesn't own that many suits, and I can't imagine there is a single one that he considers his "power suit." (How silly.) Clearly, this director hasn't met my husband.

Connie

Finally, in one more message dated August 1, 2006, campaign manager John Ryan sent this response to my e-mail:

Connie,

This was the best e-mail of the entire campaign—and the competition is fierce. It describes Sherrod the best out of anything I have ever read. It also shows why I love your husband so much. He is who he is—and we like him that way.

John

sixteen
What a Mesh

IT WAS THE THIRD WEEK IN AUGUST, AND WE WERE ON THE VERGE of getting three whole days to ourselves. Or what was left of our selves after two red-eye flights for California fundraising. This is what happens when young people plan trips for the middle-aged.

I'm always a little cranky with Sherrod after these flights, and I admit this isn't reasonable or fair of me but, honestly, try spending five long, wide-awake hours in the middle of the night sitting next to a man who falls sound asleep before most passengers have even boarded.

"How'd you sleep?" he asked, stretching as the pilot announced our descent into Cleveland.

One look at me and all thoughts of chit-chat evaporated.

"Well, baby, less than twenty-four hours," he said, rubbing my shoulders. "In less than twenty-four hours, we'll be on our vacation."

Three days may not sound like much of a vacation, but it felt like a downright retreat to us, because it was the only period of time in the

next eighty-three days in which we would have more than four con-
secutive unscheduled hours, if you didn't count the time we slept in
an actual bed. For three whole days there would be no press, no
fundraisers, and, if we were really lucky, no one who even knew our
names.

We were heading to Canada.

A four-hour drive north deposited us at Niagara-on-the-Lake,
home of the Shaw Festival, a summer-long feast of plays written by
George Bernard Shaw and authors who lived during his lifetime.
Shaw carries a special significance for Sherrod and me, but even as I
consider sharing this story I realize I am confirming our staff's glee-
ful suspicion that Sherrod and I are the biggest nerds of all time. On
our first date—at a Cooker's restaurant in Cleveland on January 1,
2003—Sherrod brought with him two typed pages of his favorite
quotations. One of them was also one of mine, by Shaw:

> I want to be all used up when I die. Life is no brief candle to me; it
> is a sort of splendid torch which I've got a hold of for the moment
> and I want to make it burn as brightly as possible before handing it
> on to future generations.

Spending a little time with Shaw in August was, we thought, the
perfect antidote to the Senate race. We were giddy as lovesick
teenagers to return to the place full of warm and fuzzy memories
from our visit there the previous summer. We checked into the bed-
and-breakfast that was within walking distance of all the theaters and
immediately set out for dinner before catching H. G. Wells's *Invisible
Man.* Over the next two days we had tickets for three other plays, including Chekhov's *Love Among the Russians,* which made Sherrod,
bless his Russian-studies heart, laugh harder than I'd seen in weeks.
Maybe months.

Between plays, we slept, hour after blissful hour. We ate, too, but
only if it didn't take too much time from sleeping. Our only en-
counter with a member of the American media took place during

intermission—Sherrod called it halftime—at a performance of George Bernard Shaw's *Arms and the Man.*

An elderly man approached me from the left.

"Excuse me," he said softly on his way to the aisle.

Sherrod and I did a double take as we let him by.

"Was that . . . ?" Sherrod said.

"Maybe," I said.

A few minutes later the man reappeared.

"I'm afraid I must impose on you again," he said.

"Not at all," I said as we stood.

Sherrod could not resist.

"David?"

"Why, yes," the man said.

"Sherrod Brown."

"Oh, yes," he said, grabbing Sherrod's hand. "Sherrod, how are you?"

Sherrod immediately turned to introduce me to *Washington Post* columnist David Broder, mentioning that both Broder and I had won the Pulitzer for commentary.

"Oh, right," he said, shaking my hand, his face blank. I'm always embarrassed when Sherrod does this, especially when it's clear the other person has never heard of me.

They talked about the race a bit. David said he'd been in Columbus, Ohio, and "It's looking good." Then he asked Sherrod if they could meet for coffee soon.

Sherrod looked at me and said, "We'd love to."

I shook my head. "I think he means you, honey."

Broder nodded.

"Oh, sure, we can get together," Sherrod said.

They never did meet for that coffee. The next month, Broder slammed Sherrod's trade policy in his *Washington Post* column.

By our third and last day, we were rested enough to stroll up and down the main drag, popping into art galleries and checking out the shore of Lake Ontario. I thought nothing of it when Sherrod said he'd wait on the bench for me outside one of the gift stores. He's not a shopper, and he smiled when I showed him the two hand-painted squares of slate I had bought for our home: "Never Too Old to Dance in the Kitchen" and "Welcome to Heaven on Earth." (The closer I get to fifty, the more I am like my mother, the Queen of Kitsch.)

Our last evening ended with the musical *High Society*, and as soon as we returned to our room, Sherrod collapsed on the bed with a groan.

"It's getting harder for me to stand or walk for very long," he said.

My hand, still holding the earring I'd just unhooked, froze in midair.

Harder? Harder than what?

This was the man who snapped the pedometer onto his sweat-pants as soon as he leaped out of bed and loved to boast that he'd logged more than nineteen thousand steps in one day on Capitol Hill during the CAFTA fight.

I turned to face him.

"What are you talking about?"

"I've been having some pain," he said, pointing to his abdomen.

"For how long?"

"I don't know. Two weeks maybe?"

"Two weeks? *Two weeks!*"

He frowned. "I think I might have a hernia."

I sat down next to him on the bed. "Why didn't you tell me about this sooner?"

"I thought three days off might make it better."

"You thought three days of walking everywhere we went would repair your hernia?"

Silence.

"Sherrod?"

"I never said I was sure it would work."

The following morning we were standing in the Buffalo airport waiting for our flight to yet another airport, JFK in New York, where we would land and then immediately catch a ride for the two-hour drive to back-to-back fundraisers in East Hampton.

"I'm calling Shana," I said, referring to our campaign scheduler, Shana Johnson. She knew my doctor, Patricia Kellner, because I had referred her there as a patient the year before. "I'm going to ask her to call Patty Kellner and see if we can get you in on Monday."

No argument from the Senate candidate, who was eyeing the long line ahead of us and wondering how long it would be before he could sit again. "That's probably a good idea," he said, smiling weakly.

When Sherrod first ran for Congress in 1992, he promised he would never take the congressional health insurance until all Americans had health care. He never dreamed that fourteen years later, even more Americans would be uninsured, but then again he never thought George W. Bush would be president, either, so life had been just full of surprises.

Anyway, a promise was a promise. When I met him in 2003, he was still buying minimal coverage every year. When we married in 2004, I insisted he get on my health care plan.

"I've got bad news for you," I told him at the time. "No matter how many times the press describes you as 'boyish,' you are getting older. It's a trend, see, and one you can't stop. So, I want you on my health care plan."

Sherrod, never one to miss a jab at the mainstream media, found this a delightful proposition. "After all these years," he said, chuckling. "*The Plain Dealer* never once wrote about how I refused the congressional health care plan, and now they're going to pay for mine."

I pointed out that I actually contributed to this health care plan, but that did nothing to mitigate his glee. He did agree, however, not to mention it at the microphone when he spoke at our wedding reception, where a fourth of the crowd was *Plain Dealer* reporters and editors. Since my leave of absence, we were paying *The Plain Dealer* for my coverage through the Consolidated Omnibus Budget Reconciliation Act, which Congress passed in 1986 to ensure that those who lose their jobs and don't have a boatload of discretionary income can still afford their insurance. The acronym for this dubious benefit is, appropriately enough, COBRA.

The next day, on Monday, we wedged Sherrod's doctor's visit between a news conference and a fundraiser. It took Dr. Kellner all of five minutes to determine that Sherrod did indeed have a hernia.

"Do you want to feel it?" she said, looking at me.

Sherrod immediately raised his gown and his eyebrows in my direction. Dutiful wife that I am, I placed my hand on Sherrod's lower abdomen, and Patty told him to cough.

"Whoa!"

"Yeah," she said, nodding. "We need to take care of this."

"How soon can we get him in?" I asked.

She went to her office to call the surgeon while her staff drew Sherrod's blood and did an EKG to spare him an extra visit. By the time she returned to the examining room, Sherrod had a Thursday afternoon appointment with Dr. Raymond Onders and a 7:15 A.M. slot for surgery the following day.

Immediately, we asked if she would be willing to talk to reporters if there were any questions. The last thing we wanted was even the suggestion in print or on the airwaves that Sherrod wasn't up for the job.

"Oh," she said with a sigh. "That's right. I guess you have to think about that. Well, of course. Have them call me."

Dr. Onders was already nationally known as the doctor who helped enable the actor Christopher Reeve to breathe better. We fell in love with him for other reasons. It turned out that Dr. Onders was that most unusual of surgeons: an ardent Democrat, and an activist one at that. He had recently helped to found Wounded Warriors, recruiting surgeons around the country to donate their time and skills to help wounded Iraq War veterans from rural and small-town America who weren't getting adequate care from their local Veterans Administration clinics.

"The majority of the troops over there come from rural areas and small towns, and they don't want to travel to the big cities, where the better VA centers are," he said after examining Sherrod. "Unfortunately, that often means they're getting inferior care, and they need major medical treatment."

Oh, and by the way, he said, Sherrod had two hernias, not one.

He started drawing diagrams and explaining the options as Sherrod let the news sink in. Having already read everything on hernias that I could find on the Internet, I had my own question.

"Why do more men have hernias than women?" I asked.

"Testicles," he said, shrugging his shoulders. "We have testicles."

I wadded up my stack of reading material and swatted Sherrod on the arm. "*Finally*, you pay for those things," I said, followed immediately by one of those moments of dead silence that illustrate exactly what I mean when I say my humor is often dramatically underappreciated in our marriage.

After more discussion, Sherrod opted for laparoscopic surgery, which requires three tiny incisions but general anesthesia. Major abdominal surgery, on the other hand, splits you open but requires only a local anesthetic.

Dr. Onders pulled out of his pocket a square of mesh that looked as though it had been cut from a screen door. "This is what we use to repair the hernia," he said, handing it to me. "You can keep it."

First I got to feel Sherrod's hernia, and now I had a sample of the foreign body that would be left in his. Why don't more people envy my life?

I pulled out my notebook and asked if I could get a quote from him for reporters, which I later dictated to Sherrod's communications director, Joanna Kuebler: "Sherrod Brown will have the same routine hernia surgery that more than a half million Americans undergo each year. He will return to a full schedule on Monday."

Like Patricia Kellner, he said he'd be happy to answer any questions from the media.

"You'll be back to work by Monday," he told Sherrod.

That night, I assured the hovering campaign staff that we didn't need a driver or an entourage to get to the hospital by 6:15 the following morning. I would take Sherrod to the hospital, I would wait for him in the reception room, and I would drive him home.

"You're sure," Shana said, sounding not even remotely convinced.

"I really am."

"Okay, well, if you change your mind . . ."

"Right."

That night, Sherrod curled up against my back in bed and whispered in my ear, "We get the whole weekend off."

I rolled over and looked at him. "You never want the whole weekend off."

He grinned and said, "Doctor's orders."

Finally, a guilt-free break from the campaign.

THE FOLLOWING MORNING SHERROD ARRIVED AT UNIVERSITY Hospitals in Cleveland at 6:13, no worse for the wear after riding in the front passenger seat of the family car driven by his wife—who, it should be noted, listened patiently as he read aloud stories from *The Plain Dealer* all the way to the hospital.

The friendly receptionist, an elderly woman with a curved spine and sensible shoes, asked Sherrod to sign in. Being in a most cooperative mood, he did just that.

We turned toward the seating area and, as if on cue, the TV mounted on the wall immediately started blaring the National Republican Senatorial Committee's latest attack ad against Sherrod.

To make the ad, the Republicans had hired four different trackers to videotape Sherrod on the road so they would have footage of him for their own ads. Three of these trackers looked like college students, but one of them was a freelance photographer who also did work for CBS News. He actually tried claiming that was why he was there, until our communications director, Joanna Kuebler, demanded to see his press credentials.

A year before, Joanna had been so timid that she wouldn't have uttered a peep if a two-hundred-pound man had stood on her foot for a six-mile ride on the subway, but the campaign—and her loyalty to Sherrod—seemed to coax out Joanna the She-Warrior. She did her best to thwart the trackers, jumping in front of their cameras, taking their photos as they photographed her, and basically just making them as miserable as possible without committing a felony.

Even so, they managed to maneuver around Joanna's bobbing head enough to catch snippets of Sherrod on tape, and now there he was, starring in an ad meant to humiliate him, courtesy of the National Republican Senatorial Committee.

He looked great in the footage if you could ignore the constant incantation, "Sherrod Brown let us down . . . Sherrod Brown let us down." Which I couldn't. A colleague from *The Plain Dealer* had gushed after seeing the ad the day before, playing silently on one of the mounted TV screens in the newsroom. "Hey, Sherrod looked really hot in the latest ad," she wrote in an e-mail, not knowing that she was describing a Republican attack ad.

"You might want to turn up the volume next time," I wrote back. Later that afternoon she responded with a single line: "I hate them I hate them I hate them . . ."

As soon as Sherrod and I sat down in the waiting room, another attack ad came on the TV. This time, it was from Sherrod's opponent, Mike DeWine. In it he was perched on a porch railing wearing a plaid shirt and talking in the folksiest of newfound twangs about O-*hiiii*-a and the "terrists" threatening us all.

"I don't believe this," I said, pointing at the screen. Sherrod, a little preoccupied with thoughts of the slice-and-dice awaiting him down the hall, just laughed.

An elderly woman sitting to our right glanced over at us, motioned toward the screen, frowned, and gave it an ardent thumbs-down.

Right after this gesture of solidarity, a woman in her fifties came out and asked Sherrod to join her for a brief intake interview. She was a polite woman who, we soon learned, had worked at the hospital for

nearly thirty years. She looked at the computer screen and did a double take when she read Sherrod's supposed date of birth.

"You were born in 1962?"

Sherrod's face lit up like the butt of a firefly. Oh-ho-ho, no, he
wasn't born in 1962, he was actually born in nineteen *fifty*-two, but,
hey, if she wanted to make him ten years younger . . .

On and on he went, which was the first indication that he was actually nervous. A five-minute interview turned into a fifteen-minute
chatfest as Sherrod talked to her about her kids, where she grew up,
how long she'd been working there—oh, and what did she think of
his doctor? When he finally walked out of her office, she all but
hugged him.

Almost immediately, Sherrod was called back to get undressed.
While I waited for permission to kiss him good-bye, the Republican
attack ad ran again, followed by DeWine's. Again.

The TV was set to WOIO–Channel 19, the station that made national headlines in 2004 after one of its news anchors stripped on the
air for ratings during sweeps week. I had criticized Channel 19's tactics in the past in my column, and I condemned her stunt, too. An an-
chorperson at the station told me that since then, everyone at
Channel 19 was under a standing order never to talk to me.

Sherrod's campaign had purchased nearly a half-million dollars'
worth of airtime the day before to run his response ad, but it never
popped up on the screen of Channel 19 that morning. Our campaign
manager, John Ryan, had mentioned that one station had refused to
run our ad until Saturday. By the fifth Mike DeWine ad, I had a hunch
I'd found the station.

It was right about then, though, that the friendly receptionist
shuffled over to me and delivered me from my suffering.

"Do you mind if I change the channel?" she said.

I grabbed her hand. "I hate this," I hissed, a little too loudly. That
sixty-something lady with the curved back and sensible shoes suddenly high-fived me with the force of a trucker chugging an energy
drink.

"Let's just get rid of those ads, shall we?" the receptionist said. She switched to CNN, and I still can't believe how relieved I was to see so many ads for Anderson Cooper.

As for the surgery, Sherrod was wheels up, as surgeons love to say, by 7:13 A.M. Surgery went extremely well, as indicated by the full-color photos of his repaired hernias that the doctor handed to me when he came to deliver the news at 8:15 A.M.

Yes, photos. Why do doctors do that?

After reviving me and lifting me back into my chair, the good doctor assured me that Sherrod would be ready to leave in no time and that I could come back to see him in just a little bit. When I asked if Sherrod was awake yet, Dr. Onders smiled and said, "Oh, he's been awake for some time now. Talking to everybody in sight, too."

About fifteen minutes later, Dr. Onders came to get me, and as soon as I walked into Sherrod's room he introduced me to the attending nurse, Jennifer, a cheerful mother of two from a city east of Cleveland who had already told Sherrod she might be moving.

"Tell her why," said Sherrod, who was sucking on an ice chip.

"Because all the senior citizens voted down the school levy and now my kids have no bus."

"No bus," Sherrod said, closing his eyes.

"He's so nice," she said, pointing to Sherrod, who quickly opened his eyes and strained his head to see the guy being wheeled into the room next to his. "And he's interested in *everything*."

I pushed Sherrod's head down onto the pillow, worried that his curiosity would roll him right out of bed and onto the floor. "Why don't you rest a bit, honey."

By 10 A.M. Sherrod was allowed to go home. I helped him dress, and as I pulled on his shoes he starting rambling like any man who's just had abdominal surgery: "You know, after our ads go up there's a good chance that some people who've given maybe one hundred or two hundred dollars might be willing to give more, and you have to figure that the *USA Today* poll numbers that just came out are really going to help with . . ."

I went to get the car.

As I walked out the side door from the outpatient clinic at University Hospitals, I couldn't help but notice there was a policeman standing there, and he knew my name.

"Ms. Schultz," he said, nodding his head.

I didn't find out until later that Joanna, ever mindful of trackers, had called the hospital to make sure Sherrod wasn't videotaped as he hobbled toward the car.

I pulled up to the cashier's window in the parking garage and handed her a stamped business card from the hospital's CEO. One of his assistants had given it to me after stopping by the waiting room to see if I needed anything while Sherrod was in surgery. He was just doing his job, but I couldn't help but think it's always the people who least need the perks who get them.

On my way out of the parking garage, I glanced at the booth on my right and recognized the woman who had insisted I fill out a due bill to pay for parking my car, minutes after my father had died. I had had a ten-dollar bill for a four-dollar fee. She said she couldn't make change. It was four in the morning.

I remembered her response when, at the end of my wits, I teared up and told her my father had just died and all I wanted to do was go home.

"That's not my problem, is it?" she had said. "You aren't going anywhere until I fill out this ticket." So I sat in my car and waited for her to record my license plate number and the make of my car.

This time, with no money at all, the congressman's wife just handed the card to the cashier and was on her way.

When I pulled up in the car, Sherrod was waiting to introduce me to the orderly who had just wheeled him to the curb.

"This is Mr. Shelton," he said. "His wife has a job similar to his at the Cleveland Clinic, but he's working three jobs so that she can go to college and become a nurse."

Mr. Shelton beamed.

"I've always voted for you," he yelled as we pulled away. "And I'm gonna vote for you again!"

By the time we got home, the campaign staff had sent an e-mail with a new TV ad that the Democratic Senatorial Campaign Committee had produced with their own footage of Sherrod captured on the campaign trail. Federal elections law now prevented us from knowing what, if anything, the DSCC was planning to do to promote Sherrod's race, and so both of us saw the ad for the first time when I opened my laptop and sat next to him on the bed.

Images of Sherrod the Regular Guy (denim shirt, wild curly hair) and Sherrod the Statesman (blue shirt, rep tie, and barely any hair at all) flashed across the screen as folksy guitar music played. Clips of Sherrod in action were augmented by a deep male voice declaring Sherrod a champion of the middle class. Then the faceless voice heralded Sherrod's decision not to take the congressional health care plan.

"And he never will," the man intoned, "until all Americans have health care."

seventeen

Wifely Duties

IT WAS THE USUAL MONDAY MORNING CONFERENCE CALL WITH senior staff and consultants, but it was far from the usual conversation.

"We're going to have to do an ad with Sherrod's ex-wife," one of the Triplets said. "We've got to be ready for an attack."

Eight other people were on the call, but nobody said a word.

Oh great, I thought. *Everyone's waiting to see how* this *wife is going to handle the news.*

From the moment Sherrod decided to run, a part of me had known this day—or at least this conversation—would come. We knew that the Republicans, under Karl Rove's reign, had already logged a long and successful track record of dirty campaigns. We also knew after DeWine's first attack ad that Rove was involved in Sherrod's race here in Ohio, the much ballyhooed "bellwether" state. Just as important, we were certain from our own opposition research on Sherrod that, aside from his divorce, there was little personal dirt to dig up on him. As one of my *Plain Dealer* colleagues, politics writer Steve Koff, once jokingly complained, Sherrod didn't even have credit card debt to expose.

"Does he really not have any debt?" Koff asked in a call to my desk in the newsroom before I took my leave.

"We have a mortgage and that's it," I told him. "Sherrod doesn't believe in credit card debt because he doesn't want to pay interest."

Koff groaned, and laughed at Sherrod's consistency, but the larger point was not lost on him. While Sherrod was extremely generous with others and donated at least 10 percent of his annual income to charity, he lived a frugal personal life that would have given a Franciscan monk a run for his prayer beads. A beagle is higher maintenance than Sherrod.

When I met him in 2003, he still drove a beat-up 1996 Ford Thunderbird assembled at a plant in his congressional district— "Made in Lorain!" he always crowed—that cruised so low to the ground I felt as if I had to pick gravel out of my backside every time I rode in it. As I write this, it still sits in our driveway, plastered with political bumper stickers that date as far back as 1999 and looking so ratty you find yourself looking for the cinder blocks.

It was hard to find much to smear in that lifestyle.

Our campaign strategists were certain, though, that the Republicans would delight in exploiting allegations Sherrod's ex-wife, Larke, had made against him during their 1986 divorce. She had initiated the divorce while he was Ohio's secretary of state.

Cleveland Scene magazine, an alternative weekly, ran a cover profile of Sherrod in 2001 that included this alarming passage about their ugly divorce:

> When Sherrod and Larke Brown split in 1986, it was a well-known secret in political circles that they parted badly. Statehouse reporters at the time were delivered anonymous brown envelopes containing court documents with claims of neglect and cruelty. Larke had sought a restraining order against her husband. . . .

Brown answered that he had never been abusive toward his wife and daughters. A divorce was granted in 1987; the court found both parties at fault.

The allegations had been in the news before. In October 1992, Sherrod, who had suffered his only election defeat in 1990, was running for Congress. In a last-ditch effort to derail his race, his opponent, Margaret Mueller, ran a radio ad with the voice of a woman—voters were supposed to believe it was Larke—reading aloud from the divorce allegations. Larke stepped up for Sherrod and demanded that Mueller pull the ad.

Mueller refused to take the ad off the air, but Sherrod won the race, and it was the last time a political opponent had tried to dredge up the old, and disavowed, allegations. Mike DeWine, though, had a history of smear tactics. In 1992, DeWine ran against Senator John Glenn, who was a decorated war hero and former astronaut. This didn't deter DeWine from accusing Glenn of being unpatriotic and soft on Communism. *The Columbus Dispatch* offered up this quote from the DeWine campaign: "If Glenn had his way the Berlin Wall still would be standing and former Soviet republics still would be enslaved." DeWine lost the race.

Sherrod regularly mentioned DeWine's race against Glenn during any "what if" discussions about potential attacks. He and most of the campaign's senior staff figured it was only a matter of time before DeWine, aided and abetted by the Republican National Committee, trotted out the divorce allegations to raise doubts about Sherrod's character. Soon after the 2006 primary, the allegations showed up on some conservative bloggers' websites.

Life had changed considerably for Sherrod since his divorce twenty years ago. He was a seven-term congressman, and after sixteen years as a single parent, he was now happily married—to me. He claimed there was a definite connection.

No one celebrated our marriage more than his daughters, Emily and Elizabeth, who were now grown and devoted as ever to him.

Their ties to their father ran deep and long. Despite the divorce, he never missed a chance to be with them, which I mistakenly once referred to as his "visitation." Whoo-boy, did Sherrod erupt.

"I hate that word," he said. "I didn't *visit* my own children. I am their *father*. I raised them too."

That was evident the first time I went to Sherrod's home. He lived in a century-old two-story colonial on the shore of Lake Erie in Lorain. The walls and most tabletops were covered with framed photographs of the girls. Every cupboard, shelf, and closet held relics of their childhood: tiny mittens and fuzzy winter caps, homemade magnets from church school, favorite stones retrieved from walks on the rocky beach. Their bedroom was frozen in time, the time when they were little girls who slept head to head in matching twin beds facing framed caricatures of their younger selves.

I smiled the first time I saw that room, imagining them rolling their teenage eyes in amusement, surrounded by memories of their previous selves. Dozens of stuffed animals and dolls still rested in a triangle of net hanging in a corner from the ceiling, and a small white bookcase by the doorway remained full of the blue-and-yellow spines of Nancy Drew mysteries. Hanging on the wall above was a framed newspaper essay Sherrod wrote in 1988 about one of the many train trips he took around the country with his daughters.

Sherrod's most prized possession from the girls' childhood was "The Funny Book," which was full of his handwritten memories of times when they said something humorous or poignant during their childhood. The only rule: If you tried to be funny, it didn't make the book. Over time, one of Sherrod's favorite bedtime rituals, before he played songs on his guitar, was to read a story or two from the book before they went to sleep.

"Read the wood story," one of them would say, and Sherrod would turn to the passage recounting the time when he told five-year-old Elizabeth, "You're a piece of work." Her response: "You're a piece of wood, too, Daddy."

When twenty-four-year-old Emily married in 2005, Sherrod

painstakingly hand-copied into a new journal the entire contents of the Funny Book. At the rehearsal dinner, he promised Elizabeth he would do the same thing for her. He gave it to her for Christmas in 2006.

Another change in Sherrod's life was in his relationship with Larke. After years of tension, they had found their way to something better. Larke and I hit it off from the beginning, unburdened with any mutual history. We celebrated graduations together, attended Emily's wedding reception at their home, and when Sherrod declared his candidacy for the Senate, Larke told the girls she wanted pins and bumper stickers. In March, she and her husband, Joe, held a standing-room-only fundraiser for Sherrod, and Sherrod could not help but laugh when he saw both of them wearing his sticker as they greeted us at the door of their Granville home.

"Did you ever think you'd see this?" he said to his daughters. I don't think Emily and Elizabeth ever stopped smiling that night.

It was a preemptive strike, a chance to let DeWine know we were a united front. Larke and Joe held a second fundraiser in October.

Sherrod dreaded telling his daughters that it looked as though the divorce that had brought so much sadness and pain to their young lives might resurface again. He warned them, and asked them if they thought their mother might be willing to film an ad to defend him. Emily offered to ask her, and within days, Larke agreed to help.

I worried what dredging up the allegations might mean for us, for Emily and Elizabeth, and for Larke and Joe, too. I also worried about the public's turning a wary eye on our marriage. I had a hard time believing that anyone who knew me or read my column would ever believe I'd marry a man capable of abuse. But publicizing such awful allegations, no matter how false, would automatically focus the lens of scrutiny on our marriage, too.

So far, I had been invisible in campaign ads and literature. While I was out stumping almost daily for my husband, his campaign literature didn't even hint at the existence of a wife, lovely or otherwise. Photos of his parents and his daughters appeared in ads, but the consultants never even suggested that I be included in the packaging. I never had the nerve to ask the consultants why they ruled me out as a commercial asset.

Besides, I was torn. As a journalist, the last thing I wanted was to appear in a political ad, even for Sherrod. Some of my friends, however, pointed out with frustration that other candidates—including the Democratic nominee for Ohio governor and also Sherrod's opponent—had ads and literature in which their wives were prominently featured. Granted, they were depicted walking alongside their husbands and glancing at them with a loving gaze, but at least voters knew they existed. DeWine showcased his entire family—they had eight children and nine grandchildren, he always pointed out to reporters—while Sherrod appeared to be the same fancy-free bachelor he'd been for the sixteen years before we met.

Occasionally, I grumbled to Sherrod, who expressed puzzlement over the strategy. But he had other things on his mind. I had said nothing to the consultants, until that morning when they announced during the conference call that they wanted to do an ad with Sherrod's ex-wife and their two daughters, just in case DeWine brought up the old allegations.

"Wait a minute," I said. "We haven't had so much as the toe of my tennies in an ad for Sherrod, but now we're going to film an entire piece with his ex-wife?"

Silence.

"Isn't there a role I should be playing in this? Do we really want the only wifely image in Sherrod's race to be that of his *former* wife?"

More silence, if you didn't count the growl of collective throat clearing.

"We'll write a couple of scripts and run them past you," Mattis Goldman finally said.

"We won't do anything until you guys sign off on it," added John Ryan. I knew he'd be calling me as soon as the call was over.

"John," I said, not even bothering to say hello, after the phone rang.

"We're not going to do anything that makes you uncomfortable," he said.

"This whole thing makes me uncomfortable."

"Okay, well, we won't do anything that will make you feel worse than you have to."

"This is your idea of reassurance?"

John sighed. "I know this hard for you. It's hard for me, too. I've never had to deal with anything like this."

"That's what you get for having a long, happy marriage."

After a lot of negotiation and dickering over the next few days, we finally agreed that a "blended family" ad would work best—or it would at least keep Sherrod's current wife from imploding, which is what I suspected was the agreement behind closed doors. The ad would include Larke and Elizabeth and Emily, and me with my daughter, Caitlin. My son, Andy, was traveling out of state and couldn't make it.

The night before the shoot, I sent an e-mail:

Dear Larke,

I can only imagine your thoughts as you bolster yourself for tomorrow's filming. It cannot be easy, no matter how much you love your daughters or believe in the cause for change, and I am grateful for your willingness to do what few others would even consider. You and I have had nothing but wonderful interactions from the day we met, and I love Sherrod so much, that it is hard even to imagine a different time between the two of you. I see both of you as such honorable, kind people, and what you are doing tomorrow for Sherrod and his race confirms all of my assumptions about you as a mother and a fellow traveler in this thing we call life.

Please thank Joe, too, for we know what this asks of him. The two of you show a commitment to something so much larger than yourselves that the mere thought of it takes my breath away.

I think someday we might laugh about all this. Not tomorrow, but someday.

Until then, I just wanted to extend my own gratitude to you. I do look forward to seeing you. And the mischief in me is enjoying the discomfort of the consultants and film crew. They've seen too many bad movies, I'm afraid, and don't quite know what to make of us.

Love,

Connie

WE FILMED THE AD IN CLEVELAND ON THE SECOND SATURDAY IN September. It was scheduled for the afternoon because I had to give two speeches that morning in central Ohio. Immediately after the second talk I hightailed it north over two and a half hours of interstate to a stranger's home to film the ad. The director had spotted the house on a tour of neighborhoods, and one of our staff members asked the owner if we could borrow it for the day. Generously, she agreed.

When I showed up she was immediately friendly, and full of opinions. She took one look at me and said, "Oh. She's going to need makeup." She delivered this verdict in front of Larke and our daughters and the twenty or so members of the production crew. Caitlin shot me a sympathetic grin.

"Well," I said, trying to smile. "I'm a middle-aged woman in the middle of a statewide campaign. This might be as good as it gets."

"Just because you're middle-aged doesn't mean you have to look like it," the owner said, frowning.

"Right."

Thirty minutes later, I was newly painted and had even managed to fluff my flattened hair with the handy-dandy set of travel hot rollers I was now hauling everywhere I went. A year ago I hadn't even known they made travel hot rollers, and now I not only owned my own set but had a variety of outlet adapters to go with them in case I decided to flee the country. Only now does it strike me as odd that I rolled my hair in the downstairs bathroom of a woman I'd met only five minutes earlier and then thought nothing of parading around with them on my head for a whole ten minutes before the shoot. Give me fuzzy slippers, butterfly hairpins, and a can of Aqua Net and I would have been my mother in 1962.

Larke could not have been more gracious. Not one of us wanted to do this, but we wanted Mike DeWine to win even less. This was about family, and our version of it, which happened to reflect millions of families in America.

The ad struck a delicate balance between Larke's need for dignity and our need to refute any ugly attack based on a twenty-year-old divorce. It also had to meet our need to do all of this in thirty seconds.

Scene One: The ad began with a shot of Larke and Elizabeth sitting on the front porch steps. Elizabeth talked about how she loved her dad but hated politics sometimes. Then Larke said divorce was difficult and theirs was no different, but that Mike DeWine's attack on their family was just wrong.

Scene Two: The screen switched to a shot of all five of us, with Caitlin and me seated on a picnic table, and Larke, Elizabeth, and Emily on the bench in front of us. I identified myself as Sherrod's wife, Connie—no last name—and said our family was united in condemning Mike DeWine's attack ad. Emily and Caitlin just had to look familial and outraged.

Originally I was supposed to end by saying, "In fact, this ad says more about Mike DeWine than it does Sherrod Brown," but Larke felt strongly that she should have the walk-off. It felt odd having my husband's ex-wife defend him in an ad that would run in every television market in Ohio, but then again, this whole venture was hardly a page from The Waltons, so what was one more moment of discomfort?

Scene Three: Sherrod, noticeably absent from the filming, appeared on the screen, courtesy of a previously recorded assurance that he approved this message.

One question gnawed at us long after the trying shoot was over: Would we have to run this ad?

We wouldn't know the answer until the weekend before the election.

eighteen

Deck 'im

A WEEK AFTER SHERROD'S SURGERY, ON SEPTEMBER 7, HIS OLDEST friend, John Kleshinski, called my cell phone from his home in Boston.

Immediately, I knew something was up. John was a sweet and gentle man who told Sherrod to marry me right after he met me, but I was just a happy sidekick on the John and Sherrod show. John had regularly sent me encouraging e-mails during the campaign, and had carved out a special place in my heart in recent times after my son was diagnosed with Type 1 diabetes at age thirty. John had been diabetic since age thirteen, and no one stepped up faster to help Andy than John. I didn't know until much later just how much John had helped Andy, and by then it was too late to thank him.

Sherrod and John were Mansfield born and bred, although John always joked that he was just a poor Catholic boy from a large herd on the other side of the tracks, while Sherrod was a pampered doctor's kid. A year older than Sherrod, John didn't really get to know him until Sherrod was running for reelection as a state representative at the ripe old age of twenty-three. John made his wealth in pharmaceuticals, retired in his forties, and was now a philanthropist—Sherrod called him "a warrior for social justice"—who was especially drawn to charities for children. He loved to say that he donated to Sherrod's first fundraiser—a three-dollar pretzel-and-beer bash at the local UAW hall—and had supported him ever since. The two shared a love for Cleveland Indians baseball and politics. "In that order," John often said.

John was the most generous man, both spiritually and materially, that Sherrod and I knew, and he also insisted on joy. I swear they were twenty years younger whenever they were together. The only thing missing was the bathroom jokes.

This time, though, John was all business.

"Hey, you know how I don't like to butt in on all this campaign stuff," John said.

"What is it, John?"

"You guys have enough unsolicited advice coming your way every day."

"John?"

"Okay, listen, I saw Sherrod last night in Washington. We had dinner. You knew that, right?"

"Yeah, he loved seeing you." And he did, too. John was always such a touchstone for Sherrod.

"Well, I'm concerned."

Immediately, I was, too.

"What is it?

"He is absolutely exhausted, Connie. I've never seen him like that."

"What do you mean?"

"Remember how you and I talked months ago? About how the only way Sherrod could lose was if he made a mistake?"

I remembered that conversation well. "We said a tired candidate is a candidate who makes mistakes."

"Right. Well, he's looking that tired. He was forgetting what he was talking about in the middle of a sentence. He kept yawning and his eyes were really red, and he was irritable. Sherrod is almost never grumpy, at least not with me. You've got to intervene, Connie. You've got to get more involved in his schedule."

That was all I needed to hear. Almost anyone else, and I would have questioned his judgment. John, though, knew Sherrod nearly as well as I did, and he would know if Sherrod was off his game.

I thanked John for weighing in, and immediately called our scheduler, Shana Johnson. We went over Sherrod's schedule, day by day, event by event, and started shaving. We decided what he absolutely had to do, what we could let go, and when he could squeeze in a nap.

Then I called John Ryan, and his response convinced me yet again that one of the smartest things we ever did in the campaign was to beg John to become campaign manager. He, too, knew how rare it was for John Kleshinski to offer advice.

"This has to change," he said. "And it has to change right now. I promise, Connie. We'll make sure Sherrod gets some rest."

Sherrod was scheduled to fly home from Washington that evening, and I knew he was supposed to land around eleven. I always waited up for him, and we had a ritual that never changed no matter what time of day he flew: As soon as he landed, he either called or e-mailed on his BlackBerry to let me know he was safely on the ground. The campaign may have made me a more regular flier, but I still knew most crashes came during liftoff or landing, and some habits were mighty hard to break.

Right around 11 P.M., my phone rang once—then stopped.

I recognized the number as one belonging to the campaign, but had no idea whose phone it was, so I dialed the number.

No answer.

Tried again. No answer.

Tried again. The call immediately kicked into an automatic voice mail recording on the second ring.

Ah, the overactive mind of a tired writer.

I imagined the plane going down, and Sherrod, his nose facing the ground, calling one last time as the plane roared toward the asphalt.

Then I imagined him frantically dialing as he tumbled down a dark, bottomless ravine in the campaign car.

"What if his last call was to me!" I cried out to Gracie as I pulled my bathrobe tight around me and kept dialing, dialing, dialing.

No answer.

No answer.

No answer.

Finally, at 11:20, it occurred to me to call Zach West, who was supposed to be driving Sherrod from the airport.

Zach answered on the first ring.

"We're ten minutes away," he said.

I could hear Sherrod's raspy voice in the background.

"It's almost eleven-thirty at night," I said. "Who is he talking to?"

"He's fundraising."

"What?"

"He's making a fundraising call."

"At eleven-thirty at *night*?"

"Yeah," Zach said. "He's calling the West Coast."

I hung up the phone and took a deep breath.

Only sixty-one days, and counting.

A FEW DAYS LATER, MY FRIEND FLEKA ANDERSON REMINDED ME why we must always keep old friends close, no matter how far away they live.

Fleka is a no-nonsense executive recruiter who has been my friend for more than twenty years. When she first met me, she nicknamed me "Miss Love the World" because, being the introvert that she is, she found my friendliness just this side of mind-numbing.

Over time, though, she got used to me, and she is the only friend I've had who would sit on my front porch with me and share a bottle of champagne and a box of Bugles. That kind of friend, you keep.

Besides, we had working-class roots in common. Her father, who died when she was seventeen, was a coal miner, a union organizer, and a steelworker before he met Fleka's mother and bought a bar in Niles, Ohio. Her mother tended bar at his side throughout Fleka's childhood.

Fleka moved to Florida a few years ago, where she is raising five-year-old Sydney, who gives me a reason to buy fairy princess dresses, cartoon underwear, and books starring strong little girls. Her grateful mother regularly sent me funny e-mails to lighten the load during the campaign—and to check up on me.

Many times, she forwarded the latest scare letter from the National Republican Senatorial Committee warning about all the disasters that would plague our country within days of the election of Sherrod and his fellow Democratic candidates. A horrified Fleka ended up on the NRSC's e-mail list after she launched a spirited defense of Sherrod on their blog.

This particular Fleka e-mail, though, titled "I am about to have a crisis," was intended to make me get a grip on the whole "lovely wife" thing. Her adoring Swedish father named her Fleka because it means "girl" in Swedish. Fleka has always claimed that this name was a source of constant misery because of one particular horse. Hence the following e-mail:

Con,

I realize that you are having a very hectic life now, things are getting rough, you have a lot on your mind. I know you have camera guys stalking you for pictures to get you at unflattering moments, people going through your garbage. Hell, you have the Republican party saying negative things nationally about your husband and your life. I get it. I admit, it is rough, but do you realize what is about to happen to ME on Friday????????

Yes, my good, solid, always-been-there-for-me friend, Hollywood, with its ever unconscionable acts, has decided to release the film version of "My Friend Flicka," simply titled "Flicka." To hell with your problems. Do you know what I am about to endure???? The book was bad enough, but it was old, Con, old. It was but a distant, foggy memory to most people. This stupid movie puts it all front and center, and they're back—all those clever people who say "Hey, did you ever realize your name sounds a lot like that horse in the movie?"

You may be "the lovely wife," but at least no one will associate you with a horse. Stop and think about that for a moment. A HORSE!!!!!!

Well, having gotten all of that off my chest, I will go to bed and pray that the movie bombs and no one sees it. As always, you are in my thoughts. My offer still stands to come up if you need me. Hey, that may be a good idea. It will take your mind off the stress of the campaign as you hold me back from punching someone for making the horse reference when you introduce me. Imagine the Republican trackers getting a snapshot of that one. . . .

Love you,
Flek

As I said, some friends you gotta keep.

By mid-September, everyone but me agreed that Sherrod needed another haircut. The idea was to do it now so that he wouldn't look newly shorn for his debate on *Meet the Press* the following week. Instead of the House barber—I still hadn't forgiven him for the shearing he gave Sherrod in July—our scheduler, Shana, scoured the city for a barber who would (a) take Sherrod on short notice and (b) promise to give him a camera-ready haircut. We ended up at Goodfellas, a shop just south of Cleveland run by Ray Calabrese.

Ray took one look at Sherrod's short, stubby sideburns and shook his head. "This is like the Nazi look. It's not popular anymore."

Sherrod's eyes shot open.

"The what?"

"The Nazi look. Your sideburns are too short."

"Could you fill them in with Magic Marker?"

Ray grinned. "Nice try. So, how'd you do this to yourself?"

"In the shower."

"You shave without looking?"

"I've had this face for a long time," Sherrod said.

"Yeah, but why act blind if you aren't blind?" Ray said. "You can get a special kind of mirror for the shower that doesn't steam up."

"I need to *see* this face?"

"Hey, who you talking to here? I'm no Brad Pitt. I've got my own problems."

Snip, snip.

"What's the deal with *Meet the Press*? Is it just you?"

"No," Sherrod said, starting to shake his head. Ray grabbed his face with both hands.

"Steady. So, it's you and who else?"

"Mike DeWine."

"Again. Here we go."

"Yeah. Well, it's a debate."

"Okay. Well, you're going to look great."

He pulled off the gown with a snap and whirled Sherrod around toward the mirror.

Both sideburns were the same length, a first since I'd known him, and he had at least a hint of curl around his temples.

"I have a good feeling about this haircut," I said.

Sherrod rolled his eyes. "You're a sucker for the curls, baby. Thanks, Ray."

Ray smiled and waved. "You bet. Remember, leave the sideburns alone."

It was a moment's levity in an otherwise heavy weekend. The next day, we traveled to Appalachia again, where we met in a storefront in Jackson with locked-out factory workers who'd been waiting for a new contract for several months. As the rain pounded the town's crowded Apple Festival, one worker told Sherrod how he was supposed to be taking medication for high blood pressure but couldn't afford it, so he prayed a lot. Another worker said his doctor told him he needed heart bypass surgery, but he had no health insurance.

"I take aspirin every day," he said. "I'm just hoping that'll do it until we go back to work."

Sherrod scribbled notes as one of the organizers laid out their predicament.

"They can't get hired elsewhere because those employers say they know they'll leave if and when the strike ends."

Sherrod looked up and asked the men, "Is that true?"

To a person, they nodded their heads.

"Can't be dishonest about that," one of them said. "The old job pays more."

"Our people just never realized this could happen," the organizer said. "This guy sitting next to me? He's a diehard Republican, and I can tell you right now he's not voting Republican. He told me, 'Things have got to change.' "

The man next to him nodded. "That's what I told him. Meant it, too."

Sherrod took down several names and promised to have one of his government staff call them about applying for Medicaid. On our way out of town, we stopped at a church booth and bought two orders of chicken and noodles and then stood under an awning to scoop up the hot broth.

"Look at what's happened to these people," Sherrod said softly, returning the smiles of townspeople as they made their way from booth to booth in the rain. "How do we fix all this?"

As we talked, I couldn't help but notice how so many more people recognized Sherrod now. The ads were working. As much as I wanted to believe that Sherrod's hard work alone—all the news conferences and media interviews, the speeches and roundtables—could get him elected, I knew better. His chances of winning were directly related to how much money he could raise for television advertising. All the rest of his efforts shaved fractions off DeWine's poll numbers, but it was the power of his message—and his photogenic image—telegraphed every day on TV screens that was swaying the voters.

Hillary Clinton had advised us early to respond directly to attack ads: Show a two-second clip of DeWine's ad, then respond and, in her words, "deck him." We took her advice to heart, and many of Sherrod's ads were direct responses to DeWine's attacks.

The ads produced by our campaign that generated the most comments from supporters and strangers alike, though, were ads featuring Sherrod talking directly to the camera. Two of these stood out during the campaign.

In the first ad, soft music played as factory workers with hard hats in hand walked in slow motion out of a factory as Sherrod's voice described their lives:

"They work hard, they love their country, they play by the rules. But the cars, steel, and appliances they used to make are now being made overseas, where workers are paid three or four dollars a day."

Then the camera cut to Sherrod, who walked in shirtsleeves along a chain-link fence with a "Closed Plant" sign as he spoke:

"My opponent supported the trade agreements that cost us these jobs. He said, 'It's just business.' I say it's wrong."

Sherrod stopped walking and stood facing the camera with his hands on his hips:

"I'm Sherrod Brown, I approve this message. In the Senate I'll judge U.S. trade agreements by this standard: Are they fair to America? Do they put Americans first?"

Everywhere we went, people commented on that ad. Sherrod looked strong, they said, like a fighter, and he was fighting for them.

The other most popular ad from our campaign came at the end, when Sherrod looked directly at the camera and, over a soft sound-track, talked directly to the voters:

"Before I ask for your vote, I owe it to you to tell you where I stand: I'm for an increase in the minimum wage and against trade agreements that cost Ohio jobs. I support stem cell research, tighter borders, and a balanced budget."

Another man's voice listed some of Sherrod's votes that reflected his stands on these issues, and then Sherrod reappeared:

"I'm Sherrod Brown, I approve this message, it's time to put the mid-dle class first."

No matter how nasty DeWine's ads got—and they got mighty ugly toward the end—we always made sure these ads ran, in addition to our response ads, at least some of the time. We knew by our polling and focus groups that voters responded to Sherrod whenever he spoke directly to them. He meant what he said, and that came through in his ads.

The DSCC ran a series of its own ads for Sherrod, which we never knew about until they were on the air. Former senator John Glenn stepped up and filmed a positive piece.

Jan Kellar, the mother of an Iraq War veteran, also did an ad for Sherrod. We had first met Jan during Sherrod's announcement tour. Out of the blue, she spoke up at our next-to-last stop in Akron in December 2005. In a strong voice, she told the roomful of people that when she wrote to Mike DeWine about the lack of body armor for her son and other troops, he responded with a form letter that didn't even mention body armor. She had heard that Sherrod was helping military families get the supplies they needed, so she called his office, even though he wasn't her congressman.

"My son got the body armor he needed," she said. She had come to Sherrod's announcement just to thank him.

"Let's make sure we get her name and contact information," I said to Joanna that day.

Joanna smiled. "Already on it."

If she was willing, Jan would be a valuable spokeswoman when—not if—DeWine attacked Sherrod for not supporting the troops, which was a common Republican tactic against Democrats who voted against the war. We are so grateful she was willing to film the ad, even though she admitted to great nervousness about such a public act of support.

To the occasional chagrin of our consultants, the DSCC paid for some clever ads produced by Mandy Grunwald, who is perhaps best known for her work for Bill and Hillary Clinton. We never saw these ads until they were on the air, and Mandy had a humorous touch that made for some entertaining moments, such as the ad that featured a photo of DeWine and Bush laughing it up as children sang:

The more we work together, together, together,
The more we work together, the happier we'll be.
'Cause your friends are my friends and my friends are your friends,
The more we work together, the happier we'll be.

That was just one of several ads that Mandy and her team came up with for Sherrod during the campaign, and Sherrod was grateful for Mandy's efforts—and the laughs.

IN THE LAST MONTH OF THE CAMPAIGN, TWO THINGS WOULD GET the word out about Sherrod Brown: millions of dollars of advertising, and televised debates. We could control the content of our ads, but debates were a whole other monster to wrestle. The race could be won or lost right there, in front of thousands—sometimes millions—of viewers, and so debate prep was crucial. Sherrod and DeWine had agreed to four debates, and the first one was scheduled for October 1, when they would debate on *Meet the Press*.

Before a campaign decides how to prepare a candidate for debate, it must decide *who* will prepare him. This was a dicier undertaking than I realized, because it quickly became clear that some in Sherrod's life clearly measured their worth to the campaign by whether they were included in debate prep. Unfortunately, some of those insisting they had to be part of the process were unlikely to help Sherrod improve. And as he kept saying, he really needed to improve. Sherrod always agreed to debate his Congressional opponents. But he had not had a real debate—or a real race—for more than a decade.

Sherrod had been in politics for more than thirty years by the time he ran for the Senate, and so he had collected a vast number of acquaintances who, in one way or another, felt they were mini-experts on Sherrod. Not coincidentally, these were inevitably men, and they were rather forceful in exerting their expertise. As Joanna joked in an e-mail to me after one round of debate prep, "I think I'll go have a big bowl of testosteroni now."

The atmosphere was mighty charged. The chance to take aim at everything the candidate says can turn into a blood sport in the wrong hands. The challenge in debate prep was to include those whose only agenda was to help Sherrod improve, not to show off how clever they could be or whose strong personalities intimidated those on staff who were less forceful but unrivaled experts in their fields.

Even the best of debate prep is grueling, amounting to one long pick, pick, pick at the poor candidate. Sometimes I would close my eyes and just listen:

Say this, but don't say it like that.

Don't say that, unless you put it like this.

Stand up. Lean in. Not that far. No, now you're too far back.

Quit blinking so much.

Remember to blink or you look like a deer.

Don't smile there, but do, yeah, right there, smile right there.

And that was a session that was going well.

Debate prep was always a delicate dance. Too much criticism, and Sherrod would end up deflated. Too little, and he'd be a pig stuck in mud when DeWine started swinging.

Sherrod wanted nothing to do with choosing the debate prep team. Ever the get-along guy, he was worried about offending friends and family members, and so he left it to two people—campaign manager John Ryan and consultant Tom O'Donnell—to decide who would and would not help.

The core group included Ryan, O'Donnell and his colleague David Doak, Joanna, our pollster Diane Feldman and her colleague Roy Temple, and our chief researcher, Anne Davis. Several others, including staffers Eleanor Dehoney, Liz Farrar, and Jack Dover and former Clinton deputy chief of staff Steve Ricchetti, also provided valuable insights.

John Ryan insisted that I sit in on all of the sessions too.

"Why?" I wasn't really looking forward to watching Sherrod get hammered by a roomful of people who thought they had a better version of my husband in their pile of notes.

He smiled and shook his head. "I keep telling you, Connie, he does better when you're with him. And he's less likely to lose his temper if you're in the room."

At first, the star of debate prep was not the candidate but his chief debate coach, former congressman Dennis Eckart. Dennis had retired from the House in 1992 and was now a practicing attorney in Cleveland. He was funny and charming and had a long history of giving national candidates a real workout in debate prep. Dennis was on board because he wanted Sherrod to win, he assured me, and that could make for some bumpy road.

"Some spouses hate me by the time it's over," he said. And then he grinned.

Dennis and Sherrod had been roommates nearly thirty years earlier when they both served in the Ohio General Assembly, and their predictable rivalry—both of them were young, smart, and handsome—had given way over the years to a camaraderie born of accomplished lives and maturing perspectives. Sherrod respected Dennis, but he also really liked him, which helps when you've got somebody pummeling you into pesto, as happened on the first day of debate prep in late September.

To prepare for the debate, Dennis watched hours of videotape of both Mike DeWine and Sherrod. Press conferences, speeches, old commercials—he watched all of them, and discerned their habits.

"Most folks have habits," he told me. "So do politicians. Styles get recognizable; they get comfortable with certain words, phrases, and the same old story, stump speech, 'magic words' right on schedule." He paid particular attention to DeWine's ugly race against Senator John Glenn in 1992, when he attacked Glenn's patriotism.

Dennis noticed that above all else, DeWine was disciplined. "I counted on him not breaking out of his predictable modes, although I concede it wasn't always clear which DeWine you would get in any given event—nice Mike, or rough Mike."

Let's just say nice Mike took a long vacation.

Sherrod and DeWine had a trial run of sorts in early August, when they agreed to a taped interview at Lakeland Community College. While not billed as a debate, it involved a back-and-forth between the two candidates that gave us an idea of what we could expect in future debates. DeWine was aggressive and bullying. Sherrod pulled punches at first, as if he were caught off guard to find himself sitting next to rough Mike and trying to figure out just how hard he could punch back.

That day I had my first, and only, conversation with DeWine's wife, Fran. It didn't go well. She shook hands only after I offered mine, and rebuffed my attempts at conversation during breaks in the taping. She had been in politics with her husband for more than thirty years, and I was stunned at her open unfriendliness. I was brand-new at this political-wife gig, but I knew one of the roles I was supposed to play was the public optimist. The mantra was always: *My husband's going to win, you betcha.*

Fran DeWine's silence told me everything I needed to know about the DeWine mind-set.

"They know they're in trouble," I told Sherrod on the ride home. It was the first time I thought DeWine knew he could lose.

Dennis wrote in an e-mail to me that the Lakeland interview

showed him how far Sherrod had to go to be ready for a real debate with DeWine:

> I knew Sherrod wasn't that serious about this yet, and that was probably also true about DeWine. It is *so* hard to get candidates and campaigns to give them the time they need to make prep work right. That's why I wanted an early free-form opportunity, both to assess our opponent and scare our guy into taking this seriously.

It worked.

"Man, I need real debate prep," Sherrod said on the drive home that day.

"Yeah," said Eckart.

"I need a real team to get me ready."

"Yeah."

"You already know this."

"Uh, yeah."

We set aside two full days of prep for each of the four debates. In the prep sessions, Eckart played DeWine—better than DeWine played DeWine, as it turned out. DeWine never had the one-two punches that Eckart delivered with the grace of a prizefighter.

The first day of prep was the worst. As Sherrod put it, "Eckart kicked my ass."

Dennis was aggressive and relentless, and on issue after issue, Sherrod fumbled. Then he stumbled. Then we got to watch it all on videotape.

"Ohhhh," Sherrod groaned as everyone else in the room laughed. "I look awful."

It was a place to start, and Tom O'Donnell made the ground rules clear. When Sherrod took a bathroom break, Tom lectured us like the patriarch of an unruly brood.

"Look," he growled in his strong Brooklyn accent as he laid eyes on each and every one of us. "I don't want everyone beating him up. Dennis just did that, and that's his job. (Dennis beamed.) Now we have to help him get better, and we're not going to do that if everyone starts showing off and criticizing every little thing about him."

Sherrod and I both had a real soft spot for grumpy Tom. My crush began when we interviewed him with his colleagues, David Doak and Mattis Goldman, for the consulting job back in the fall of 2005. I will never forget his answer when we asked why he wanted to work for Sherrod: "I've been waiting a long time for a candidate to fight, to really fight, for what I believe in," he said, his face folded into one long scowl. "Sherrod is on the right side, and I want the right side to win for a change."

O'Donnell later told me that he'd never seen a candidate more willing to improve than Sherrod. While I winced at all the criticism, Sherrod took notes. When he didn't feel comfortable with an answer, he'd practice until he felt he knew the material cold. He drew stick figures at the top of his notes to remind himself to stand up straight during the debates. And he learned how to turn his anger at predictable jabs from DeWine into opportunities to nail him.

DeWine, for example, loved to describe Sherrod as being "on the fringe of his own party."

"Respond, pivot, and deck 'im," O'Donnell yelled.

"Are you calling workers fringe?" Sherrod said in the last debate prep before *Meet the Press*. "Are the majority of Americans who oppose the Iraq War on the fringe? Are our senior citizens who want affordable drugs on the fringe?"

"There you go!" O'Donnell said. "Don't you *dare* let him get away with that."

The women in the room helped to give Sherrod balance. When the topic of school violence came up, the men immediately grilled him on what he would do to prevent future shootings. Liz Farrar, from Sherrod's D.C. office, politely interrupted.

"Shouldn't his first comment be to express sympathy for the families whose children have been wounded and killed?"

"Oh, right."

"Sure, absolutely."

"Well, yeah, that goes without saying."

Throughout debate prep, we encouraged Sherrod to start with broad points, then zoom in on specifics. O'Donnell said that, unlike a lot of candidates, Sherrod really understood policy. He couldn't tell you how to play a CD or imitate the robot on *Lost in Space,* but he could give you a rundown of Will and Ariel Durant's entire *History of Civilization* because he'd read all eleven volumes. He loved talking about the lessons of history, and his memory—and enthusiasm—for numbers, which started when he was a young boy calculating batting averages of Cleveland Indians, had served him well throughout his career.

As the hours progressed, Sherrod got better and better. At the end of Day Two in debate prep, I turned to him and said, "You're going to have fun on *Meet the Press* tomorrow."

Dennis nodded. "As the Pentagon would say, it's a target-rich environment."

And Sherrod was ready to take aim.

nineteen

Bananajuana

As soon as the camera lights dimmed on the set of *Meet the Press,* Sherrod turned to me and said, "I didn't want it to end."

His debate with Mike DeWine would set the tone for the rest of the campaign. In less than an hour on that Sunday morning of October 1, 2006, Sherrod proved he was more than up to the challenge of being a United States senator. And others took notice. Potential donors who'd ignored his calls for weeks were suddenly sending checks. Some reporters and columnists started writing about how, short of an October surprise, Sherrod looked unbeatable. And it wasn't long before the Republican National Committee virtually abandoned Mike DeWine.

Most reporters declared all the debates to be slugfests that nobody won. We didn't agree, but we didn't waste any energy lobbying, either. What mattered was how Sherrod felt after the debates, and he was flying high after *Meet the Press.*

It was becoming clear to even the most jaded reporters that Sherrod's race was gaining momentum. Sometimes, they actually acknowledged it, such as in Dayton, which was the site of the second televised debate.

As Sherrod made his way down the hall and into the studio, Joanna, Dennis, and I hummed the theme song from *Rocky*. Dennis jogged behind Sherrod, rubbing his shoulders like a trainer, and I jogged backward in front of him, throwing imaginary punches to warm up our prizefighter. Sherrod was laughing, as were most of the journalists around us.

"Okay, I shouldn't tell you this," one of them said, pointing toward the room where DeWine was getting ready. "But the mood down there is *real* different from the mood right here."

The crowds were another indication that Sherrod was pulling ahead. Sherrod Brown supporters easily outnumbered DeWine supporters two to one at the third debate in Toledo, and the DeWine people were getting desperate. During that debate, Sherrod stopped midsentence and asked his supporters not to boo and hiss as DeWine's supporters in the audience did every time Sherrod spoke. That only made the DeWine people jeer louder.

In the last two weeks of the campaign, Sherrod got another boost. His dear friend John Kleshinski joined us on the trail. This was Jack Dover's idea, and someday we'll stop thanking him. Sherrod had warned me that the last two weeks of any campaign will drive even the most decent person to make a deal with the devil if only he'll promise to bring it all to an end. By then, you've eaten so much bad food and had so little sleep even your earlobes are bloated. Your pets sniff you as if they've never seen you in their entire lives. And everywhere you go, you're accosted, either by people who wear your opponent's T-shirts and taunt you, or by well-wishers who wear your T-shirt and want a picture with you, which you readily agree to because they've often waited two hours or more just to see you.

John was the perfect antidote to all of this. Where we saw another grinding sixteen-hour day, he saw one long party. Every morning, he'd show up at our home, clap his hands, and say, "Okay! Everybody ready? Let's go campaign!" I'd pour him a strong cup of my French roast coffee and off we'd go, our new driver, Nick Watt, leading the way.

"Hey, guys, can you believe this?" John said over and over as we traveled one last time through southern Ohio, then back through central Ohio on our way to Cleveland. "Can you believe we get to do this?"

He was, as he said, "one happy puppy."

In Gallipolis: "Wow, how 'bout that crowd!"

In Chillicothe: "Did you *see* all those homemade signs?"

In Wapakoneta: "My God, this is history in the making!"

John had been a diabetic since he was thirteen, and his wife, Emily, worried about him constantly. She had agreed to his coming to Ohio as long as he promised to call her regularly. So four, five, six, eight times a day, he'd dial his cell phone and give her updates on the trail from the backseat of our Pacifica. "Em, I'm not kidding," I heard him say at one point, "this is one of the most exciting things I've ever done."

After our third day of campaigning with John, Sherrod turned to me and said, "John sure makes it a lot of fun, doesn't he?"

He made it easier, too, and I told John that as he and I were standing in the back of the room at a Democratic Party dinner in Lima.

"His step is lighter because you're here, John."

He looked at me and smiled gently. "You think so? Really?"

"I really do."

"Well, let me tell you something, Connie. He could not have done this without you. He knows it, we all know it. I've known Sherrod for thirty years, and he's a different man because of you."

Now I was the one tearing up. I gave him a big hug, and then we congratulated each other for not having to sit at the head table like Sherrod. When Sherrod got up to speak, John and I gave him our full attention—even when he started talking yet again about his canary pin.

"He sure likes that pin," John whispered.

"Mm-hmm."

A couple of times in those last two weeks we stayed in a hotel, and on one of those nights a housekeeper popped in on John to ask if he wanted his bedclothes turned down.

"No, I can do that myself," he said, handing her a twenty-dollar tip. She insisted that she could not take that money without doing something for him.

"Okay," he said. "Would you say a prayer for me?"

She nodded, and asked his name. When he told her, she smiled.

"I will pray for you, John."

"Isn't that the nicest thing?" he said the next morning, recounting the story. "Who can't use an extra prayer?"

As October marched on, two of Sherrod's fellow Ohioans in Congress, Stephanie Tubbs Jones and Tim Ryan, started stumping for Sherrod throughout their districts—and beyond. A lot of Democratic heavy hitters had come to Ohio to help, too. Senators Hillary Clinton, Dick Durbin, Barack Obama, Tom Harkin, Barbara Boxer, Blanche Lincoln, Chuck Schumer, and Harry Reid and former senators Max Cleland and John Edwards all came to Ohio for fundraisers and rallies. So did former president Bill Clinton, Congresswoman Linda Sanchez, and political pundit James Carville. John Kerry raised more than $100,000 through two e-mails sent to supporters around the country, and Senator Dianne Feinstein raised nearly that same amount for Sherrod at a single fundraiser in her home.

Al Franken drew a huge crowd at Ohio State for Sherrod. Actor Adam Brody of the TV show *The OC* volunteered for Sherrod, as did Luke Perry, who starred on *Beverly Hills 90210*. Brody said he had been following various candidates' races on the Web and chose Sherrod's. Wherever the slight, polite young actor went, girls screamed and swooned.

Perry had a more personal tie to Ohio. He was born in Sherrod's hometown of Mansfield, and Sherrod's dad, Dr. Charles Brown, delivered him. Doc Brown was his family physician for many years, and Sherrod hung on Luke's every story about his father, who had died in February 2000.

Luke pointed to the scar on his forehead and told Sherrod, "That's where my brother stuck an arrow in my head. Your father pulled it out for me. He was always having to rescue me from something."

We also enjoyed swapping stories with Luke about others' misperceptions of Ohioans. Whenever Sherrod and I went to California for fundraisers, inevitably someone would comment on how young and energetic we seemed. "It's like they were expecting Aunt Bee and Otis from Mayberry," I told Luke.

"I know what you mean," he said, grinning. "Every time someone hears I'm from Ohio, they expect me to pull out a banjo and start playing."

Singer Carole King, a longtime friend of Sherrod's, came to Ohio for several days. She insisted that in addition to playing a fundraising concert, she would campaign for Sherrod in small rural communities. And that's exactly what she did, drawing crowds and headlines everywhere she went. My favorite moment with Carole, though, was during her concert for Sherrod in Cincinnati. We were sitting in the balcony, within view of the three hundred or so attending. When she sang "You've Got a Friend," she asked everyone to sing along. The lights went up, and she pointed right at Sherrod. The entire crowd turned to face him as they sang the chorus, assuring Sherrod that he was not alone.

J. D. Souther and Jackson Browne came, too, for a fundraiser for the Ohio Democratic Party. When Jackson performed "I Am a Patriot," many of those in the room wiped their eyes. It had been a long few years, full of right-wing attacks on our family values and our patriotism, and it felt so good to sing along as the nighttime breezes washed over us.

That was the fun stuff, but we squeezed it in around a full schedule of campaigning and fundraising. Sherrod was still doing a minimum of four radio interviews every weekday morning before 7:00, and then hitting the road most days by 8 A.M. for as many public appearances as possible in front of large groups. Whenever he was in the car or between meetings, and before events started, he continued to make fundraising calls. That goal—a minimum of two hundred calls a week—did not change until the last week of the campaign.

What did change was my schedule. John Ryan had called me during the last week in September with a specific request.

"This is countdown time," he said. "This is when Sherrod will be monitored closely at every single public event in the hopes that he'll screw up and one of the Republican trackers or a reporter can catch the mistake."

"I thought we'd been worried about that for months," I said.

"Well, yeah, we were, but back then we always figured we'd have the time to recover. Now, he makes a mistake, we don't have enough time to turn it around."

I was reminded of a story one of our consultants told us early in the campaign. Right after the 1972 presidential race, the consultant was dining with a friend in a Washington restaurant. The friend pointed to a man sitting nearby and said, "There's the person who made Edmund Muskie cry."

"That's William Loeb, the newspaper editor?"

"No," his friend replied. "His scheduler."

Loeb's newspaper had attacked the character of Muskie's wife. Muskie launched an emotional defense of her right outside the newspaper's office during a snowstorm. Reporters later said Muskie had cried during his speech. Muskie insisted that snowflakes had melted on his face, but the damage was done.

Our consultant's friend said Muskie broke down because he was exhausted from his unrelenting schedule.

That sort of story was why I worried about Sherrod throughout the campaign, and it was why I immediately responded to John Ryan.

"What do you want me to do?" I asked him.

"I want you to be with Sherrod on the road as much as possible."

"What about things I'm already scheduled to attend?"

"I always told Shana to tell anyone requesting you in October that your schedule could change."

"And now it has?"

"Yeah. He does better when you're with him, Connie. He laughs more, he relaxes more, he's more confident. You know it, and so does he. I think that's where we need you most."

Shana cleared my calendar of all but the bigger events where I would be speaking to large, nonpartisan crowds. An AARP luncheon stayed on the schedule; so did a senior citizens group of about two hundred in Strongsville. I also kept my commitment to speak at a house party in Knox County after the organizers won a contest sponsored by the campaign. Whoever could guarantee the largest crowd got—ta-dah—me. Sherrod and I were always reunited as soon as possible, and staff often joked that Sherrod was quick to complain if he felt we were apart too long.

On the evening of October 15, *The New York Times* broke the story that the GOP was pulling out of Ohio.

Adam Nagourney's story, posted on the *Times*'s website and then on the newspaper's front page the following day, gave us all we needed to know in the first sentence:

> Senior Republican leaders have concluded that Senator Mike DeWine of Ohio, a pivotal state in this year's fierce midterm election battles, is likely to be heading for defeat and are moving to reduce financial support of his race and divert party money to other embattled Republican senators, party officials said.

DeWine, and RNC chairman Ken Mehlman, quickly scrambled to refute the claim, but the damage was done. From that moment on, reporters started covering the DeWine campaign as if it were the band on the *Titanic*.

Sherrod sent this e-mail to his campaign, titled "To the Best Campaign Staff in the History of the World":

The news in Monday's *New York Times* is incredible. All of us need to step back, take a breath, and realize what has happened: We are running against a two-term incumbent who is popular among the elite and the opinion-makers in Ohio—an incumbent who has showered so many with tax money, who outspent us on television this summer by a two-to-one margin, who has savaged us as anti-patriotic and tax-and-spend liberals (not to mention "Far Out Brown"—my favorite).

Yet the Republican National Committee has made the decision to leave our state.

This is all about what YOU have done. You have out-organized them, out-fundraised them, out-worked them. You have hit back every time he has hit—and always harder and smarter and with way better research. . . . You have out-scheduled them. You have beat them on the Internet and on the ground. You have beat them with fundraising and with free media. You have—I actually heard about this—shown up at his press conferences and, while acting courteously, stolen the spotlight or at least dimmed his.

You have, in a nutshell, run the most amazing campaign in the country. And John Ryan has been a superstar.

But—while I rarely quote any Yankee [Sherrod's an ardent Cleveland Indians fan]—it ain't over till it's over.

We have to be even better in the next 23 days. We have to continue to be aggressive and smart. We have to raise more money and continue to work for earned media. We have to organize even better than we have already.

The bigger our margin—and we haven't even won yet, so get that out of your mind—the bigger our margin, the more down-the-ballot races we win. The bigger our margin, the stronger national message we send that an unapologetic progressive—who cares about the poor and the middle class, who cares about social justice, who cares about globalization—can win anywhere.

Remember that David Brooks of *The New York Times* said that this was the most important political race in the country. We need to show him and everyone else watching that this is also the best campaign in the country. So far, it has been; that's why Karl Rove pulled the plug. We need to continue—only better—for the next 23 days.

Thank you; Connie and I are so proud of ALL of you.

Sherrod

In October, all the Ohio newspapers' editorial boards announced their endorsements. Of all the major daily newspapers, Sherrod got only one endorsement—from the Toledo *Blade*. Both Cincinnati papers, the *Dayton Daily News, The Columbus Dispatch,* the Canton *Repository,* the Youngstown *Vindicator,* the *Akron Beacon Journal,* and even *The Plain Dealer* endorsed Mike DeWine. We found out about that last one just as we were leaving for dinner on Sweetest Day, which we normally never celebrated, but we were grateful for the excuse to spend a few hours alone. I was signing off my computer when I noticed the e-mail from a *Plain Dealer* colleague. I read it, and my heart sank. I'd always known this would happen, but it still felt awful.

Sherrod walked up just as my computer screen went dark, but he could tell by the look on my face that something was wrong.

"*The Plain Dealer* is endorsing DeWine tomorrow."

Sherrod looked at me, gave me a hug. "Of course they are. Let's go eat."

What we didn't know that evening was that *Plain Dealer* columnist Dick Feagler, a Cleveland treasure, would counter the *Plain Dealer* editorial with his own endorsement in the same issue titled

"I'm for Sherrod Brown." If I had to choose between the readership of the editorial page and that of the popular Feagler, it wasn't even a contest.

That night at dinner, Sherrod gave me a new pack of Moleskine notebooks, which is what I used to take notes during the campaign, and after our meal the waitress delivered a bouquet of fall flowers to our table. Immediately, I was a blubbering fool.

"Happy Sweetest Day, baby," he said, clearly pleased with himself.

We pulled on our coats and started to leave, but another couple stopped us. The woman smiled at Sherrod. "I was going to vote for you anyway," she said. "But seeing what you just did for your wife seals the deal."

Sherrod threw me a sheepish grin. "I swear," he said as we walked to our car, "I swear, I swear, I didn't mean for that to happen." I just laughed and buried my face in those flowers, grateful that the campaign was almost over.

The newspaper endorsements had an interesting effect on the campaign trail. Naturally, Sherrod's supporters were angry, but a lot of reporters talked to me about them, too. A few said it was making their job harder, because most readers don't know there is a difference between the editorial board that endorses candidates and the reporters who work hard to stay neutral. They were getting hammered by readers who now accused them of bias. One photographer was so upset with his paper's DeWine endorsement that he slapped one of Sherrod's stickers on his jacket at an event he was assigned to cover.

Long before I knew Sherrod, I thought newspapers should not endorse candidates. Unlike editorial writers, reporters are out on the trail, working long and hard to cover these races fairly, and they often feel undermined when their own newspapers come out at the last minute favoring one candidate over another. Even more troubling, most readers don't know that some editorial endorsements don't even reflect the vote of their board. Sources later told us that three editorial boards had voted to endorse Sherrod but were overruled by their newspapers' owners. That was never disclosed to readers, which is disingenuous, if not unethical. I wish more newspapers would adopt the policy of Al Neuharth, the founder of *USA Today,* when it comes to endorsements. In all the major races, his editorial board abstains, trusting the voters to make up their own minds.

Sherrod assured me the editorial boards were out of touch with Ohio's voters. In just a few days, we would find out just how out of touch they really were.

SHERROD'S FINAL DEBATE WAS SCHEDULED FOR FRIDAY, OCTOBER 27, in Cleveland. Dennis Eckart had negotiated the debate dates and venues with the DeWine camp, and we were surprised—and thrilled—that DeWine agreed to do the last one in Cleveland, our home base.

By then, the RNC had pulled its money from DeWine's race, and his attack ads had reached a new low, including an accusation that Sherrod had promoted an unnamed employee who dealt drugs out of his secretary of state office more than twenty years ago. DeWine refused to name this employee, and Sherrod had no idea who he could be talking about. Several newspapers deplored DeWine's tactics as unfair and desperate, but he refused to pull the ads.

Before the debate, my friend Meg Driscoll, who worked in the flower department at Heinen's grocery store near our home, sent an e-mail she hoped I would forward to Sherrod. I first met Meg when she came up to me to thank me for advocating for hourly workers in my column. She had watched the Toledo debate on television and wanted to pursue one of the questions a reporter had asked DeWine:

The reporter asked what DeWine did with the $73,000 he got in tax cuts over five years. That comes out to $14,600 per year. That is more than people working at 40 hours make at minimum wage, per year. Probably they don't get health coverage and many don't get the 40 hours, but rather just under that so they are considered part time. I am furious that he insults our intelligence. That we working people making even more than minimum wage would be [placated] by a mere $500 to $2,000 while he is raking in such profit and voting against people working so hard for so little. I can't tell you how this cut to the quick in me. So, I am writing to you in hopes that you will pass this response from a voter on to Sherrod.

Sherrod printed a copy of Meg's e-mail to take with him to the debate. "I don't know if I'll use it, but I don't ever want to forget it," he said.

Sherrod woke up early for the final debate, which was sponsored by the City Club of Cleveland. A record crowd—more than eleven hundred—was expected, so the City Club had moved the debate from its usual venue to the ballroom of the Renaissance Hotel on Cleveland's Public Square.

Make-up artist Kylee Cook, who was practically family now after dabbing our cheeks and noses for television appearances all over the state of Ohio, showed up at our home around ten that morning. The debate would be telecast, and we wanted to make sure Sherrod didn't look pale under the hot lights. He was in his usual good temper about this, grumbling the entire time she patted him with pancake, but Kylee cheerfully assured him that this was the price of fame.

Dennis joined us and our driver, Nick Watt, for the half-hour trip to downtown Cleveland. Charlie Anderson, a retired Iraq War veteran and veterans liaison for Sherrod's campaign, had told us that a traveling antiwar exhibit, "Eyes Wide Open," would be set up across the street from the hotel. Charlie knew we'd want to stop there.

Sherrod and I had opposed the war from the beginning. By our first date, in January 2003, Sherrod had already voted against the war, and I was regularly writing columns against it. I had first written about the "Eyes Wide Open" exhibit in 2004, when more than eight hundred pairs of empty military boots filled row after row on a grassy hill in Cleveland Heights to represent the American troops who had died in Iraq. Now, in October 2006, the exhibit, which was sponsored by the Quaker-based American Friends Service Committee, displayed more than three thousand pairs of boots, and included rows of children's shoes to represent the tens of thousands of Iraqi citizens who had died. Throughout the campaign, the war was always there, always hovering, and by the day of Sherrod's final debate, Ohio ranked fifth in the number of troops killed.

We crossed the street to the exhibit, but well-meaning supporters started following us, chanting, "Sher-rod! Sher-rod!" Immediately, Sherrod asked them to stop. Silently, we walked alone among the many boots, sometimes kneeling, sometimes holding hands as we read the names of the dead.

By the time we entered the hotel lobby, the place was packed. Hundreds of supporters gathered around Sherrod, shaking his hand, pulling on his sleeve, wishing him well before the debate. Finally, Joanna came up and whisked us off to a private corner in a banquet room. She knew it was our practice to pray before each debate.

Sherrod and I sat facing each other, our knees touching as we held hands.

"Will you start?" Sherrod said.

"Sure." I took a deep breath and squeezed his hands. "Dear God, thank you for giving Sherrod the strength and the wisdom . . ."

That was as far as I got. Sherrod had started to cry.

"Sherrod?"

He put his face in his hands.

"Sherrod? What is it?" I had never seen him like this, certainly not right before a debate, and it scared me.

"Sherrod, what's wrong?"

"What if I let them down?" he said.

"Who?"

"All those people out there. Did you hear the things they were say- ing? They said they had hope again, they were thanking me for giving them hope. I don't want to let them down. Think what it took for them to come through for us after what happened in 2004."

Now I got it. This was the Sherrod I knew—and an exhausted Sherrod, too—never wanting to fail anyone who believed in him.

"Sherrod, there is no way that anyone will ever doubt that you did everything you could to win this race," I said. "And you did it by taking the high road."

He nodded, but he still looked troubled—and this was not the mood we needed right before he took the stage for the final debate, which would start in just a few minutes. Time for desperate measures.

"Sherrod?"

He looked up, his blue eyes focused on mine.

"You know I love you."

He nodded.

"Well, I'm going to have to say something I never thought I'd have to say to my husband."

His face grew alarmed. "What?"

I took another deep breath. "If you don't stop crying, you're going to smear your makeup."

We were sitting with our foreheads pressed together, laughing like crazy, when Dennis Eckart walked into the room.

"Are you two just going to goof around or are you ready to go win a debate?"

Sherrod stood up and shot him the biggest of grins.

"I'm ready to win."

The final Senate debate of 2006 will forever be known in our house by John Kleshinski's description of DeWine's lowest moment.

It came right after DeWine raised, yet again, the phantom of Sherrod's unnamed employee from more than twenty years ago and then insisted, before an astonished crowd, that the employee had laced a banana with marijuana.

A *banana*. He meant a brownie, but he never corrected himself, and in fact insisted "I'm not making this up." Even the tables with DeWine supporters started laughing and shaking their heads.

John Kleshinski immediately dubbed it the "Bananajuana Scandal"—and we knew the race was over.

After Sherrod opened the debate with his plan for the future, DeWine launched a litany of personal attacks. Sherrod's response to these attacks was quoted in newspapers across the state: "You have just watched a two-term incumbent senator morph into a desperate candidate."

By the time it was over, even many Republicans I recognized in the audience were clapping for Sherrod.

That evening, we had five more events, and Sherrod was so tired that he started to doze off during a radio interview from the car. I called John Ryan and told him we had to shave the schedule again, and he readily agreed. Then I checked my voice mail and found this message from my sister Toni:

"Hey, Con, just wanted you to know: We put Sherrod's sign in Dad's front yard today. He'd want it that way, you know?"

Sherrod was in the backseat with me, and, even in the dark, he could tell something was up.

"What is it?" he said.

"Nothing, really," I said, and then told him what Toni said.

"Oh, baby," he said. He grabbed my hand, and held it tight for the rest of the drive home.

THREE DAYS AFTER THE CLEVELAND DEBATE, WE WERE IN A PACKED auditorium at The Ohio State University with Michael J. Fox for a rally in support of stem cell research.

Michael suffers from Parkinson's, and he was campaigning for candidates who supported the research that could save countless lives. Michael had taped a campaign ad for Missouri Senate candidate Claire McCaskill, and after the ad hit the airwaves, Rush Limbaugh raised a firestorm of criticism by imitating Michael's involuntary jerking movements and accusing him of faking.

It is heartbreaking to watch this gracious, talented actor and father of four struggle to perform the simplest of tasks—like sitting still, for example, or completing a sentence. He has made it clear, time and again, that he does not expect to live long enough to benefit from the research he is championing—and yet there he was, sitting onstage with Sherrod along with a number of other people afflicted with diseases that stem cell research might cure.

I got a healthy dose of humility from Michael Fox that day. Sherrod and I sat on either side of Michael, watching as a sixth-grade boy with Type 1 diabetes gave a speech. He was going on a bit, and I smiled nervously at Sherrod. I was worried that all this waiting would tire Michael.

Michael leaned over and whispered in my ear, "You know, it is going to make him feel so good to get his whole story out." He smiled at me, and I was appropriately reprimanded. When it was Michael's turn at the microphone, he turned to the boy and said, "At any age, you feel the need to tell your story, and I consider you an inspiration."

The standing-room-only crowd cheered, and I spotted my son, Andy, who had been diagnosed with Type 1 diabetes just two years earlier. Nearby, there was John Kleshinski, who'd been injecting himself with insulin since he was thirteen. They watched Michael, their faces brimming with hope, and once again I was struck by what a blessing this campaign had been for Sherrod and our entire family.

All of our kids were working hard for the campaign. Sherrod's older daughter, Emily, made the greatest sacrifice. She took a leave of absence in July from her union organizing job to help run, as a volunteer, the coordinated campaign in Ohio. Her husband, Mike Stanley, a community organizer, took an unpaid leave of absence to join Emily in Ohio, but as it turned out they were constantly separated in those last weeks. Mike organized outreach to faith-based groups and coordinated get-out-the-vote efforts. He also helped Wendy Leatherberry compile a list of more than fifty political, religious, and civic activists in Ohio who were committed to vouching publicly for Sherrod's character if he needed their support. They were part of our planned response if DeWine stooped to using the divorce allegations against Sherrod.

Andy and Stina regularly volunteered in our Columbus headquarters and canvassed numerous neighborhoods—all around full-time jobs. One of their more sobering accounts from the trail was finding entire blocks of houses where no one was registered to vote.

Elizabeth, a gifted orator, gave speeches for her dad throughout the summer. In the fall, she flew home on weekends from Columbia University to speak in more than thirty counties. We often say that if another Brown family member runs for office, it will be Elizabeth. Liz also helped to organize more than forty Columbia students who came to Ohio in the last days to volunteer for the campaign.

Caitlin, who was attending college in Ohio, had registered voters on campus and was now always armed with a roll of Sherrod stickers, pasting them on anyone who crossed her path. She was our youngest and least experienced politically, but she got into the campaign spirit. She wore makeshift "Sherrod earrings"—hoops plastered with stickers—and hosted an entire table of classmates (most of them Republicans) at the City Club debate. All of them later declared their support for Sherrod.

On so many days, Sherrod and I would hear yet another story about one of our children on the campaign trail, and it was so humbling to know these were our kids, sacrificing so much of their daily lives for a common cause. We never browbeat them into helping, never told them that they, too, should put the rest of their lives on hold. But all of them, including Michael and Stina, stepped up in ways that Sherrod and I only now fully comprehend. What a difference they made in the campaign—and in these parents' lives.

Sherrod's entire family was involved, too, and he never tired of supporters telling him about an event where they met his mother or one of his brothers. Throughout the campaign Bob represented Sherrod, giving speeches at dozens of events. Charlie organized the seven counties around their hometown of Mansfield. Charlie's wife, Anne Swanson, came from Maryland to Ohio, too, passing out Sherrod Brown emery boards bundled with helium balloons to dozens of hair salons. Anne also raised significant money for the campaign.

The only thing distracting us from all the mounting excitement was our fear that DeWine might still go up with an ad recycling the old divorce allegations against Sherrod. We had our own ad, of course, with Sherrod's ex-wife, Larke, our daughters, and me, but we were still hoping we wouldn't have to use it. After the City Club debate, one of DeWine's staffers told the Toledo *Blade,* "The divorce is on the table." After that, John Ryan, Joanna, and Dennis had called every television station in the state, and nearly all of them agreed that we could switch to our divorce ad if DeWine went up with his.

It was only on the Friday evening before the election that John Ryan could put our fears to rest. The deadline had passed, he said. Mike DeWine had run out of time. There would be no divorce ad.

That weekend, I finally lost my temper with a TV reporter and cameraman who chased us out of a church service in Columbus to ask Sherrod about the unnamed employee from his secretary of state days. We had discussed how Sherrod should answer this, and decided that he should take the offensive and ask, "Who is this employee? Why isn't DeWine naming this person?"

The reporter pushed, insisting that she was just reporting the news. When the camera turned off, I turned on her.

"You should be ashamed of yourself," I said. "This is not reporting, this is regurgitating unfounded, anonymous attacks from a desperate candidate."

"I'm just doing my job," she said.

"I'm a journalist, and I say you're not doing your job," I said.

"Okay," she said, laughing, and then made quotation marks in the air with her fingers: "You're a 'journalist.'"

A *Dayton Daily News* reporter was standing with us, and she immediately reprimanded the TV reporter. "Actually, she really is a journalist, a Pulitzer Prize–winning journalist."

The TV reporter blanched. "Look, this wasn't my idea. It was another reporter and she couldn't come so I had to come in her place . . ."

I felt a tug on my sleeve. It was poor John Kleshinski, trying to rescue me. "We gotta go, Connie."

"In a minute."

"No, now. We gotta go *now*."

He all but dragged me to the car.

"Did you hear what she said?"

"Yup," said John, as Sherrod chuckled in the front seat.

"That is so wrong!"

"Yup," said John. "It really is."

"I could have taken her, John."

John smacked his forehead in mock horror. "Think of the headlines, Connie," he said. "Think of the headlines."

twenty

The Middle Class Wins

WHEN I WOKE UP EARLY ON ELECTION DAY, MY FIRST SURPRISE was that I had ever fallen asleep. The second surprise was finding that, after all we'd been through, I wasn't so much nervous as just excited. Finally, the day we'd been working toward for more than thirteen months was here.

For most of the campaign, whenever I thought about Election Day my chest would tighten and—poof!—my appetite would disappear, and I'd look for the nearest chair. I imagined a day of excruciating length, full of horror stories about voter intimidation and malfunctioning voting machines. I saw myself sprouting gray hairs like sea oats and wringing my hands into putty as the results trickled in.

Sherrod and I had fielded hundreds—really, hundreds—of questions, not just in Ohio but across the country, about Secretary of State Ken Blackwell's attempts, real and imagined, to suppress voter turnout. Blackwell had gained a national reputation for himself by

2006. Several times, he had changed the rules for casting a provisional ballot, which is used when a voter shows up at the wrong polling place, and then he fought efforts to count them. He also tried to stop independent groups, including the League of Women Voters, from registering people to vote.

Far too many Americans doubted that Ohio could have a fair election. It was impossible to dismiss their concerns out of hand, and not just because of Robert F. Kennedy Jr.'s troubling piece in *Rolling Stone* magazine in the summer of 2006 that detailed these and other problems in Ohio's 2004 election. I'd seen firsthand Blackwell's attempts to disenfranchise voters. In 2004 I had wanted to run a reprint of Ohio's voter registration form with my column. The goal was to encourage voters of every political ilk in northeastern Ohio to register. Blackwell, though, clearly didn't want more people registering in the most Democratic part of the state. He was a Republican, and also George W. Bush's Ohio campaign chair—just like his political counterpart in Florida, Katherine Harris.

Blackwell had said he would not accept any completed voter registration forms on newsprint because the paper "wasn't heavy enough." I called all seven county boards of elections in our circulation area, and to a person they said they would defy Blackwell and accept the form. I'll never forget what one of them said: "We just want to encourage as many people as possible to vote."

Blackwell backed down in 2004 as soon as he counted heads and realized his own crowd was against him. Thousands of voters registered using the *Plain Dealer* form.

During the 2006 campaign, Sherrod always acknowledged concerns about election fraud, but then insisted that he and all the Democratic candidates on the state ticket would win by a large enough margin to thwart any attempt to taint the tally. That didn't always assuage the fears of those who couldn't help but wonder how secure any election could be when the guy overseeing it was also the Republican candidate for governor.

Now, two days before the election, John Ryan e-mailed his final words of encouragement to the campaign staff, which included this cautionary note:

Election Day—For those who have not been through the drill before, get ready to hear 1,000 rumors on Election Day. Normally none of these turn out to be true. Just take a breath before passing on something you hear as the truth. Make sure you report things to the person you are reporting to that day but keep focused on bringing people out to the polls.

Election Protection—This year we have an effective vehicle to pass along any potential voter problems. Have voters call 888-DEM-VOTE. We have a bank of lawyers in Columbus who will help follow through.

By Election Day, our own polls showed that Sherrod was going to win. Since mid-October, Sherrod had been telling me he would win by double digits. The morning of the election, he told me he'd win by 12.68 points. He said it exactly like that. The process he used to conjure up that number involves a lot of political acumen and a little bit of magic.

First, Sherrod tallied what he called his *W* and *L* days. Starting March 1, Sherrod asked himself every single day, "What do I have to do to win?" At the end of the day, he'd evaluate his efforts. By his measure, he usually had either a winning day or a losing day. Winning days got a *W*. Lots of good press coverage earned a *W*, for example, as did any day when he raised a lot of money with a single event. Losing days were marked with an *L*, such as when DeWine got a newspaper's endorsement or whenever Bush came into Ohio for a fundraiser. *W* days made for a chirpy Sherrod. *L* days made for long nights as he rehashed mistakes and missteps. Fortunately, the *W* days far outnumbered the *L* days.

This was only the beginning of Sherrod's equation for victory. He also looked at polling trends—his numbers had steadily climbed as DeWine's steadily fell; then he weighed other factors from March 1 to

November 5: his 411 TV hits, 668 radio interviews, and the 7,277 handwritten letters he'd sent to a wide range of Ohioans, from anyone turning ninety or celebrating more than fifty years of marriage to newly minted Eagle Scouts. (By the way, once you're an Eagle Scout, you're always an Eagle Scout, which I learned after I spoke to a roomful of men and mentioned that Sherrod "used to be" an Eagle Scout. Oh, the furor. Learn from me.)

After Sherrod calculated those numbers, he did that thing he does in his head that I don't understand and he can't explain, and decided he would beat DeWine 56.34 to 43.66, a 12.68 percentage margin. He wrote this equation in his calendar the night before the election.

How accurate was he?

To quote a postelection e-mail from John Kleshinski:

"Don't break your arm patting yourself on the back."

OUR TWO YOUNGEST KIDS, CAITLIN AND ELIZABETH, WENT WITH us on Election Day to vote at 9 A.M. at the Avon Public Library, which is about a half-hour's drive west of downtown Cleveland. Lots of cameramen, photographers, and reporters followed us around, which made me wince for all the other residents in our precinct who were just trying to cast their vote. Liz, who grew up with such hoopla, took it in stride. Cait, not to be outdone by her sophisticated (and beloved) stepsister, also acted as if it were the most normal thing in the world to have a gaggle of strangers document your every *tap-tap-tap* of the electronic touch screen.

Joanna, our intrepid communications director, stepped up when they tried to photograph Sherrod and me voting in plain sight.

"Hey, sorry, but the voting booth is still private, even if there isn't any, well, *booth*," she said, shooing them off to a safe distance. I heard Sherrod talking to someone and looked up to find my husband, seized by the spirit of Gandhi, shaking the hand of our neighbor with the DeWine sign in his yard. Unable at that moment to be the change I wanted to see in the world, I looked back down and kept voting.

We later learned that out of seven hundred or so votes cast in our Republican precinct, Sherrod won by fifty. I sleep a little better knowing that.

Soon after voting, we parted with our daughters. Liz went to work the phone banks at one of our campaign headquarters while Caitlin canvassed neighborhoods in the rain with our driver, Nick Watt. Emily was still in Columbus and Mike was in Marion, both of them coordinating the get-out-the-vote efforts. Andy and Stina canvassed in Columbus. All of our children would later join us at our hotel.

After visiting two more polling places, Sherrod and I arrived around 1 P.M. at our hotel room at the Crowne Plaza in downtown Cleveland. The Crowne was directly across from Cleveland Public Hall, where Sherrod's victory party was scheduled to take place later in the evening. We never let ourselves call it anything other than that. Dennis Eckart headed up the planning.

"You're going to love it," he kept saying throughout the weekend, without ever providing any details. When we asked our scheduler, Shana Johnson, she just repeated his assurance. "Really," she said, "you're going to love it."

We had decided just before the weekend not to join the coordinated campaign celebration in Columbus, the state capital, because the Ohio Democratic Party had not reserved a big enough space to accommodate all who wanted to attend. We didn't want so many volunteers and contributors closed out after a long year of such hard work. Besides, we lived in northeastern Ohio, where Sherrod had been a congressman for fourteen years and I had worked nearly as many years at *The Plain Dealer*. If we held the party in Cleveland, supporters throughout the northern part of the state—many of them union members who'd worked on Sherrod's campaigns for more than a decade—could join in the celebration.

Our press secretary, Ben LaBolt, initially balked at the switch, insisting the media would abandon us for the party in central Ohio. After a few calls to the press, though, he laughed at his own anxiety.

"They'll be here," he said, beaming. "Media coverage definitely *won't* be a problem."

We left the chaotic hotel lobby for our suite on the twenty-second floor. The campaign staff reserved a suite, which had two bedrooms, three bathrooms, and a living and dining area, as well as three televisions. No matter how many people joined us in the next few hours, we would have one bedroom reserved just for us. For two whole hours, we had the place to ourselves before dozens of family members, staff, and volunteers—not to mention a number of people we'd never seen before—found their way to our room.

Shana had ordered some food for us, and both of us started laughing when we spotted a dish of cold baked potatoes piled amid the cheese and crackers. Sherrod always asked me to bake extra whenever I made them for dinner, so that he could bring the leftovers on the campaign trail the next day. I'm afraid I've never developed a taste for the cold spuds, but Sherrod eats them like apples—much to the amusement of staff members. Apparently Shana thought he preferred his potatoes like this, and so there they were: a small mountain of stone-cold tubers.

I looked out at the overcast skies and spotted the sole wind turbine—I mistakenly called it a windmill until someone corrected me—spinning at Cleveland's Science Center. So many times Sherrod had mentioned the wind turbine in speeches as a promise of what could come to Ohio if only we focused on creating alternative energy solutions. It was a sign of the future, and I found it oddly reassuring as I watched it twirl.

Public Hall, surrounded by quiet streets, looked lifeless and abandoned. That would change, and soon. In less than three hours, the polls would close and the crowd of activists, staff, and political junkies would convene in the cavernous auditorium. Sherrod expected the networks to start calling the race a half-hour or so later.

"By eight o'clock," he said. "They'll know it by then, unless it's close—and it's not going to be close."

The day before, Sherrod and I had brainstormed the beginning of his victory speech. We knew that at best he had maybe two minutes to capture the attention of the media, and I encouraged him not to start with a litany of the people he wanted to thank. Politicians do that all the time, and even the objects of their gratitude start to swoon with boredom around the fourteenth name.

First, we tried a little humor. The Toledo *Blade* was the only major Ohio paper to endorse Sherrod, so we toyed with this beginning:

> To the editorial boards of the *Akron Beacon Journal, The Cincinnati Post,* the Cincinnati *Enquirer,* the *Dayton Daily News, The Columbus Dispatch,* the Canton *Repository,* the Youngstown *Vindicator* and *The Plain Dealer:* I gratefully accept this endorsement from the hardworking men and women of Ohio.

When we ran it past Joanna, she laughed like crazy. Oh, ho, ho, ain't we funny?

Then she shook her head.

"Okay, I know you guys are having a little fun, letting off a little steam, but do we really want this to be our message on election night?"

Whenever Joanna started talking about "we," the real "we" knew that we'd just found ourselves a fish that couldn't be more dead in the water.

Sherrod had scribbled some notes, but four hours before the polls closed, he had hovered but not landed. He pulled off his suit and tie and changed into a pair of his rattiest sweats in the time it took me to kick off my shoes.

"I need to write my speech," he said, frowning as he sat down at the large wooden dining table. "I still don't know what I'm going to say."

"Yes, you do," I said, grabbing the notes he'd read to me a little earlier. "And it's not this."

He looked at me and sighed.

"Think about what this means," I said, "to you, to Ohio—and to the country."

"Was that supposed to make me feel *less* nervous?"

I put down my own notebook and sat across from him at the table.

"Tell me a story," I said, and that was all I had to say.

Less than thirty minutes later, Sherrod knew exactly what he wanted to say to the people of Ohio.

OUR SUITE BEGAN TO FILL SHORTLY AFTER 5 P.M. JOANNA, SHANA, Wendy, and John Kleshinski were the first to show up, mainly to go over last-minute details. Soon after that, Liz and Caitlin arrived, followed by my sisters, Leslie and Toni, who had driven together from our hometown of Ashtabula, about an hour east of Cleveland. I really wanted them with me on Election Night, and to my delight they immediately agreed. My brother, Chuck, joked that while he was a Republican willing to vote for Sherrod, he had to draw the line at sharing a stage with the guy who took on the pharmaceutical companies—one of which is his employer.

Les and Toni hugged me, then pulled me aside.

"We have something for you," Les said.

"We knew Dad would want you to have it," Toni added.

When they pulled it out of the bag, I recognized it immediately: Dad's beloved old suede jacket, the tan one he'd worn at Sherrod's rally in Ashtabula. It was the same jacket he had on in the last photo I took of him, the picture that popped up on the television screen during my interview on the *Today* show only four days after he had died. That same photo was in a frame in our center hallway, and I never walked past it without silently saying, "Hi, Dad."

I held up the jacket and noticed that his "Sherrod Brown" sticker was still over the left pocket.

I barely got out the words "Thank you," then walked into a nearby bathroom and closed the door. I pulled on Dad's jacket, sat on the counter, and had a good cry.

Soon after that, Jackie and Kate showed up, and I nearly teared up again at the sight of our two close friends. Jackie took one look at me and said, "Oh, dolly, can you believe it? You're almost there." She hardly ever left my side throughout the rest of the evening.

By 7 P.M. or so the place was buzzing. All of our kids and Sherrod's family had arrived. I watched as Emily and Elizabeth, veterans of so many campaigns, hovered around their dad like butterflies. Repeatedly they patted his back, whispered in his ear, and leaned on his shoulder. They had waited a long time for this night, this victory.

John Ryan called on my cell phone to let us know that a close friend of Mike DeWine's had called Ryan and asked for Sherrod's private cell phone number.

"Why?" I asked.

To his credit, Ryan pretended I hadn't just asked one of the more stupid questions of the campaign.

"Well, probably so that Mike can call him," he said.

Silence.

And then the heavens opened up and the choir began to sing.

"Oh, oh, right," I said, finally catching on. "So that he can concede."

"Right."

"Wow."

"Yeah."

"You gave him the number?"

"Yeah," said Ryan, who was really earning overtime with this call. "I gave it to him, but maybe you should hold on to Sherrod's phone to make sure he gets the call."

"Which phone? One of the BlackBerries, or the cell phone?"

"The cell phone. I figured you could fit that one in your pocket."

That was John Ryan, always thinking of the candidate's wife, even when she wasn't thinking at all.

I shared Ryan's news with Sherrod, who nodded silently and handed me his phone. Then we excused ourselves from the increasingly crowded part of the suite and went into our bedroom so that we could shower and change.

At about 7:40, ten minutes after the polls had closed, Sherrod and I sat down on the edge of our bed and said a prayer before rejoining the group, who were already in a celebrating mood.

As always, we faced each other and joined hands, then bowed our heads as we thanked God for getting us through this challenging year. We prayed for strength, ours and Mike DeWine's, and then we held each other for a moment, until we heard a cheer swell up outside our bedroom door.

Sherrod looked at me quizzically. The clock on the bedside stand said it was only 7:45.

We opened the door and found Joanna standing inches away.

"Okay," she said, smiling, "it's premature, but CBS has just declared you the winner." We looked up at the large-screen TV and saw the check mark under a portrait of Sherrod. We turned to each other, and as soon as I saw the tears in Sherrod's eyes I wrapped my right arm around his neck and buried my face in his shoulder, as I so often do in our more private moments.

Then we heard it: the *kachick-kachick-kachick* of cameras, their lights flashing over and over.

We looked at the group of photographers crouched in front of us, then looked at Joanna, whose own eyes were on the brink of flooding.

"I forgot to tell you they were here," she said. "Remember? They wanted to come up for a few minutes? We talked about this."

Sherrod and I both shook our heads and started to laugh. The next day, versions of that photo—capturing us clearly overcome with emotion—ran in newspapers across the country, including *The New York Times.*

The *Dayton Daily News*'s Jessica Wehrman best described that moment, and what it meant for me, a few days later:

> It was a familiar and comfortable stance for Schultz and Brown, who've been married two years; one Schultz knows viscerally.
>
> Until she opened Wednesday's paper, though, she'd never seen what that familiar pose looked like to the outside world.
>
> It was a second when both realized that their long hours campaigning had resulted in a victory, and it was duly recorded and put on the wires for all newspapers to run in their morning editions.
>
> And it made Schultz realize, yet again, what a different sort of marriage hers is—where a moment of victory or defeat can be captured by the cameras; where crowds press against them at campaign events, people taking pictures with cell phones; where perfect strangers recognize her and her husband.
>
> "It wasn't our moment," Schultz said. "We don't get that anymore."

It was merely an observation of how much our lives, and our marriage, had changed.

MINUTES AFTER CBS DECLARED SHERROD THE WINNER, SENATORS Harry Reid and Chuck Schumer called Sherrod to congratulate him. Shortly after that, Hillary Clinton was on the phone.

"Tell Connie not to let anyone tell her she can't have her career," she said to Sherrod, who immediately repeated her advice. Several women in the suite applauded. Granted, they were my friends or relatives, but still. Shortly after that, our Jos. A. Bank salesman, Allen Roy, called. "Whatever you do," he said, "don't forget to straighten Sherrod's tie before he gives his victory speech. The entire nation will be watching. Let's not have them focused on the crooked tie."

Even though DeWine's friend had called early in the evening for

Sherrod's phone number, by 10 P.M. he apparently still hadn't persuaded DeWine to make the call. We were waiting for even a hint of a concession. The crowd across the street was growing, but Ryan was worried we'd lose a number of them if Sherrod didn't show up soon. Joanna fretted over losing precious television airtime before the eleven o'clock news. "Once the news starts, we lose them," she said.

Ryan looked at his watch and gave us a rare order. "We wait until ten-thirty. If we don't hear from DeWine by then, we're going over to the hall and Sherrod's going to give his speech." Ted Strickland had already delivered his victory speech as Ohio's next governor.

Meanwhile, we crammed around a TV set, watching as one Democrat after another captured a congressional seat. Sherrod leaned in and whispered, "This could have turned out a lot differently, baby." I grabbed his hand and squeezed. We always knew it was a gamble, but once we made the decision, we never let ourselves look back. Until Election Night, that is, when we watched the best-case scenario play out before our eyes.

The Democratic Senate victories were starting to pile up, too. Bernie Sanders took Vermont; Bob Casey beat Rick Santorum in Pennsylvania; Amy Klobuchar won in Minnesota; Sheldon Whitehouse took the Rhode Island seat from Lincoln Chafee. Claire McCaskill's race against incumbent Jim Talent was still too close to call, but we were confident she would win because the votes in heavily Democratic St. Louis had not yet been reported. Jon Tester of Montana and Jim Webb in Virginia, both of them locked in neck-and-neck races, were destined for all-nighters. Harold Ford in Tennessee was the only certain Democratic defeat.

As our suite grew louder, I set Sherrod's cell phone to ring-and-vibrate and then held it in my hand throughout the evening. I had only one job that night, and I wasn't going to screw it up. Around 10:20, Ryan pulled us aside. "I think we'd better head on over. We can't wait forever for DeWine to call."

It took several elevator rides to get everyone down to the lobby, and we were walking across East Sixth Street in downtown Cleveland when my hand started to vibrate. I looked in the cell phone window: The area code was from DeWine's home county. Immediately I pulled Sherrod back to the sidewalk.

"It's DeWine," I said, handing him the phone. Ryan and Joanna began shushing everyone as Sherrod flipped open the phone.

"Hello?" Pause. "Mike. Thank you for calling."

For the next few minutes, we stood silently around Sherrod as he talked with the man we'd known only as his opponent for the last thirteen months. Sherrod listened as DeWine congratulated him on running a strong race and told him, twice, "You're going to love this job."

"I know how hard this call is, Mike," Sherrod said. "I had to make this kind of call to Bob Taft in 1990, and it wasn't easy. I appreciate that you did this."

DeWine asked Sherrod to wait until he delivered his concession speech before he took the stage. Sherrod agreed, and we headed over to the hall to wait.

Sherrod's colleague and cherished friend Stephanie Tubbs Jones effortlessly segued from preacher to stateswoman to stand-up comedienne. We arrived just as she was pantomiming DeWine's lockstep with Bush to uproarious applause. As soon as the large video screen over the stage began televising DeWine's concession speech, though, the hall grew silent. Sherrod and I watched on a small TV monitor backstage.

Against the backdrop of a large American flag, surrounded by his family, DeWine delivered a somber speech.

"In this race we fought hard," he said. "We did everything we could do, but it just wasn't meant to be. This was not the year. We could not win."

He spoke for a few more minutes as his wife, Fran, stood by his side. While some on the stage were wiping away tears, she looked the way I'd hoped I would if the roles had been reversed: already poised to be the rock her husband would need. As I watched, I couldn't help but feel I had more in common with Fran DeWine than with anyone standing around me. We are different women, as others too often had gleefully pointed out, but we both love our husbands and had stood by them through a grueling race. Nobody else really understood what we had been through, but our loyalty to our husbands also meant that those were stories we would never share with each other.

During the campaign, some reporters and columnists had predicted political death for the loser in this race, but DeWine clearly wasn't buying that theory. He ended his speech by suggesting he would be back:

"There is unfinished business in this state, and I believe, the good Lord willing, that I have unfinished business, too."

He never mentioned Sherrod.

As soon as DeWine finished, the stage at Public Hall went dark. Dennis Eckart gave us last-minute instructions: We were to wait until his son, Eddie, introduced us over the loudspeaker. Sherrod and I would then walk out on center stage together, followed by our family and friends. I was to stand to Sherrod's left.

"You won't be able to miss your marker," Dennis said, grinning. "I marked a strip of tape on the floor just for you." He seemed awfully excited about a strip of tape, but then again, we were excited about everything that night.

Sherrod and I walked behind the black curtain. I closed my eyes, trying to will myself to live in the moment, in this moment, to breathe it all in so that I'd never forget everything that was about to happen.

Somewhere, drums started to beat the prelude to Aaron Copland's *Fanfare for the Common Man* as a booming, faceless voice (that of Eddie) announced with high drama:

"He fights for the middle class."

Sherrod looked at me and grinned.

"He'll stand up for Ohio."

We both started giggling.

"Ladies and gentlemen, the next senator from the great state of Ohio—the Honorable Congressman Sherrod Brown, and his wife, Connie Schultz!"

The curtains parted, and out we walked into the blinding lights. The ceiling rained confetti as the music blasted and hundreds of supporters clapped, cheered, screamed, and even cried at the sight of their next senator.

Fighting tears, I turned to Sherrod and shouted the first thing that came to mind.

"Doesn't this music remind you of the scene in *The Natural* when Robert Redford hits the home run and smashes the lights and the crowd goes crazy?"

"Robert Redford?" Sherrod shouted.

"Yeah."

"Robert Redford is here?"

"No," I yelled. "He was in *The Natural.*"

"Right here?"

"No," I said, suddenly realizing how ridiculously *out* of the moment I had just traveled. "Never mind!"

The crowd started chanting, "Sher-rod! Sher-rod! Sher-rod!" which made the object of their affection turn a fetching shade of fuchsia.

"All right, all right," he said, laughing as he gestured for them to stop. This only inspired a louder round of "*Sher-rod! Sher-rod! Sher-rod!*"

He opened the leather binder that held his notes, and I looked down to find my stage marker. As soon as I saw the writing on the foot-long strip of tape, I knew why Eckart had been so pleased with himself: "THE LOVELY WIFE."

Finally, the room grew quiet, and Sherrod uttered the twelve words that would be repeated in stories and video clips around the country: "Today, in Ohio, in the middle of America, the middle class won."

The room exploded.

He praised their progressive values and the work they did to help change the country, and then he repeated what had become the mantra of all the Democratic candidates in Ohio: "As Ohio goes in '06, so goes the nation in '08."

Again, the crowd erupted, which it continued to do throughout his ten-minute speech. Sherrod reminded them that most politicos thought he could not win when he got into the race, that they had advised him to abandon his progressive politics for the middle of the road.

"They warned us to be cautious. They advised me not to be myself. . . . But you know, it's a risk worth taking to stand up for what you believe in, and it's a risk worth taking to fight uncompromisingly for progressive values. . . . This year, we knew the politics of fear wouldn't work, and we knew the politics of smear wouldn't work. What people needed was hope, and you gave people hope by making it clear what we stand for."

Then he repeated the principles of his entire campaign, each one of them greeted with cheers and applause:

"We're for a higher minimum wage and embryonic stem cell research.

"We're against an energy policy dictated by the oil industry . . . but we want to make Ohio the Silicon Valley of alternative energy.

"We want affordable health care for all Americans.

"We're against job-killing trade agreements that betray our values and destroy our communities.

"We want to fix No Child Left Behind and make tuition affordable for middle-class Americans."

He paused, then leaned into the microphone and said, "We all want an end to the war in Iraq," which drew the loudest applause.

He told once more the story behind his canary pin—he just couldn't help himself—rattling off many of the laws championed by progressives that have saved American lives. "That's why we are such a great people, because we're in this together, we've fought together, we've worshipped together, and we've worked together."

Suddenly, a corner of the room near a video screen erupted into cheers. Someone yelled the news to Sherrod. Gesturing toward the audience, he asked, "They know it yet?" When it was clear that the word hadn't spread, Sherrod turned back toward the crowd and made an announcement that brought down the house: "The networks just said the Democrats won the House of Representatives!"

Then, in a rare moment of abandon, one that the kids and I still tease him about, Sherrod leaped into the air, pumping his arm and yelling, "All right! All right! Change is on the way!" For a few more weeks, he was still a House member, and one who'd spent most of his congressional career there in the minority.

He wrapped up by reminding his supporters what he had learned the hard way: "As progressives, don't ever let them question your values, don't ever let them question your faith, and don't ever let them question your patriotism!"

One more time, the crowd erupted, chanting "Sher-rod! Sher-rod! Sher-rod!" as the house lights went up.

JOE TONE, THE TWENTY-EIGHT-YEAR-OLD REPORTER FROM THE weekly *Scene* magazine in Cleveland who touched base with me fairly regularly during the campaign, provided his own insights from that night in an e-mail a few weeks later. He had called me after the election asking whether I was planning to return to *The Plain Dealer*, and in the course of the conversation I mentioned his coverage of election night.

Of all the journalists and columnists covering Sherrod's campaign, the ones who demonstrated time and again their eye for the telling personal details of life that illustrate a bigger story were Jessica Wehrman of the *Dayton Daily News*, Peter Slevin of *The Washington Post*, and Joe Tone of *Cleveland Scene*.

Tone included this passage in his election coverage:

[T]he kids' faces said it best. They were kind of blank. Joy and pride and the rest would come later, it seemed, when this guy of theirs—dad, step-dad, dad-in-law, uncle—started getting introduced as U.S. Senator. But for the moment, they simply seemed relieved. Relieved that the whole damn thing was over. Relieved that they didn't have to hold their breath every time *Grey's Anatomy* went to commercial, wondering what they might hear about their guy. Relieved not so much that their guy had won, but that, thank God, he didn't lose.

Weeks later, that passage about our children still made Sherrod and me misty. Our kids had invested so much of themselves in Sherrod's race.

"You were right," I told Tone later in a phone conversation. "Our children *were* relieved that it was over, particularly Caitlin. She was so worried that Sherrod would not win, because she'd never been in a campaign with him. She was all hope and no experience."

Before hanging up, I told Tone that I wished I had seen him at the victory party. "Well, it was a crazy night," he said, adding that my face as we worked our way through the election-night crowd reflected "total shock and amazement."

He was right, of course. I really didn't even see who was in front of me that night. I remember recognizing at the time almost everyone who grabbed my hand across the crowd control barriers, but now I can name only a handful of the people who shook my hand. I recall Wendy Leatherberry standing behind me, her hands alternately hovering around my waist or pulling me back with a tug on my jacket as well-wishers pulled me by the arm. I remember John Kleshinski, in tears as Sherrod spoke and later without his usual grin as he stood next to Sherrod, performing the same body-check for Sherrod that Wendy did for me, tugging hard on occasion to rein Sherrod in when supporters yanked on him with too much enthusiasm.

I also remember having to muscle my way through the lock grip of reporters and cameramen surrounding my husband so that I could stand near him as he answered the onslaught of questions. I remember squinting into the bright lights, and grabbing a fistful of Sherrod's suit coat so that I didn't lose my balance amid all the jostling by television crews competing for the same sound bite. I remember Jackson Browne's "I Am a Patriot" blasting from the loudspeaker as Sherrod descended from the stage, and singer-songwriter J. D. Souther rushing up to us with hugs of congratulation.

There's so much I don't recall, though, despite my intention to remember it all. I don't remember confetti falling from the ceiling *after* Sherrod's speech, even though a videotape of that night shows it landing on our heads and shoulders like fat snowflakes of red, white, and blue. I don't recall seeing our kids or our other relatives in the sea of faces after we left the stage, but somehow they all ended up with us in our hotel suite, hugging us good night before leaving for their own rooms. I don't remember who poured the champagne into the flute in my hand, but I can still see Sherrod smiling at me when I giggled as the first bubbles tickled my throat.

My final memory of Election Night, though, is seared in my brain. It was past one in the morning, and Sherrod and I were lying in bed, wide awake.

"I can't sleep," he said, his eyes a map of red lines.

"I can't either," I said, my own eyes on fire from fatigue.

"Tell me a story," he said.

We talked past three before falling asleep holding hands.

Neither of us remembers a single word.

twenty-one

An Offer You Can't Refuse

THE SATURDAY AFTER THE ELECTION, SHERROD SNAPPED SHUT HIS flip cell phone and shot me a sheepish grin.

"We have to go to the White House."

"No, we don't," I said.

He frowned.

I called his frown and raised him a scowl. "You *said* so."

An e-mail invitation had arrived the day before at Sherrod's office:

THE WHITE HOUSE IS PLEASED TO
INVITE YOU AND YOUR SPOUSE TO A

RECEPTION FOR NEWLY ELECTED
MEMBERS OF CONGRESS

MONDAY, NOVEMBER 13, 2006

5:00 P.M.–6:00 P.M.

THE WHITE HOUSE
STATE FLOOR

Sherrod had forwarded the e-mail to me, adding, "Connie? I assume the answer is no." I immediately responded with praise for his uncanny insight on how to preserve a marriage and thought the issue was closed. After a year on the campaign trail, I'd had it up to my feathered bangs with frozen smiles and good behavior. I didn't want to spend another millisecond pretending the Republican efforts to annihilate my husband were just fine, really, if you don't count all the character assassinations, living for months on end under the threat of a "divorce ad," and that whole Bananajuana scandal.

"Forget it," I said.

Soon-to-be Senate Majority Leader Harry Reid, however, had other ideas, which we soon found out when Joanna called Sherrod on Saturday.

"Harry wants us to go," Sherrod said after the call. "It's a gesture of good intention, it shows we want to work with the other side, that we're putting all the nastiness of the campaign behind us and will work together to get things done."

Add a good soundtrack, and we would have had ourselves another campaign ad.

Even as I sighed, though, I knew Sherrod—and Reid—were right. It was time to build bridges, not lob grenades. I also knew I needed to make this easy for Sherrod, to show my unequivocal support if he was willing to stand face-to-face with the man who'd spent the last six years steering our country in the wrong direction, not to mention raising $2 million for Sherrod's opponent. This, I realized, was my first test as a senator's wife.

"I'll hate every minute of it," I said, on the brink of flunking.

"But you'll go?"

"I'll go."

(C for effort, maybe?)

THAT MONDAY MORNING, WE FLEW TO WASHINGTON. AS WE DEscended, the butterflies did their usual flap-and-flutter around my heart at the sight of the Capitol dome, but I resisted my usual in-air ritual of whispering, "Hi, honey," mainly because my honey was sitting right next to me. Most times when I fly to Washington, Sherrod is already there, already working, and the sight of that dome always makes me think of him. At such moments, I'm reduced to this act of silliness, but then I always tell myself there's not a happily coupled person alive who doesn't do something goofy on a regular basis in the name of love. That's what I tell myself, anyway, and so far, it's worked.

Sherrod blissfully rejected any notion that his life should change on the brink of senatorhood, even as we agreed to stay at the same hotel with all the newly elected senators rather than in our Washington apartment. He had under-packed as usual, throwing into his duffel bag two days' worth of socks and underwear for a four-day stay. He planned to wash them out in the shower as he always does.

I, on the other hand, packed for a two-week trip to just about any climate you could imagine. Whenever I feel my life is spiraling into chaos, I focus on the one thing I can still control: my clothes.

It speaks to the growth in our marriage that Sherrod no longer puts me through his speech about how he learned during his Eagle Scout days to pack only what he could carry on his back—"and then you cut that in half," he loved to say. Even he could see that I was forever cured of the supposed wonders of that neat trick after taking his advice for a seven-day trip to Moscow, where I spent far too much time trying to dry my sodden clothes with a hair dryer.

Our first event was a photo op with Senators Harry Reid and Chuck Schumer and all the senators-elect, except for Claire Mc-Caskill, who had the nerve to take care of herself and go on vacation with her husband. Apparently, spouses were not supposed to attend, but nobody told me that, and so I showed up at Reid's office with Sherrod and immediately was introduced to Bernie Sanders's wife, Jane O'Meara Sanders. Sometimes you just know God did you a favor, and that's how I felt the moment I met Jane in the reception area. She is kind and down-to-earth, and not afraid to admit when she's nervous, which is a nice balance to someone like me. When I'm nervous I'm a toddler behind the wheel of a tank, which can really mislead others into thinking you know what you're doing at the precise moment when you have no clue. Sometimes it works, sometimes it gets you the night shift.

Jane smiled, shook my hand, and whispered, "I don't think we're supposed to be here."

"Why not?"

"They said this is only for the senators."

Oh, those pesky "they" again. I'd had my fill of people half my age telling me what I could and couldn't do. As Sherrod headed back to join his future Democratic colleagues in the Senate, he turned around and motioned for me to join him.

"C'mon," I said to Jane, looping my arm through hers. "We're not going to miss this. We're going in."

It was quite a sight, seeing all of those newly elected senators together for the first time. Sherrod kept shooting me grins as he shook hands with Jim Webb of Virginia; Jon Tester of Montana; Ben Cardin of Maryland; Amy Klobuchar of Minnesota; Bob Casey of Pennsylvania; Bernie Sanders of Vermont; and Sheldon Whitehouse of Rhode Island. We met two other renegade spouses, too, Myrna Edelman Cardin and Sharla Tester; apparently they hadn't gotten their marching orders, either. Amy Klobuchar pointed at me and joked that her husband, dutifully ensconced back at the hotel, had been "outspoused" again.

After a few minutes, Reid and Schumer said it was time to meet the press. The doors opened to our left and out the senators walked, greeted by an onslaught of camera firepower as they settled into chairs arranged in a tight semicircle.

"Let's get the wives out here," Reid said after a few moments, and the four of us joined them. I stood behind Sherrod, put my hands on his shoulders, and tried to ignore the cameras and not cry with pride. Multitasking as usual.

Most newspapers that ran the shot the next day used one without the wives, which didn't surprise me after a year of campaign coverage.

It also was an appropriate record of such a historic moment. My favorite photo from the shoot, by Melina Mara, ran in the next day's *Washington Post.* In it, Sharla Tester was pressing her cheek against her man's head, beaming as she wrapped one arm around his wide, laughing face. I'm to their left, behind Sherrod, standing stiff as a fencepost. I admired and envied Sharla's unabashed glee.

The still photographers were ordered out for the TV cameras, and as they lighted up the room, Sherrod pointed to our dear Joanna, who was standing against the wall smiling and blinking back tears. She had already left the campaign staff and was back in Sherrod's office on Capitol Hill, setting up interviews with other senators' communications directors to prepare for the transition from the House to the Senate. When we teased her later, she shook her head and welled up again.

"I just can't believe you're here," she told Sherrod. "I can't believe we did it."

After the shoot, we headed for a shuttle van, which stopped at the Madison Hotel to pick up the spouses who knew how to follow instructions. We were also joined by the only Republican senator-elect, Bob Corker, and his wife, Elizabeth. In a spirit of bipartisanship, the whole busload of Democrats reached across the aisle and welcomed them. Emily Reynolds, performing her final duties as secretary of the Senate under Republican leadership, counted our heads and recited our names, and then the driver pulled away from the curb.

We were on our way to the White House.

PILING OUT OF A VAN LIKE A BUNCH OF SUMMER CAMPERS CAN ROB you of dignity even when you're dropped off in front of the White House, but we managed to straighten up and walk sedately through the North Portico entrance. A string quartet played as we entered the State Room, where a table the length of a football field held enough finger food to feed the entire Congress—which, as it turned out, was a good thing, since about thirty newly elected members of the House of Representatives, many of them with spouses, soon joined us.

It was nice to see them, mainly because we had spent our first twenty minutes or so staring at one another under the watchful gaze of the dozen or so young White House staffers hovering on the periphery like mothers-in-law keeping an eye on the silver. It was only after the room was brimming with the buzz of a crowd that we were instructed to join a reception line to meet George W. and Laura Bush.

The president seemed weary and deflated. He congratulated Sherrod. "You ran a good race," he said. Mrs. Bush was guarded and frosty, but I didn't blame her. She had watched her husband become the most lethal arsenal for Democratic candidates across the country, including my husband, and she couldn't even let off steam by taking on her husbands' attackers the way I did on the campaign trail. I wanted to lean in and whisper, "I know, I love my husband too," but decided against it.

We wound our way back to the reception, and that's when I saw Karl Rove.

Karl Rove: the man who pushed DeWine to run the "Twin Towers" attack ad against my husband.

Karl Rove: the man who ordered DeWine to get more aggressive and personal in his attacks against Sherrod, or the Republican National Committee would pull its support for his race.

Karl Rove: the man who has made a career of winning campaigns by turning Americans against one another and trying to scare them to death.

"Look," I said to Sherrod, already starting to walk away. "There's Karl Rove."

"No."

"Yes."

"Where?"

"*There*," I said, turning his head in the right direction.

"We've got to go meet him."

"You've got to be kidding."

But he wasn't. Sherrod didn't want to gloat; he didn't want to challenge Rove. He just wanted to make Rove look him in the eye and shake his hand. So he waited and waited, until Rove finished a conversation with another couple and looked up at my husband.

"Mr. Rove? I'm Sherrod Brown," he said, thrusting out his hand. Rove shook it and said, "Congratulations, Senator."

Sherrod introduced me.

Rove smiled, took my hand, and asked, "You going to go back to your newspaper column?" I told him that was the plan, and then answered a series of questions about my column and the book I was writing.

What struck me most about Rove was how harmless he looked. If I saw him at an airport or standing in line at the drugstore, I'd take him for a middle-aged guy who spent his days in a cubicle wishing he had more hair and more time with his kids.

I waited, wondering if he'd say a word about his role in Sherrod's race.

I didn't wait long.

"Well, nice to meet you," he said, and then he walked away.

After that, we decided to make it a trifecta and introduce ourselves to Vice President Dick Cheney. I'll give him this: He didn't even try to be friendly. No "Congratulations." No "Glad to meet you." Just a gruff "Hello" and quick handshake, and then he turned away.

Soon, all of the senators-elect and their spouses were back on the bus, heading for a dinner at the Capitol. As Sherrod and I made our way through the marble halls of history, we ran into Representative John Boehner, a fellow Ohioan and a Republican whose time was running out as the House majority leader.

Boehner, tanned and wound tighter than a Jheri curl, darted over as soon as he saw Sherrod and pulled him a few feet away from me before whispering in his ear. Sherrod laughed, and then introduced me. Boehner, whom I had never met, wrapped his arm around me and said, "Should I tell her what I just said to you?" He looked me in the

eye and shook his head. "Nah, you tell her. I might embarrass her."
Then he dashed off.

"What did he say to you?"

Sherrod hesitated.

"What?" I said.

Sherrod sighed and then repeated Boehner's words of insight regarding Sherrod's victory. Something about being lucky, and a dog's genitalia.

Let's just leave it at that.

twenty-two
Starting Over

WHEN SHERROD AND I FIRST AGREED THAT HE SHOULD RUN FOR the Senate, we made several promises to each other.

Sherrod would run a progressive race, championing the working men and women of Ohio who felt betrayed by their own government. By the end of the campaign, we knew that voters didn't care about labels, about liberal versus conservative. What they cared about was who was on their side. By a margin of 12.4 percent, they decided it was Sherrod.

We also agreed that whenever DeWine and the Republican National Party attacked Sherrod, Sherrod would fight back—and he did, every time, often with the help of the Democratic Senatorial Campaign Committee. We stayed on the high road, too, no matter what DeWine alleged. In the last few weeks of the campaign, people stopped us everywhere we went and said they noticed the difference. So many of them thanked Sherrod for making them proud.

We had promised ourselves that, unlike John Kerry's 2004 race in Ohio, Sherrod's campaign would be in all eighty-eight counties, no matter how conservative or supposedly pro-Bush. We had coordinators and phone banks in every county, thanks in large part to the organizing efforts of our field director, John Hagner. Sherrod carried forty-six of those counties, which was thirty more than John Kerry had won in 2004.

Just as important as all of these promises was the one about our marriage. We vowed this middle-aged couple's young marriage would remain a priority throughout the campaign, and we kept that promise. We were together at least every weekend, and talked and e-mailed throughout the day. Whenever possible, Sherrod slept at home. Most mornings, he still made my coffee, and just the way I like it. He took out the dog, collected the day's newspapers from the driveway, and fed the cats, too.

A single memory of us as a couple on the campaign has crystallized in my mind. We were at Dulles International Airport, waiting for a late-night flight to Cleveland that would end up being more than two hours late. It was around ten, and we were exhausted. We moved away from the blaring television screen and found an empty bench. I laid my head on Sherrod's lap, and it wasn't long before he leaned over and laid his head on my hip. We slept that way for an hour, cocooned like twins in the womb.

This campaign would not have become such a strong and fluid operation had we not tended the marriage, too. Sherrod waited until I was ready for him to run, which cemented us as husband and wife, united for the same journey. So many have now declared Sherrod's race one of the best run in the country. Whenever they say that, I think of how we ended as many nights as possible in each other's company. Most nights, we were all we had for each other, and every night, that was more than enough.

May Sarton once wrote, "The fact remains that, in marrying, the wife has suffered an earthquake and the husband has not." That tumbled through my mind a lot, as there was no denying that marriage to Sherrod had changed virtually every aspect of my life. But the earnest wish of Winnie-the-Pooh also floated around me. His words are stitched on a pillow I gave to Sherrod after he once pulled me tight and said, "I sure hope we live long and die together." He was lamenting that we had married later and didn't know how much time we had together. But then again, who ever knows that?

The pillow, now on our bed, reads: "If you live to be a hundred, I want to live to be a hundred minus one day, so I never have to live without you."

AFTER THE ELECTION, SHERROD AND I HAD HOPED THAT THE REST of 2006 would settle into something resembling a normal life—our version of normal, anyway, which would include a lot of evenings at home by the fire with our pets cuddled up beside us as we mapped out the next course of our life together.

My first order of business was deciding when, not if, I would return to *The Plain Dealer*. Nearly a year away from my job had stoked a real fire in me to continue writing. I used to joke that whenever I had a column idea on the campaign trail, I'd hit Sherrod with a pillow. So many opinions to write, with nowhere to put them. I was eager to return to work.

While I was away, *The Plain Dealer,* like so many newspapers around the country, had tried to shave its expenses by offering buyouts. A total of sixty-four staffers in the newsroom alone took early retirement. I scheduled a meeting with Doug Clifton, *The Plain Dealer*'s editor-in-chief, during that time to make sure we agreed on when and how I would return to writing my column. It was a thrill to drive my own car for a change, although I couldn't remember which side the gas tank was on. But I knew how to find my way back to *The Plain Dealer,* and I knew what question to ask. If there were going to be a lot of new limitations on what I could write, there was no point in my going back.

"What will be the parameters?" I asked Doug.

"You'll write the same column you used to write," he said.

That was all I needed to know. We agreed I would return in late January, which *The Plain Dealer*'s reader representative, Ted Diadiun, announced in a November 12, 2006, column titled "Connie Schultz's Fans—and Others—Have Reason to Cheer." Ted and I rarely agreed on politics, but we had found our way to an abiding friendship nonetheless, and he said he was glad I was coming back. He told me he was already getting complaints from some conservative readers who insisted I had no business writing a column now that Sherrod had been elected. Ted's lead sentence in the column was "Connie Schultz often drives me crazy."

It was good to be home.

Sherrod was busy organizing his transition team and hiring Senate staff. Some key members of the campaign, including John Ryan and Joanna Kuebler, would stay with Sherrod. Several from his congressional offices would also transfer to the Senate staff. Jay Heimbach came on as his chief of staff, and Ngozi Pole agreed to be his deputy chief administrator. Once they were in place, Sherrod relaxed a little and let the reality of all the changes in his world sink in. For a few days, we actually felt that we might have life under control.

Two weeks after the election, though, life reminded us who was in charge.

On November 29, hours after Sherrod and I both received e-mails from him, our dear friend John Kleshinski died in his sleep of a heart attack. John had almost single-handedly made the last two weeks of the campaign bearable, and we had just had dinner with him and Emily earlier that month in Boston. John was in the middle of organizing Sherrod's swearing-in events for January, and many on the campaign staff had come to adore him. At the age of fifty-five, he was gone.

Bob Marotta, another longtime friend of John's, forwarded to Sherrod an e-mail that John had written right after the election. It was John as we remembered him in those last days of the campaign:

My two weeks in the car with Sherrod and Connie were the adventure of a lifetime. I could write a book about all the TV stations I visited, radio station interviews, tense scheduling moments, schmoozing local public officials who Sherrod couldn't get to, union guys asking for a photo op, courthouse steps I climbed with all the statewide candidates, early mornings and late hotel arrivals, aggressive press, adoring crowds, famous people (Obama, Cleland and Michael J. Fox) and simply good decent people from Cleveland to Gallipolis just looking for somebody to act like they mattered. I'm still fairly overwhelmed by what my old buddy has achieved and the convincing manner in which he has done so. We made a bet at the beginning and I said it would be under 4 percentage points. . . . I got my ass kicked. I'm certain he will do the great state of Ohio proud.

Jk

At home, Sherrod could barely say John's name before his eyes filled and he repeated what became his mantra: "I can't believe this, I can't believe John is gone." Publicly, he did what John would have wanted. Sherrod delivered eulogies for his oldest friend at services in their hometown of Mansfield and again in Boston, where John had lived with Emily.

"It's going to be like this from now on," Sherrod said on the flight home from John's memorial service in Boston.

"What is?" I asked.

"The longer we live, the more of our friends we'll lose."

No one, though, will be missed more than John.

TWO WEEKS AFTER THE ELECTION, I ATTENDED HARVARD UNIVERsity's Nieman Narrative Journalism Conference, where I was scheduled to give several talks.

Sherrod tagged along, and it felt great to be back among what I always joked were "my people"—in this case, about eleven hundred fellow writers and journalists. Sherrod looked like one of us, what with his rumpled shirts and scuffed shoes. We're a ragtag bunch, we journalists.

While I relished the chance to talk about the reporting and writing I love, I often found myself responding after my talks to questions about how I was going to fit in with the "Stepford Wives" of the Senate. I was surprised at how much this depiction of my counterparts troubled me. By then, I had met many of these wives, and this stereotype of the robotic wife was such an unkind and unfair depiction of the women I was getting to know.

One of the wives, whose husband has been a longtime senator, told me she spent the first two years of his Senate career constantly angry. "I hated what had become of my life," she told me, "and I was trying to figure out where I belonged, especially since we had moved to Washington." Another Senate wife, who sat next to me during a dinner, said that she, too, was trying to figure out exactly who she was since her husband's election. "We work so hard for our husbands to get them elected," she said. "Then they win and get these great jobs, and so many on the campaign move on to great jobs, too, and we're the only ones who don't really have anything at the end of it all."

These were not Stepford Wives, nor were any of the other women I met. For the most part, they were bright, articulate women who were navigating the land mines of political life, with varying degrees of success. I was grateful for my career, but I could also see what I had in common with many of these women, rather than focusing on our differences, which was what I did when Sherrod was a congressman. Regardless of where we live or what we do in our daily lives, all of us are married to men who belong to one of the most exclusive bodies in the world. There's no denying that, and the challenge is how to keep intact our own identities and still support them in these high-profile jobs. I do not think of myself as a Senate spouse. I am Sherrod's wife, happily so.

I am asked a lot, "What's it like to be a senator's wife?"

My answer is always the same: *I'll let you know.*

Twelve days after the election, Sherrod agreed to an interview on CBS's *Face the Nation,* his first with this Sunday-morning talk show. As usual, he buttoned himself into a starched blue dress shirt that had passed my inspection for a frayed collar or cuffs. He chose his dark blue pinstripe suit and pulled on two pairs of socks for warmth, black over brown, before slipping into a pair of the scruffy dress shoes he'd logged so many miles in during the campaign.

"What happened to the new shoes they gave you?" I asked, referring to the post-election gift from two fundraisers who thought Sherrod's shoes needed an upgrade now that he was about to become a senator.

"These have worked for me so far," he said, not even looking up until he finished tying them. "That okay with you?"

I didn't bother answering as we headed downstairs. He knew it was more than okay.

"Which tie?" he asked, holding up several that he'd wrapped around the banister at the foot of our stairs. Two of them were red, including his "lucky tie" that he'd worn for three of the debates. Another was the familiar blue tie used for too many television interviews, but the fourth tie was always one of my favorites. One of the consultants had warned us away from it because "many voters see it as a cowardly color." I'd rolled my eyes then, but now I just grinned at the memory. The things we worried about only two weeks ago.

"Wear the yellow striped," I said.

Sherrod pulled it around his neck and we headed for the studio a few miles from our home.

Over the years we'd both sat for televised interviews at this particular studio, and we knew everyone who worked there. We were surprised to see the owner there on a Sunday, and he hugged me when
we walked through the door, full of praise for the race we'd run. The
crew fluttered around Sherrod like ducklings, congratulating him and
assuring him they'd voted for him.

He sat more patiently than usual for the obligatory plastering of
makeup—fatigue is a wonderful sedative—and as he sat under the
lights I couldn't help but notice signs of life sprouting all over his
head. His curls were coming back, declaring their freedom in every
direction around his collar and brow. I fought the urge to reach over
and ring one of them around my finger.

"Your hair's coming back," I said.

"Just for you, baby," he said, and everyone laughed.

I sat on a nearby stool as another staff person helped him adjust
his earpiece and clipped on a microphone. Then Sherrod sat in silence for a few minutes, jotting down notes before the show began.

The cameraman pulled off his headset, leaned out from behind
the lens, and pointed to the canary pin on Sherrod's lapel.

"You gonna start wearing a flag pin now that you're a senator?" he
asked.

Sherrod hesitated for a moment, then looked at me with raised
eyebrows. We both grinned and shook our heads.

"No, I like this one," he said, tapping his lapel. "I'm going to keep
wearing the canary. As a reminder."

I walked over to him and kissed his forehead, then reached down
for the pin.

"Let's just make sure it's straight," I said, aligning it between two
pinstripes. He grabbed my hand and kissed it.

The cameraman slid on his headset again and silently motioned
to Sherrod.

"Senator?"

I stepped back, returned to the stool, and pulled on my own head-set. Sherrod sat up in his chair. The canary pin gleamed.

Silently, the cameraman began to count down with his fingers for Ohio's next senator.

Five.

Four.

Three.

Two.

One.

acknowledgments

SO MANY PEOPLE HELPED SHERROD IN HIS SUCCESSFUL RACE FOR the Senate that it is impossible to list them here. Instead, I want to thank those who were supportive in a personal way during the campaign and the writing of this book.

Many women formed their own organizations in Ohio after the 2004 election, and they welcomed me with open arms. What an inspiring—and growing—group of women.

Doug Mitchell pulled into town to help Sherrod and became my dear friend, too. It will be a long time before I forget windshield baseball.

John Ryan could not have worked so many miracles for us without the countless sacrifices of his wife, Jeanne, and their daughters, Megan, Colleen, and Erin.

Jack Dover guided and goaded us with equal measure, and made us better. To his wife, Agi: Thank you for the loan of your husband.

Numerous dynamic duos helped us keep perspective: Brian and Kim Baker, Subodh Chandra and Meena Morey Chandra, Joe and Pam Kanfer, Woody and Peggy Chamberlain, Sue and John Bender, Cheryl and Stuart Garson, Helen and Vic Stewart, Gloria and David Brown, Jennie and Allan Berliant, Melissa and Herb Hedden, Peter and Alice Lassally, Chuck and Shirley Fair, Ses and Maggie Kleshinski.

Wendy Hoke, Jill Miller Zimon, and Cindi Zawadzki blogged

their way onto my A-list. Jeff Coryell took a stand for integrity. Chris Baker cleared new road with his wisdom and passion.

No one shared our commitment more than Joanna Kuebler—and, oh, that laugh! Anne Davis kept us armed and ready. David Doak, Mattis Goldman, Tom O'Donnell, and Diane Feldman made all the difference. Tom, in particular, understood Sherrod as few have. Diane calmed us down and worked us up with impeccable timing.

Dr. Patricia Kellner stepped up in every possible way, as a stellar family doctor—and as a trusted friend. Dr. Ray Onders repaired Sherrod in record time, and we are also grateful for his work to help injured Iraq War veterans. Joe Mackall reminded me why I do what I do. Dennis Eckart always knew what I needed to hear. Robin Davis Miller helped me celebrate the synchronicity of it all. Nannette Bedway saw only the best in me. Cool-hair Ryan DiVita shared the vision. Kylee Cook worked magic.

Sheila Dwyer treats political wives as if we have a brain in our head—and does it with such style. Kathleen Gallagher must never stop writing. Donna Caudill lightened the load with her wit. Rick Brunner's enthusiasm wiped out every urge I had to whine. Sharon West egged on the journalist in me. Amy Budish's certainty was emboldening. Annie Glenn talked me off more than one cliff. Emily Paul was the embodiment of grace.

I am grateful to Senators Harry Reid and Chuck Schumer for their kindness and respect.

Guy Cecil was a crucial link. Patrick Anderson delivered the tough talk with grace. Kimberly Wood was the spark that set the flame to roaring. Kim Kauffman knew when to push—and when to make a joke. Nick Watt made the home stretch much easier to bear.

Peggy Zone Fisher set the precedent. Lana Moresky reminded me by example why I must never give up. Meg Driscoll always reminded me why the fight mattered. Barbara Gould was wise when times were tough. Michael Naidus helped me set my compass, time and again. Russ Ayers was unforgettable. Susan Hagan wrote my favorite campaign song. Deborah Read moved mountains. Craig Ferguson made me laugh when I thought I couldn't. Michele Young reminded me that it's always about others. Romi Lassally insisted that I had something to say.

Memories of other people float up like snapshots. Lauren Spector's hugs were such a boost. Davis Filippell made me proud to be his godmother. Steve "Later Leiber" was better than a jolt of caffeine. Lisa Scheer always looked out for me. Jennie Geise's warm welcome was a crucial jump start. Debbie Skettle saved me from the chaos. Luke Perry proved it's cool to be from Ohio. Carole King brought hope with her. Sabrina Singh was strong for me in a difficult moment. Michael J. Fox showed us what real courage looks like.

Russ Goodwin has changed many lives, including one very close to me. Thank you for mining the treasure, and sharing the wealth.

Several colleagues were friends throughout the campaign: Regina Brett, John Campanelli, Debbie Van Tassel, Andrea Simakis, Sheryl Harris, Bill Livingston, Chuck Yarborough, Harlan Spector, and Merlene Santiago. Tom Feran, with his collection of go-get-'em e-mails, is in a category by himself. On so many nights I read aloud Tom's notes, just to watch the exhausted candidate laugh.

Stuart Warner's faith in me kept me afloat. He is my greatest mentor.

Other journalists supported from afar. The fight in the Newspaper Guild–CWA's Linda Foley kept me swinging. Anna Quindlen long ago set the standard, and her gentle support guided me more than she knew. Dotty Lynch was a public champion. Mary McCarty caught me mid-stumble. Leonard Pitts was as kind as he is talented.

Peter Slevin affirmed my pride in our profession. Joe Tone keeps me hopeful about its future.

Several Ohio newspaper writers deserve special mention: Carl Chancellor, Jack Torry, Steve Koff, Mark Naymik, Jonathan Riskind, Jim Tankersley, and Jessica Wehrman. I didn't always like what they wrote, but I've got no quibble with their fairness and their passion for our profession.

I cherish the friends who've been with me from the beginning. Throughout the campaign, they reminded me that shared history transcends all: Hope Adelstein, Stanley Adelstein, Fleka Anderson, Jackie Cassara, the Reverend Kate Huey, Dr. Gaylee McCracken, Buffy Filippell, Mark Filippell, Gloria Goldstein, Laurence Goldstein, Clem Hearey, Sue Klein, Dr. Patricia Kellner, and Bill Lubinger. If you don't know what you mean to me by now, then I've got some explaining to do.

Patient friends oversaw various drafts of this book: In addition to Fleka, Jackie, Gaylee, Joanna, and Sue, I got big assists from Joan Klein, Wendy Bonds, John Ryan, and Jeanne Ryan. Wendy Leatherberry deserves special mention, not only for her many pages of copyediting notes, but for her relentless faith in democracy.

This is my second effort with the same team of talented and dedicated people at Random House. Kate Medina knew I had another book in me before I did, as is her habit. No one has had a greater impact on my career. Robin Rolewicz eased my every worry even as she pulled every last shred of effort from me. Abby Plesser kept the train roaring. Beth Pearson is that unsung hero of publishing—the production editor. Managing editor Benjamin Dreyer was a constant source of wit and wisdom. Copy editor Emily DeHuff saved me from myself. And I could always count on Sally Marvin for a pep talk.

Finally, there is family.

Theresa Congdon loved my father and tended to us all. My sisters, Leslie Schultz Perkoski and Toni Schultz, bore more than their share of burdens and never once complained about my absences. They are my heroes. Les's husband, David Perkoski, was also incredibly supportive. Thanks to my brother, Chuck, for voting his conscience. (Feels good, doesn't it?)

Two sets of parents raised their children so well that they lost them for a year to our family, as they devoted every spare moment to changing the direction of the country. To Nancy and Snowden Stanley, and Angie and Noel Torres: Thank you for the gifts of Michael and Kristina, and for understanding more than should have been asked of you.

Sherrod's family—his mother, Emily Campbell Brown; brother

Bob and his wife, Catherine Scallen; brother Charlie and his wife, Anne Swanson—were tireless champions for Sherrod. Tara Brown has clearly inherited the passion for politics, and Marcia Grace Brown was the brightest spirit on any day of the campaign. Anne kept a particularly watchful eye out for me, and I appreciated the concern.

Marriage to Sherrod has brought many blessings. Three of the greatest are my two stepdaughters, Elizabeth Clarke Brown and Emily Montgomery Brown, and Emily's husband, Michael Stanley. They supported Sherrod with breathtaking devotion, which bolstered me on many a day. They bring so many gifts to my life.

Four years ago, my two children, Andy Gard and Caitlin Schultz Gard, gave Sherrod a chance because they loved me. It didn't take long before they, too, loved him, and they proved it throughout the campaign. They also looked out for me. Andy was forever checking up on me, and Caitlin never let me forget who I am. Kristina Torres has had little downtime since she joined this family. She is a kind and gentle soul. Stina's sister, Marisa Torres, often joined us, and with her came a lot of joy.

As for Sherrod, my husband: Honey, I just wrote an entire book about you. What a ride, my love. What a ride.

index

about the author

CONNIE SCHULTZ, a biweekly columnist for the Cleveland *Plain Dealer*/Creators Syndicate, won the Pulitzer Prize for Commentary in 2005. Her other accolades include the Scripps-Howard National Journalism Award, the National Headliners Award, the James Batten Medal, and the Robert F. Kennedy Award for social-justice reporting. Her narrative series "The Burden of Innocence," which chronicled the life of a man wrongly incarcerated for rape, was a Pulitzer Prize finalist. Connie Schultz is married to Ohio's junior senator, Sherrod Brown, and has two children and two stepchildren.

about the type

This book was set in Minion, a 1990 Adobe Originals typeface by Robert Slimbach. Minion is inspired by classical, old-style typefaces of the late Renaissance, a period of elegant, beautiful, and highly readable type designs. Created primarily for text setting, Minion combines the aesthetic and functional qualities that make text type highly readable with the versatility of digital technology.